Also by Master Denise Liotta Dennis

Classical Feng Shui for Wealth & Abundance
Classical Feng Shui for Romance, Sex & Relationships

Classical Feng Shui for Health, Beauty & Longevity

About the Author

Denise Liotta Dennis is one of less than a hundred genuine Feng Shui Masters in America today. She has studied with four noted Feng Shui Masters from China, Malaysia, and Australia including Grandmaster Yap Cheng Hai (1927–2014), and belongs to his 400-year-old *Wu Chang Pai* Feng Shui Mastery lineage. Born to an entrepreneurial family, Denise possesses more than thirty years of business ownership experience and is among a rare breed of Feng Shui consultants. Denise lives in Houston, Texas.

To Write to the Author

If you wish to contact the author or would like more information about this book, please write to the author in care of Llewellyn Worldwide, and we will forward your request. Both the author and the publisher appreciate hearing from you and learning of your enjoyment of this book and how it has helped you. Llewellyn Worldwide cannot guarantee that every letter written to the author can be answered, but all will be forwarded. Please write to:

Master Denise Liotta Dennis
℅ Llewellyn Worldwide
2143 Wooddale Drive
Woodbury, MN 55125-2989

Please enclose a self-addressed stamped envelope for reply, or $1.00 to cover costs. If outside the USA, enclose an international postal reply coupon.

Many of Llewellyn's authors have websites with additional information and resources. For more information, please visit our website at www.llewellyn.com.

Classical Feng Shui for Health, Beauty & Longevity

Transform Your Space to Enhance Well-Being in Body & Home

MASTER DENISE LIOTTA DENNIS

Llewellyn Publications
Woodbury, Minnesota

First Edition
First Printing, 2016

Book design by Bob Gaul
Cover art by iStockphoto.com/11028056/©pixhook
iStockphoto.com/20031332/©xiepeng
iStockphoto.com/18898488/©MeiKIS
Cover design by Ellen Lawson
All interior art by Llewellyn art department except Figure 9: A Chinese Luo Pan (compass) on page 60 and Figure 17: The 24 Mountain Ring on page 139 © *Guide to the Feng Shui Compass* by Stephen Skinner, published 2010 by Golden Hoard Press/Llewellyn Publications
Editing by Laura Graves

Library of Congress Cataloging-in-Publication Data
Names: Liotta Dennis, Denise, 1954– author.
Title: Classical feng shui for health, beauty & longevity: transform your space to enhance well-being in body & home / Master Denise Liotta Dennis.
Description: First Edition. | Woodbury: Llewellyn Worldwide, Ltd, 2016. | Includes bibliographical references.
Identifiers: LCCN 2016024835 (print) | LCCN 2016033972 (ebook) | ISBN 9780738749006 | ISBN 9780738750989
Subjects: LCSH: Feng shui. | Health—Miscellanea. | Well-being—Miscellanea.
Classification: LCC BF1779.F4 L575545 2013 (print) | LCC BF1779.F4 (ebook) | DDC 133.3/337—dc23
LC record available at https://lccn.loc.gov/2016024835

Llewellyn Publications
A Division of Llewellyn Worldwide Ltd.
2143 Wooddale Drive
Woodbury, MN 55125-2989
www.llewellyn.com

Printed in the United States of America

I dedicate this book with great love
to my beautiful mother, Rosalie Marie (née Liotta)
Dennis, who was a cancer survivor of thirty years

Notice: This book is not intended to prescribe, diagnose, treat, or cure any condition for readers, who are advised to seek local and professional medical care for conditions that may be unique. Cases and studies cited by the author support a personal view and are meant to inform only. Always be mindful when following generally stated medical advice; a reader's personal history, habits, and condition may alter results.

Contents

Part II: Feng Shui Systems to Enhance Healthy Living

Part III: Design & Arrange Your Space for Vibrant Health

Acknowledgments

I'd like to acknowledge my brilliant and generous teacher, Grandmaster Yap Cheng Hai (Kuala Lumpur, Malaysia, lived 1927–2014). Without his willingness to pass on his extensive knowledge, it may have been lost; I'm eternally grateful and deeply thank him.

I'd like to recognize my extraordinary family and thank them for their love and support, including my beautiful mother to whom this book is dedicated. My mother taught me courage. I extend the deepest love to my son, Mark Weightman, my daughter-in-law Mandy, and their three gorgeous children—Makenzy, Kaitlyn, and Grayson. I'd like to express much love and appreciation to my most beloved sister, Linda Dennis; and her son, my favorite nephew, Madison Smith. Tremendous thanks to all my clients who for the past two decades have been a continual source of knowledge and inspiration.

It is with enormous pride that I salute my remarkable core students who are now Feng Shui Masters: Jennifer Bonetto, Katherine McClerkin, Peg Burton, Marianne Kulekowskis, Kristy Coup, Peggy Lanese, Kristie Yeckel, and Nathalie Ekobo. I also wish to recognize my colleagues around the world whose association I value greatly; these Feng Shui Masters' consulting and teachings are a gift to the world: Jennifer Bartle-Smith, Australia; Maria Santilario, Spain; Bridgette O'Sullivan, Ireland; Cynthia Murray, Colorado; Jayne Goodrick, England; Di Grobler and Christine McNair, South Africa; Scheherazade "Sherry" Merchant, India; Nathalie Mourier and Helen Weber, France; and Birgit Fischer, Petra Coll-Exposito, Nicole Zoremba, and Eva-Maria Spöetta, Germany.

And finally, I'd like to extend gratitude to Llewellyn Worldwide for their continued confidence and support!

Denise A. Liotta Dennis, Feng Shui Master
Houston, Texas

Introduction

Traditional Chinese healing practices such as acupuncture, herbal cures, massage, and martial arts focus on energy/chi. Naturally, Feng Shui does as well, but it involves the external surrounding environment and your interior living space, not just the body. The concept of chi is based on the belief that all things in the Universe possess the mysterious consciousness of energy. Therefore, every cell in your body and every room in your dwelling have their own unique energy.

The Chinese also believe that when we live in a state of harmonious energy (Feng Shui), we'll naturally enjoy good health. Not only that, when illness does strike, there's always the *Tien Yi* or "Heavenly Doctor" to make you well again. In fact, my teacher, Grandmaster Yap Cheng Hai, began his journey into Feng Shui in the 1950s due to the persistently ill health of his four young children. He told us that in those days, about half of his salary went to doctors and medicine. Frustrated, he hired a Feng Shui Master to come to his home; the results were so remarkable *and* immediate, he embarked on learning the secrets of Feng Shui himself.

Without question, health is a gift to be more treasured than wealth. What would Apple founder Steve Jobs have given to have his health back? Most likely *all* his wealth; he was a genius and could have created new fortunes—especially with vibrant health! I personally became interested in health when my mother was diagnosed with uterine cancer when I was eighteen years old; she was only thirty-nine. While she was a long-time survivor, her health was neither optimum nor vibrant. I watched her suffer through severe treatments and ill health on and off until her passing. Determined to find out how best to take care of my health because cancer was present on both sides of my family, I experimented with a variety of natural techniques and dietary modalities, many of which I discuss in the book. In the eighties and nineties, I owned a day spa and upscale clothing boutique in Houston, Texas, and was very familiar with Western and Eastern techniques for beauty and health; many of which we offered to clients.

I've been blessed with excellent health all my life and attribute much of it to good habits, good attitude, and good Feng Shui. Americans in particular are in a sorry state of health; we rank much lower compared to the health of other developed, wealthy countries. Prescription drugs aggressively marketed by the American medical industry compromise our health, *and* we must endure polluted air, food, and water; something's gotta give!

I am very pleased to introduce this subject as there has been very little written about health and Feng Shui; there are so many methods to secure it. As one of my students put it so aptly: "People always ask how Feng Shui can enhance money and love—health just isn't that sexy of a subject." While she may be right, health is at the top of my list and millions more who desire to live well and in good health. Therefore, my goal was to make *Classical Feng Shui for Health, Beauty & Longevity* the most comprehensive book available on Feng Shui and health to include both ancient and modern techniques. The book is a culmination of the Classical Feng Shui series on wealth, relationships, and health. The recommendations in the book focus primarily on health, but you will activate all three—wealth, relationships, and health—with the precise instructions in chapters 6 and 7.

We'll start in chapter 1 exploring the Taoist view of health and longevity and the relentless search for the "golden pill" of immortality. Before we get into the actual Feng Shui systems, we'll delve into ancient Chinese and East Indian techniques for health as well as some very high-tech ones such as nanotechnology, the latter of which is putting China in news headlines around the world; they are the leaders in this new technology research. That's no big surprise, as they have a very long history of highly valuing health as one of the most desirable things in life. Perhaps the obsession with discovering the secrets of immortality has never been completely abandoned. However, the Taoist masters may roll over in their graves when health-nanotechnology methods are integrated into Traditional Chinese Medicine. In addition to advanced medicine/technology, I will introduce the *extraordinary* benefits of two *ordinary* elements—water and salt. This simple approach to better health is the brainchild of Oxford-educated American-Iranian Dr. F. Batmanghelidj and his 24-year-long research into the water-salt relationship and human life; I think you'll be as fascinated as I was.

In chapter 2, a review of the roots and premise behind this fascinating science/art known as "wind-water" is revisited. In chapter 3, unhealthy formations such as modern-day devices like cell phones, microwaves, high-tension towers, and harmful environments are discussed with recommended cures to protect the body and mind.

Using the potent Eight Mansions system, chapter 4 reveals the profound secrets of the "Heavenly Doctor" position and its importance in enhancing health. Eight Mansions is a more personalized Feng Shui system, much like an astrology report; the chapter contains insights into your personality and personal directions that will empower you. Flying Stars is discussed in chapter 5 and how it's used to identify the potential for illness and disease in your *unique* Natal Star chart. Furthermore, Flying Stars is all about timing and the annual stars that "visit" your home, denoting sickness and pernicious energy; you'll have all the cures to protect yourself against them. In this chapter, you'll also be able to peruse the famous eighty-one combination of stars and their *predictive* abilities; very cool and heady stuff!

Everything comes together for health, wealth, and relationships in chapters 6 and 7, the most hands-on section of the book; there you'll really be moving the energy for excellent Feng Shui. No need to be a master of Feng Shui, just grab a compass or your smartphone and you'll be on your way to better health, longevity, money, and relationships. Why a compass? All Classical Feng Shui methods and systems are based on using the energy of the eight compass directions: north, south, east, and so on.

Feng Shui is multidimensional: it has many layers and a collection of rich, profound techniques offering a wide variety of options. To be successful in adjusting the energy of your home, it's important to understand that the unique variations of the land, floor plan, and your birthday will greatly affect how you will orientate things. However, please relax with the knowledge that these multiple layers have all been factored into the recommendations; you need only to implement them. Once you have found the section that applies to your home, the rest is great reference material to assist your family, friends, and coworkers. In other words, not everything in chapters 6 and 7 will apply to your home and unique situation. If you move into a different home, simply refer to your *new* facing direction, and you'll be on your way to arranging the space to perfection.

Part I
Longevity, Health Modalities & Feng Shui Roots

One

A Taoist View of Longevity & Health Modalities

When he ingests the Medicines, let him fly as an immortal, have audience at the Purple Palace, live an unending life, and become an accomplished man!
Book of the Nine Elixirs

The Taoists were philosophers, revolutionaries, scientists, specialists of rituals, masters of astronomy and astrology, physicians, and health specialists. They were preoccupied with all facets of life and science. They maintain the view that humans and the universe are from the same source energy; the inception of Taoism dates back more than five thousand years.

In *Teachings of the Tao*, author Eva Wong surmises that it was Taoism, not Buddhism or Confucianism, that formed the spirit and soul of the Chinese people that has sustained its inherently scared and spiritual traditions. The Tao (also spelled Dao) is the absolute principle underlying the universe, combining within itself the theory of yin-yang and codes of behavior that are in harmony with the natural order, often referred to as "the Way." The famous philosopher Lao Tzu was one of the first great Tao thinkers, helping it later become a religion.

The *Tao Te Ching*, a famed thousands-year-old text that has survived to present day, attempts to explain the unexplainable, indescribable, and that which cannot be named. It is still the most widely translated Chinese book valued for its philosophies on non-action *(wu wei)* and harmonious living. In Feng Shui we refer to the Tao as "the Great Void" or "Nothingness" *(wu chi)* where all possibilities and limitless phenomenon is contained. From the Great Void, "ten thousand things" materialize into the physical world. The ultimate aspiration of Taoism is to become one with the Great Void or Source via daily meditation, specific disciplines, and moral practices. There is a massive collection of texts (more than 1,400) dedicated to this timeless wisdom and philosophical study, much of it written by Lao Tzu. One fascinating aspect of Taoism is alchemy; the first allusions to Chinese alchemy began in the second century BCE.

Chinese alchemy is one component of the larger tradition of Taoist body-spirit cultivation that developed from the traditional Chinese understanding of medicine and the body. From the ancient text of the *Cantong Qi*, the body has the ability to attain greater alignment with the Tao through spiritual development. The traditional view in China is that alchemy focuses mainly on the purification of one's spirit and body in hopes of gaining immortality through the practice of qi gong and/or consumption and use of various concoctions known as alchemical medicines or elixirs, each of which has different purposes.

Eventually, the practice of Taoism morphed into two main disciplines of alchemy known as the "external" and "internal." The external was a systematic approach designed to support the physicality of the human body through creating and ingesting elixirs composed of herbs and minerals. This was supposed to ensure superior health, increase longevity, and even grant one immortality. The quest for immortality was the powerful impetus to experiment with alchemical elixirs; however, it often actually resulted in death by poisoning.

This was not uncommon at intermittent junctures in its long, trial-by-errors history. In fact, the failure to produce a bona fide "pill of immortality" led to more oftentimes extreme experimenting so much so that during the Tang Dynasty Taoist alchemist used criminals condemned to death as guinea pigs. The most avid supporters and patrons of alchemy's pursuits were emperors, royal families, and the upper echelon of society; they sanctioned any and all research concerning the pill of immortality (aka the "golden pill"). Without say, the poor had no desire to prolong their plight with extended longevity or worse, immortality. Chinese history has it that more emperors died from ingesting poisonous minerals during the Tang Dynasty than any other.

What were the deadly ingredients that caused such lethal results? The most popular minerals used in the mixtures came down to twenty-seven: some were lead, mercury, zinc, nickel, sodium, sulfate, rock salt, mercuric sulphide, silver, cinnabar, various forms of malachite, and arsenious oxides. No degree in chemistry is needed to see that most (except salt) are extremely harmful to the human body. Those who ingested a "golden pill" were indeed slowly poisoned, most suffering from liver or kidney failure, nervous system damage, or the development of mental disorders, even insanity.

Some of these minerals were refined into a faux gold; it was believed that is was superior to real gold when ingested as it went through a burning process that gave it a spiritual quality. Gold and cinnabar were the most sought-after substances to manipulate and ingest, as the alchemist believed that gold and cinnabar could prolong life. Cinnabar is a mineral with a reddish brown color often found near deposits of mercury. The two were assumed related and indeed they are; cinnabar is mercuric sulfide. It was used in the search for immortality because of its color, and the difficulty with which it had to be refined. The color of the cinnabar is significant because the Chinese venerate red believing it the pinnacle of all colors representing the sun, fire, royalty, and energy. When cinnabar is fired, it produces a liquid we know as quicksilver (mercury).

Although the majority of immortality elixirs were combinations of golden elixirs, many others were formed by combining metallic bases with natural herbs or animal byproducts. The rhinoceros' horn was commonly used in medicines and elixirs and was held to have fertility-increasing abilities. Rhino horn has been used for thousands of years and continues to be one of the mainstays of Traditional Chinese Medicine, claiming to cure everything from cancer to hangovers, including purging poisons from the liver. Its harvesting has been responsible for the death of tens of thousands of rhinos around the world. There is no scientific data proving that it has any health benefit at all, but followers and practitioners in Traditional Chinese Medicine believes it does—therefore its cachet.

The Chinese government officially banned all imports in 1979; however, rhino horn is still being smuggled in from Macao, Burma, Indonesia, Malaysia, India, Taiwan, and South Africa. The retail price, after the horn has been shaved or powdered for sale, has at times in certain East Asian markets reached $20,000–$30,000 per kilo. Currently, Vietnam is the biggest consumer/offender of this illegal substance. The country's appetite for rhino horn is so great that it now commands prices up to $300,000/kg.[1] Absolutely this is something that needs to be stopped.

After three hundred years of abject failure to successfully produce the golden pill, Taoists began to question whether immortality was even possible; by the end of the Tang Dynasty (618–906 CE), the age of striving for the pill of immortality ended. Nowadays, external alchemy focuses on strengthening the physical body with moving meditation

---

1. Gwynn Guilford, "*There's a Country That Will Pay $300,000 Per Rhino Horn to Cure Cancer and Hangovers and It's Wiping out Rhinos*" at qz.com/82302/theres-a-country-that-will-pay-300000-per-rhino-horn-to-cure-cancer-and-hangovers-and-its-wiping-out-rhinos/

and various herbal formulas—no noxious, lethal chemical concoctions in sight.

The Song Dynasty (960–1279 CE) was the golden age of internal alchemy. This aspect of alchemy is that of refining one's energy through cultivation of the Three Treasures: ***Jing*** (reproductive energy), ***Qi*** (life force energy), and ***Shen*** (spiritual energy). In this discipline, the body's subtle energies are the laboratory and the refined energy itself becomes the "elixir." The *internal* alchemy's approach purported that immortality and longevity could be attained by transforming body and mind from within, not ingesting mineral potions. This practice also advocates that spiritual development requires a balance of both physical health and mental clarity—in other words, an integration of mind and body.

Some practices of internal alchemy involve martial arts such as qi gong, breathing exercises and breath control, massage, herbs, and harnessing sexual energy and static postures similar to yoga. Taoism does not require one to become a vegetarian; however, after the body is cleansed and energies refined, practitioners report that this is a natural outcome. Internal alchemy is a rigorous path of spiritual training, shrouded in secrecy even today. Asia's learned teachers guard their secrets and do not openly accept students; theirs is a lifelong discipline and practice, not simply learning qi gong or taking herbs. The true objective of internal alchemy is to prepare the mind and body to make the great return to the limitless Tao when our time as mortals has ended on earth.

Feng Shui's Roots in the Tao and I Ching

Feng Shui is deeply rooted in the philosophy of Taoism, and is the science of living in harmony with the natural and man-made environment. The *I Ching*, China's most ancient book predating even Taoism, is Feng Shui's true roots and premise text significantly predates Taoism.[2] The *I Ching*

2. Dating back to more than four thousand years, the *I Ching* aka the *Book of Changes* was authored by Confucius, King Wen, the Duke of Chou, and Fu Zi. Both Taoism and Confucianism have roots in this timeless classic.

documented the mysterious symbols of the trigrams and hexagrams, and they are used extensively in the practice of Feng Shui. It's very interesting that modern science has now discovered that the sixty-four hexagrams of the *I Ching* correspond exactly to the sixty-four DNA genetic codes, the basis of all life on earth.[3] Symbolism and traces of Feng Shui have been discovered in the Henan province (1988) that date back four thousand years; this means that Feng Shui predates any major Chinese religion, namely that of Confucianism, Taoism, and Buddhism.

Chinese religion and cosmology interconnect with much of Chinese culture, so it was natural for Feng Shui to be partly influenced by all three of China's greatest religions, but it happened primarily with Taoism. Therefore, it is important to distinguish where religion ends and Feng Shui begins. Let's briefly examine China's "three teachings" which had a great impact on how they view the world. The three main religions of ancient China were Confucianism, Taoism, and Buddhism. They were so interwoven that even today a Confucian temple might have images of the Buddha and that of Taoism's eight immortals. To a large extent, these three religions have become one in the mind of the Chinese people.

Confucianism is based on the writings of K'ung Fu-tzu (551–479 BCE), a philosopher of the Spring and Autumn period of Chinese history. Its central doctrines are the Analects as well as the Five Classics and Four Songs. The former are a compilation of Confucius's sayings, and the latter are a collection of historical and cultural works varying from poems to speeches. Indeed, the *I Ching* is one of the Five Classics. Philosophically, Confucianism's focus was on societal and personal relationships, right conduct, and revering one's parents. It served as a valuable system to cultivate moral virtues and social values among the population as it deals with practical and earthly affairs. Its highest aim was

3. From the *Tao of Abundance* by Laurence G. Boldt.

encouraging proper behavior and social harmony, and it became so influential that it was taught in Chinese schools from 206 BCE up to 1949 in the PRC.

Taoism, by contrast, is concerned with spiritual and intuitive insights; it is believed that one could evolve and attain true knowledge by communing with the natural world and to recognize one's true spiritual nature. Almost assuredly, the savant Lao Tzu (born sixth–fifth century BCE) was the founder of Taoism's profound philosophies.

Buddhism is a religion brought to China from India; the founder was Prince Siddhartha Gautama (566–486 BCE). The Mahayana tradition of Buddhism did not spread to China until the Han dynasty and it would be much later before it was embedded. The golden age of Buddhism was in the Sui and Tang dynasties. Buddhism *is not* a source of Feng Shui. Despite various books and commentaries to associate Tibetan Buddhism with Feng Shui, the truth is that Feng Shui is not a Buddhist practice. Additionally, Feng Shui is uniquely a Chinese practice even though many believe that its early beginnings came from India. India has its own "form" of Feng Shui called Vastu Shastra; a practice vastly different from Classical Chinese Feng Shui and is neither as exhaustive nor as formalized.

Since its inception in Neolithic China, its people have relied on Feng Shui to build their homes and cities for centuries. In modern times, where there are large Chinese populations such as Hong Kong, Malaysia, Taiwan, and Singapore, Feng Shui is part of everyday life. Consulting a Feng Shui Master is not only part of the business community in their small to large projects but also used by homeowners to either find a home or build one. In recent times, Westerners have come to value this ancient wisdom with Europe's and North America's architects, interior designers, real estate agents, developers, and homeowners using or looking into the benefits of Feng Shui.

Despite the fact that Feng Shui is more popular than ever, few people, including those from places where it has been practiced for generations, know much about its beginnings and the numerous approaches available. With popularity comes many claiming to be experts and practitioners, and it's often difficult to separate fad from tradition. Known as *Kan Yu* in olden times, Feng Shui became a professional skill during the Han Dynasty (206 BCE–220 CE); since the late 1800s, the term *Feng Shui* (literally "wind-water") began to refer to this science of geomantic evaluation. By the Tang Dynasty, after a three-hundred-year era of peace and creativity, Feng Shui formulas and the Luo Pan (compass) became more complex and advanced. It continued to present day uninterrupted until the communist ruler, General Mao Tse-Tung, took office in 1949 and made the open practice of Feng Shui forbidden. With the advent of the Great Leap Forward and the Cultural Revolution, things became more dangerous for practitioners, so many fled to Hong Kong (under British rule until 1997), Singapore, Canada, Australia, Taiwan, Indonesia, and Malaysia. This emigration helped Feng Shui spread around the world but resulted in generations of Chinese people who know little about authentic Feng Shui. Even after the Communist Party declared the Cultural Revolution a failure and Mao's death in 1976, it's still not legal to openly practice or register your Feng Shui business in China. That said, the Chinese government does not object to Feng Shui being used when practitioners collaborate with Southeast Asian companies/governments in business deals that insist on its inclusion.

When Feng Shui was introduced to America in the mid-1970s, it was not its traditional form but an imitation with Buddhist overtones; my teacher was fond of calling this style "the Hollywood version," brought to the United States by Tibetan Buddhist monk/professor Lin Yun of the Black Hat sect Buddhist order collaborating with his student of the

"Dharma," Sarah Rossbach, an interior designer. By selectively extracting from traditional Feng Shui and adding his own Buddhist beliefs, Lin Yun created a simplified system that was well received by the New Age community. It later became mainstream but never really attracted many Chinese fans; Americans had mostly never heard of Feng Shui and didn't know the difference. By the late 1980s, Classical Feng Shui was gaining popularity in Europe, Australia, and Canada.

Black Hat Sect Feng Shui makes use of Buddhist prayers and chants, red packets for money, beads, decorations, crystals, bamboo flutes, mirrors, coin-choked frogs, and other culturally recognizable symbols or articles of Buddhist practice. Lin Yun's style also misuses the Ba Gua (designed to represent the eight directions and its energy) by placing everyone's home as facing north even if it doesn't.

This style was eventually named *Black Hat Sect Tantric* Buddhist *Feng Shui* (BTB); Classical Feng Shui is not rooted in either Buddhism or the Tantra.[4] BTB does not use traditional Feng Shui formulas and systems developed over thousands of years, nor does it use the Luo Pan, the quintessential tool of traditional Feng Shui. BTB also found its way to Europe, Canada, Australia, South Africa, South America, and India. Noted for its "spiritual" aspects, this style has been very effective in commercializing Feng Shui and marketing retail items promoted as "cures." More Westernized versions popped up in America and elsewhere looking very much the same as Lin Yun's new-fangled style without the Buddhist underpinnings.

While I consider myself to be very spiritual, Classical Feng Shui is not a religion and does not belong in this realm. Feng Shui is a geomantic science while Buddhism is a religious practice; the two are mutually exclusive and should not be considered one and the same.

---

4. Tibetan Buddhism is one body of Buddhist religious doctrine and institutions; there are many sects and divisions much like Christianity has. The different sects are *Black Hat Sect* (Karma Kagyu), *Red Hat Sect* (Nyingma, Sakya, and Kagyu), and *Yellow Hat Sect* (Gelug).

It was virtually impossible to attend any sort of class on Classical Feng Shui until the late nineties anywhere in the world; masters were secretive and not inclined to share their knowledge, especially with foreigners. However, many masters became willing to teach interested parties when America and its considerable worldwide influence was spreading the wrong message about Feng Shui. My own teacher, Grandmaster Yap Cheng Hai, did not offer public classes until the late 1990s and rarely in the United States. He was introduced to the Western world via Lillian Too's numerous Feng Shui books published in the mid-1990s of which he was either the source or co-author. See his complete bio in the Glossary of Terms.

Why Feng Shui for Health?

Eventually, Classical Feng Shui came to address three important areas of life: wealth and prosperity, health and longevity, and relationships and romance. In order to accomplish this, it investigates the energy both inside and outside your living space. It was considered so potent and effective that in ancient days it was forbidden to anyone other than the ruling class. It is rumored that dynasties rose and fell with the assistance of Feng Shui Masters.

Even though the principles were conceived thousands of years ago, incorporating Feng Shui in our modern world is more important than ever. Never in human history have we so burdened our planet's natural resources. Moreover, we are bombarded with electromagnetic energy, microwaves, and toxins in our food, air, and water that make it a challenge to stay strong and healthy. We live in a time when technology is increasing at such a pace; it's hard not to be excited by the possibilities of our future, and concerned as well.

Therefore, applying the principles of Feng Shui is more vital than ever. Designed to improve the quality of life and how we experience it, gathering key pieces of information about your site is crucial. These are the home's orientation (facing direction), move-in date, water on the site such as pools or fountains, surrounding landforms, and magnetic energy fields. Next, the evaluation of important rooms such as the master bedroom, home office, the kitchen/stove, and the door you come and go from will reveal if the structure supports you.

If the energy is good and positive, it can bring wonderful relationships, vibrant health, business opportunities, speedy recoveries from surgeries, and promotions at work. If the home has negative energy and does not offer support, then cancer, divorce, scandals, poverty, bankruptcy, disease, heart attacks, extramarital affairs, and a host of other bad events can manifest. While much of the book will deal with the health aspect, we will discuss relationships and prosperity as well.

Using Classical Feng Shui to enhance longevity and support good health will not take away from the fact that you'll need to sustain your body by eating well and engaging in regular exercise; this is simple common sense and how the body works. However, Feng Shui is invaluable in altering the energy of your home or workplace to support vibrant health. We'll talk more about this later when we'll explore all the methods and techniques used in Classical Feng Shui to ensure you're experiencing the best energy to improve or secure your health beginning in chapter 3.

Health Modalities

Before we delve into the foundation and function of Feng Shui's role in health, let's discuss some simple modalities that can support your health in other ways. This will also provide perspective in how Feng Shui fits into a larger system for well-being.

Longevity and a healthy life have always been of prime importance in Chinese culture. The expectations for a long, healthy life are part of their societal psyche, and it is very easy to find traditional doctrines and techniques that address this aspiration. We discussed earlier the obsession with the golden pill sought by Taoist masters but at the same time, legend has it that the Yellow Emperor (Huang Di) sent three thousand virgin girls and boys into the eastern seas to find the island where the "peach of immortality" was alleged to grow; they never returned. This frustration finally gave way to more practical methods, and the Chinese have been famous for their holistic approach to health ever since.

The state of American health is indeed frightening; research has consistently shown that for some time the United States fared much more poorly in comparison with other developed nations, a trend established in the 1980s. Humanity's search for a fountain of youth and the pursuit of eternal life have been going on for centuries. Ponce de Leon searched for the fountain of youth in the fifteenth century. When King Ferdinand and Queen Isabella of Spain sanctioned Christopher Columbus's voyages to find new lands and gold, the real, hidden agenda was in search of the legendary "rivers of Paradise and everlasting youth."

Luckily, we have at our disposal many methods in the twenty-first century for securing our health—some are very ancient wisdom indeed, and others will sound a bit like science fiction. Added to this, having excellent Feng Shui is essential as well.

To start, let's investigate some very ancient methods for enhancing our health and bodies with wisdom from ancient China and India; two cultures with continuous histories dating back almost six thousand years. We'll discuss nanotechnology, the latest health-related scientific development in the twenty-first century that has been making headlines worldwide. And finally, we'll investigate some ancient and modern therapies to enhance health and beauty; two so simple you won't believe it.

I. Chinese Arts for Health and Life Extension

Chinese Medicine/Herbs, Acupuncture, Massage, and Martial Arts

Giving way to more practical methods of extending life than the pill of immortality, the ancient Chinese developed excellent practices to secure health still in use to this day. The underpinnings of them *all* are that the human body is fueled by chi; if the body's chi is balanced and strong, there is no disease or illness. If it's imbalanced, then ill health ensues and longevity is compromised.

Traditional Chinese Medicine (TCM)

Traditional Chinese Medicine (TCM) is a broad range of medicinal practices that share common theories developed in China more than two thousand years old; they encompass dietary therapy, herbs/herbal concoctions, acupuncture, massage therapy, and exercise (including martial arts).

The doctrines of Chinese medicine are embedded in books such as the *Yellow Emperor's Inner Canon* and the *Treatise on Cold Damage*, as well as in the yin-yang theory and the five elements/phases.[5] Since the 1950s, these precepts were standardized in the People's Republic of China, including attempts to integrate them with modern notions of anatomy and pathology.

TCM's view of the body places little emphasis on anatomical structures, instead mainly concerned with the identification of functional entities regulating digestion, breathing, and aging. Vibrant health is perceived as a harmonious interaction with these entities, while disease is interpreted as a disharmony.

A TCM diagnosis includes identifying symptoms and patterns of any underlying disharmony; this is accomplished by measuring the pulse, inspecting the tongue, skin, and eyes; and examining the eating and sleeping habits of the patient along with a host of other methods to discover the patient's overall well-being. The approach addresses the *whole* of the individual, not just the area of complaint or concern.

---

5. The five elements are wood, fire, earth, metal, and water; there are three phases or cycles. For more information, see chapter 2.

Chinese Herbs

Herbal medicine is an extensive part of TCM; Chinese physicians have identified thousands of plants and herbs associated with the treatment of ailments. In practice, physicians would analyze the plants' nature/properties and label them either as cold/hot, yin/yang, use a variety of raw materials, and mix them to cure diseases. In the *Compendium of Materia Medica* written by Li Shizhen during the Tang Dynasty (618–907 CE), there are more than 1,892 classifications of herbs listed, complete with detailed information on each.

Acupuncture and Facial Revitalization Acupuncture

The healing art of acupuncture is one that can be traced back at least two thousand years, while others insist that acupuncture has been practiced in China closer to four thousand years. The first known acupuncture text is the *Nei Ching Su Wen*, and there is great controversy about its exact origins and authorship. The book is also known by a variety of alternative titles such as the *Yellow Emperor's Classic of Internal Medicine* and the *Canon of Medicine*, but all these titles refer to the same treatise.

Acupuncture involves the insertion of extremely thin needles through the skin at strategic points on the body. It's a key component of Traditional Chinese Medicine, and is a technique for balancing the flow of energy or life force (chi) believed to flow through energy pathways known as meridians in the body.

When inserting needles into specific points along these meridians, acupuncture practitioners believe that energy flow re-balances. You may wish to try acupuncture for symptomatic relief of a variety of diseases and conditions, including chemotherapy-induced nausea and vomiting, fibromyalgia, headaches, labor pain, lower back pain, menstrual cramps, migraines, dental pain, tennis elbow, and osteoarthritis.

Cosmetic Acupuncture, also known as *Facial Rejuvenation Acupuncture*, is a safe and effective non-surgical treatment to reduce the signs of aging, or at least slow it down. Facial Rejuvenation Acupuncture involves the insertion of extremely thin needles into various points on the face. This increases local circulation and blood flow, stimulating the production of collagen and elastin. Also, increased blood flow results in the skin being nourished and oxygenated; it can makes it firmer, younger-looking, and the complexion glow. It's been reported that Facial Rejuvenation Acupuncture can erase as many as five to fifteen years from the face after a round of treatments.

Acupuncture's use for certain conditions has been recognized by the U.S. National Institutes of Health, the National Health Service of the United Kingdom, the World Health Organization, and the National Center for Complementary and Alternative Medicine.

Massage for Health

Massage is another of China's great contributions to the field of medicine. Like acupuncture, this remarkable treatment as a discipline of Chinese medicine also has a long history. The earliest records regarding massage can be found in the writings on bones or tortoise shells of the Shang Dynasty (1766–1122 BCE). Then there's the famous story of a doctor, *Bian Que* (770–476 BCE), who treated a prince who fainted with massage therapy. The account was documented with illustrations and the treatment's amazing results. During the Northern and Southern dynasties (386–589 CE), six techniques of hand massage evolved and became more refined, such as to strand, shake, twine, twiddle, knead, and roll—all of which are still widely used.

The massage itself depends on the strength and direction of hand; consequently some only reach the skin, while others affect the pulses, muscles, and even the marrow. The positive effects of massage have been acknowledged by people as relieving pain and stiffness in the bones and muscles, adjusting dislocation of the joints, and the removal of muscle spasms. In addition to massage for curing, there are techniques used for keeping fit.

For example, kneading the acupoints around eyes can improve eyesight, massaging three specific acupoints on the head can quickly relax you, and massaging the feet (known as reflexology in the West) can have a positive effect on the entire body. So important are the feet and their unique acupoints, that they are together known as the "second heart." Today, massage has developed into more than twenty different techniques; the study and practice of massage is still thriving all over the world.

Martial Arts for Health

According to ancient lore, Chinese martial arts originated during the semi-mythical Xia Dynasty more than four thousand years ago. Legend has it that the Yellow Emperor Huangdi (legendary date of ascension 2698 BCE) introduced the earliest fighting systems to China. Huangdi is described as a famous general who wrote lengthy treatises on medicine, astrology, and the martial arts before becoming a unified China's leader.

Colloquially referred to as *Kung Fu* and *Wu Shu*, China's martial arts comprise a number of fighting styles developed over many centuries. The different fighting styles are classified according to common characteristics, identified as families, sects, or schools.

Does the practice of martial arts have a positive effect on health? Several studies have been done and the final analysis included twenty-eight papers: one on general martial arts, one on kung fu, sixteen on tai chi, six on judo, three on karate, and one on taekwondo. Research topics varied extensively, including health, injuries, competition, morals and psychology, and herbal medicine. Most studies found that martial arts did indeed have positive effects on health.

Tai Chi

Tai Chi is an internal Chinese martial art practiced as defense training as well as for its health benefits. It is typically practiced for a variety of other personal reasons: its hard and soft martial art technique, in competitions, and for longevity. Due to its extreme popularity, a multitude of training forms exist both traditional and modern. Some of Tai Chi training forms are especially known for being practiced with what most people would categorize as slow movement, which is why it is often referred to as "meditation in motion." Today, Tai Chi has spread all over the world. The majority of modern styles of Tai Chi can trace their development to at least one of the five traditional schools: Chen, Yang, Wu (Hao), Wu, and Sun. Medical research has found evidence that Tai Chi is good for improving balance, psychological health, and has numerous benefits to older people.

Yan Shou Gong *(Martial Arts for Longevity)*

In addition to being a very skilled Feng Shui master, Grandmaster Yap Cheng Hai was equally respected for his genius and accomplishments in the area of martial arts. In fact, Master Yap said he first met famous Feng Shui author Lillian Too (then in her early twenties) while attending his martial art classes in Kuala Lumpur.

Master Yap, along with Grandmaster Datuk Chee Kim Thong devised a simple martial art system called Yan Shou Gong, "Martial Arts for Longevity," that is not as rigid as the conventional styles; it suits those who are anxious to learn the art but don't have the time or perseverance for the discipline required. Yan Shou Gong's focus is on extending longevity and good health; it encompasses select movements from a number of schools/styles, including Wu Ji Quan and Lohan Ruyi Quan. Master Yap has written a series of three books on Yan Shou Gong to take the reader through mastering the thirty-six sets of movements.[6]

---

6. You can find the book series *Yan Shou Gong: Martial Arts for Longevity* at www.ychacademy.com/htdocs/products-book-yanshougong.shtml

During our Feng Shui classes, sometimes Master Yap would have us stand up and lead us through some simple yet powerful marital art movements. Usually this was after lunch when we were getting lethargic, digesting our food. You can watch Master Yap demonstrating select movements of the Yan Shou Gong style on YouTube.[7]

II. East Indian Practices for Life Extension and Optimum Health

Ayurvedic Medicine/ Herbs and Yoga

Ayurvedic Medicine

Ayurvedic medicine (also called Ayurveda) is a system of traditional medicine native to the Indian subcontinent and a form of alternative medicine. The oldest known Ayurvedic texts are the *Suśrutha Saṃhitā* and the *Charaka Saṃhitā.* These Classical Sanskrit texts form Ayurveda's foundational works. One of the world's oldest medical systems, it originated in India more than three thousand years ago and remains one of the country's traditional health care systems. Its concepts about health and disease endorse the use of herbal compounds, special diets, and other distinctive health practices. The government of India and other institutes around the world support clinical and laboratory research on Ayurvedic medicine within the context of the Eastern belief system. However, Ayurvedic medicine is not widely studied as part of Western styles of medicine.

By the medieval period, Ayurvedic practitioners developed a number of medicinal preparations and surgical procedures. Practices that are derived from Ayurvedic medicine are regarded as part of complementary and alternative medicine along with Siddha and Traditional Chinese Medicine together they form the basis for systems medicine. There are several major areas in Ayurvedic medicine: general medicine, pediatrics, surgery, dentistry, mental illness, toxicology, anti-aging, and aphrodisiacs.

---

7. www.youtube.com/watch?v=XXBQZ0u9Jrw

According to Ayurveda, each of us has a unique mix of three mind and body *doshas* or principles that create specific mental and physical characteristics. Most of us have one or two more dominant doshas with the remaining one(s) less expressed; basically, they describe your constitution. The three doshas are Vata, Pitta, and Kapha. There are a number of free, online self-tests you can take to determine your type. What follows are descriptions for all three types courtesy of the Chopra Center (www.chopra.com):

Vata governs bodily movement as well as the nervous system. It is governed by the element of air. ***Pitta*** controls digestion, metabolism, and energy production. It is ruled by the element of fire. ***Kapha*** governs bodily structure, including muscular formation, cell and bone formation, as well as fat accumulation. It is considered ruled by the earth element.

Yoga

Yoga is another wonderful body movement modality that originated in India within Hindu culture. Nobody knows exactly who invented it; though all the details of the ancient civilization of India are not available to us, sacred texts collectively referred to as the Vedas contain accounts of yoga in the *Rig Veda*, which began to be arranged into a systematic code between 1500 and 1200 BCE. Even still, it would not be accurate to establish the date of yoga from this, as the Rig Veda was orally transmitted for at least a millennium beforehand.

The first yoga text dates to around the second century BCE by Patanjali, who prescribes adherence to "eight limbs" (the sum of which constitute Ashtanga Yoga) to quiet one's mind and merge with the infinite. The first full description of the principles of yoga is found in the *Upanishads*, thought to have been written between the eighth and fourth centuries BC.

The Upanishads are also known as the *Vedanta* since they represent the end or conclusion of the Vedas. Archeological discoveries in the Indus Valley Civilization (c.3300–700 BCE) have been made that depict figures in yoga postures. In modern times, there are fourteen types of yoga. Six of the most popular are described here: [8]

Ashtanga Yoga is six established and strenuous pose sequences, e.g., the primary series, secondary series, tertiary series, and so on, which is practiced sequentially as progress is made. Ashtangis move rapidly, flowing from one pose to the next with each inhalation and exhalation.

Bikram Yoga poses are performed in a sauna-like room. The heat is turned up to nearly 105° F and 40 percent humidity in official Bikram classes; this is to reduce injury by warming the muscles. Bikram yoga (named after its inventor, Bikram Choudhury) is comprised of a series of twenty-six basic yoga postures, each performed twice.

Hatha is one of the six original branches of yoga, encompassing nearly all types of modern yoga. Today, classes described as hatha (alongside vinyasa and prenatal) are typically very basic and traditional in their approach to yogic breathing exercises and postures.

Kundalini is a yoga in which the practitioner is in constant, invigorating poses. The fluidity of the practice is intended to release the kundalini (serpent) energy, located at the root chakra (the base of the spine) in the body and move it upward through the body.

Prenatal Yoga postures are carefully adapted for expectant mothers. Prenatal yoga is tailored to help women in all stages of pregnancy—even getting back in shape post-baby.

---

8. The fourteen types or practices of Yoga to improve health including muscle tone, flexibility and circulation are Anusara, Ashtanga, Bikram, Hatha, Iyengar, Jivamukti, Kripau, Kundalini, Power, Prenatal, Restorative, Sivananda, Viniyoga, and Yin Yoga.

Sivananda Yoga is a slow yoga practice based on a five-point philosophy that proper breathing, relaxation, diet, exercises, and positive thinking work together to form a healthy yogic lifestyle. One of the world's largest schools of yoga, Sivananda was brought to the West by Swami Vishnu-devananda in 1957 and now boasts nine ashrams, seventeen centers, and more than ten thousand teachers worldwide.

III. Medicine of the Future

Nanotechnology and Other Life-extension Strategies

Nanotechnology

Nanotechnology is the science of the *extremely* small, and it holds enormous potential for health care—everything from delivering drugs more effectively, diagnosing diseases more rapidly and accurately, health monitoring, cures for cancer, anti/reverse aging, and delivering vaccines via aerosols and patches.

Nanotechnology is the science of materials at the molecular or subatomic level. It involves manipulation of particles smaller than 100 nanometres (one nanometre is one-billionth of a meter) and the technology involves developing materials or devices within that size—invisible to the naked eye and often many hundred times thinner than the width of a single human hair. The physics and chemistry of materials are radically different when converted to the nanoscale; they have different strengths, conductivity, and reactivity; making use of this discovery could revolutionize medicine.

Because of the variety of potential applications (including industrial and military), governments have invested billions of dollars in nanotechnology research. Through its National Nanotechnology Initiative, the United States has invested 3.7 billion dollars, the European Union has invested 1.2 billion dollars, and Japan 750 million dollars.

The influence of nanotechnology extends from its medical, ethical, legal, and environmental applications to fields such as engineering, biology, chemistry, computing, materials science, and communications. Some significant benefits of nanotechnology include improved manufacturing methods, water purification systems, energy systems, physical enhancement, nanomedicine, better food production methods and nutrition, and large-scale infrastructure auto-fabrication.

China is the leader of nanotechnology research among developing countries; they have registered the most nanotechnology patents and have had a national nanotechnology program since the early 1990s with a huge number of new nanotechnology companies being set up every year. India is also very serious about nanotechnology; more than thirty institutions involved in its research have appeared recently. Other Southeast Asian countries are particularly active, with Malaysia, the Philippines, Thailand, and Vietnam all engaged in nanotechnology research. In Africa, meanwhile, South Africa has both its private and public sector working on nanotechnology research and development. In Latin America, Brazil is leading nanotechnology research and has partnered with South Africa and India, promoting a "South to South" collaboration through the IBSA Nanotechnology Initiative.

What are the other indications for health and longevity using this technology? According to scientist Ray Kurzweil, humans could become immortal in as little as twenty years' time through nanotechnology and an increased understanding of how the body works. He says our knowledge of genes and computer technology is accelerating at such an incredible rate that theoretically, nanotechnologies are capable of replacing many of our vital organs and could be available in the next decade. Mr. Kurzweil adds that although his claims may sound far-fetched, artificial pancreases and neural implants are currently available. In *The Sun*, January 26, 2013, Mr. Kurzweil said:

> "I and many other scientists now believe that in around 20 years we will have the means to reprogram our bodies' stone-age software so we can halt, then reverse, ageing. Then nanotechnology will let

us live forever. Ultimately, nanobots will replace blood cells and do their work thousands of times more effectively. Heart-attack victims—who haven't taken advantage of widely available bionic hearts—will calmly drive to the doctors for a minor operation as their blood bots keep them alive. Nanotechnology will extend our mental capacities to such an extent we will be able to write books within minutes. So we can look forward to a world where humans become cyborgs, with artificial limbs and organs."[9]

While these possibilities are extremely exciting, I'm hoping they will discover other ways to extend our lives without becoming cyborgs; perhaps a *real* golden pill is yet to be produced.

IV. Twenty-first-century Health and Beauty Treatments

Dating back to antiquity, humans have found countless ways to feel and look better, as we have always wished to prolong youth and beauty as long as possible. Some methods are as simple as the use of water. I've experienced many of the following therapies described having owned a day spa in the 1980s and 1990s; they are superb in rejuvenating the body and spirit. Some of them are ancient and others are based on a new understanding of the body, detoxification, and the revitalization of health; let's start with water therapies.

Hydrotherapy

The use and benefit of water to enhance health has been around for centuries. Hydrotherapy is a modern term that involves the use of water for pain relief and various treatments for health benefits. The term encompasses a

---

9. From the articles "Immortality Only 20 Years Away Says Scientist" by Amy Willis of *The Telegraph*, Sept 22, 2009, and "Futurist Ray Kurzweil Predicts In-body Computers and a Potential War with Machines" by Eli Segall of *The Sun*, Jan 26, 2013

broad range of approaches and therapeutic methods that take advantage of the physical properties of water, such as temperature and pressure, for therapeutic purposes, to stimulate blood circulation and treat symptoms of certain diseases.

Various therapies used in the present-day hydrotherapy employ water jets, underwater massage, mineral baths and/or whirlpool bath, hot Roman bath, hot tub, Jacuzzi, cold plunge, and mineral baths. Here are a few popular water techniques used to enhance health that are offered in modern-day health spas around the world; most will offer numerous services:

Roman Bath House: Dating back to 200 BCE, Roman bathhouses are believed to have been one of the first known places of treatment for the immune and circulatory systems. The bath house normally featured a number of hot and cold areas, including warm salt-water pools, cold water pools, steam rooms, and ice-water showers.

Russian Baths: These baths are located in a wooden room heated by rocks that radiate intense heat, while ice cold water is provided to douse your entire body; eliminates toxins while encouraging blood circulation, in addition to boosting your immune system.

Scotch Hose Therapy: Scotch Hose is an invigorating hydrotherapy treatment. The use of alternating warm and cool water, through a high velocity water wand (or hose), is controlled by a body treatment specialist. Scotch Hose units work to speed up the client's metabolism through hot and cold pressurized water and direct contact to the client's specific points of pressure.

Vichy Shower: A kind of shower in which large quantities of warm water are poured over a spa patron while one lies in a shallow wet bed similar to a massage table but with drainage for the water. The city of Vichy, in France, contains five natural mineral springs; these springs inspired the design of the Vichy shower. Some spas use the shower as a complement to massages, wraps and scrubs, while other spas use the Vichy shower as a stand-alone therapeutic treatment. As the showers massage, they stimulate circulation in the body, encouraging the transportation of fluids and blood components to the lymph nodes and back to the heart. This process detoxifies the body, helping it fight infection. The Vichy shower, therefore, can eliminate the negative effects of lymphatic blockage, which include migraine headaches, menstrual cramps, arthritis, fatigue, loss of appetite, depression, acne, and cellulite.

Mineral Spring Baths: Natural mineral springs are located all over the world and have been used for centuries to cure just about everything. There are several notable springs located throughout the Americas, although the traditions surrounding them are much stronger in Europe and Japan.

There are still many to be found in the Americas, such as Desert Hot Springs in California; French Lick, Indiana; Hot Springs, Arkansas; Mineral Wells, Texas; Mount Clemens, Michigan; Saratoga Springs, New York; Steamboat Springs, Colorado; Warm Springs, Georgia; Warm Springs, Virginia; Caxambu, Brazil; Harrison Hot Springs, Canada; Tabacón, Costa Rica; Milk River Bath, Clarendon, Jamaica; Agua Hedionda, Mexico; Termas del Arapey, Uruguay.

Mineral baths are pleasant, relaxing, and perhaps, health-enhancing because they relieve stress. Much of the current research on the health benefits of mineral baths comes from Russia and Eastern Europe, and while treatment (called *Balneotherapy*) is mentioned in Western medical literature, few studies have been translated into English. In both Europe and Japan, hot spring therapy is an accepted and popular treatment for musculoskeletal problems, as well as for high blood pressure, eczema, and a variety of other complaints.

Modern-Day/Ancient Massage Therapies

There is much archaeological evidence that massage has been found in many ancient civilizations, including China, India, Japan, Korea, Egypt, Rome, Greece, and Mesopotamia; however, the Chinese likely have the most primordial recorded history of the therapy. The ancient *Nei Jing* is a compilation of medical knowledge and it's the foundation of Traditional Chinese Medicine; massage is referred to in thirty different chapters. It specifies the use of different massage techniques and how they should be used in the treatment of specific ailments and injuries. So beneficial are they to health and healing, modern-day massage therapies still enjoy a status as highly developed and extremely popular; here are some examples of what is available:

Thai Massage: An ancient Asian practice incorporating the principles of yoga, meditation, and acupressure techniques.

Lymphatic Drainage Massage: A type of gentle massage intended to encourage the natural drainage of the lymph from the tissues space body. In 1936, after four years of research, they introduced this technique in Paris, France.

Maori Massage: This is an ancient art passed down from the Polynesians; some of the forms are Romiromi and Mirimiri. Traditional Romiromi massage and healing combine deep tissue massage, pressure points, and body alignment to help release blocked energy. Mirimiri is a therapeutic massage using native kawakawa oil, which encourages the body to heal itself.

Shiatsu Massage: Shiatsu or finger pressure massage (sometimes called Zen shiatsu) is a Japanese form of physiotherapy. It is often described as the equivalent of acupressure, but this comparison is not entirely accurate because the technique looks beyond specific pressure points, incorporating other methods such as stretching, breathing, and rotating for a more whole-body approach to restoring energy balance.

Lomilomi: This is the word used today to mean massage therapist or more accurately, a Hawaiian massage practitioner. Lomilomi practitioners use the palms, forearms, fingers, knuckles, elbows, knees, feet, and even sticks and stones during treatment.

Ashiatsu: This is a type of massage practiced with one's feet that uses deep compression as well as acupressure to relieve the discomfort and strain of tight muscles.

Champissage: This type of massage is also known as Indian Head Massage. Champissage has been practiced in India for more than a thousand years. It is a form of massage that focuses on the face, head, neck, shoulders, and upper arms.

Lulur: A Javanese body treatment that combines a coconut oil massage, herb and rice exfoliation, a flower-scented bath, and a yogurt-based moisturizer.

Hot Stone Therapy: The application of smooth, basalt mineral stones are heated and combined with oil for a massage designed to relieve muscle stiffness and fatigue while restoring the body's energy.

Myofascial Release Massage (MFR): Fascia is a connective tissue that ensheathes the body's organs, bones, joints, and muscles. It can be damaged by falls, poor posture, repetitive movements and can cause pain and inflexibility. An MFR Massage is very deep and is specifically designed to relax the fascia through the entire body.

Vistasp Therapy: An advanced Ayurvedic (East Indian) technique that uses very precise movements to stimulate nerves and maximize the flow of nutrient-rich blood to the affected areas.

Additional Beauty and Health Techniques

Dead Sea Mud Treatments: An application (as in a wrap or soak) of mineral-rich mud from the Dead Sea used to detoxify skin and body, as well as to ease painful symptoms caused by such conditions as rheumatism and arthritis.

Reflexology: Originating in Egypt and China, this ancient healing therapy makes use of pressure points in the hands and feet to stimulate corresponding organs within the body. This stimulation taps into energy resources, thus creating a balance of the body's energy. The practice has been effective in strengthening the immune system and identifying potential weaknesses within the body.

Reiki: A gentle Japanese technique that employs the laying on of hands to align the individual charkas to assist with the proper flow of energy.

Dry Skin Brushing: Dry brushing is the brushing of the skin with a natural-bristle brush to remove dead skin and impurities while stimulating circulation and the lymph system. It's often used in the preparation of the body for massages, wraps, or body masks.

Sweat Lodge: A spiritual ceremony linked with several Native American cultures taking place in a small, enclosed hut or other structures, and following the tradition of mind, body, and spirit purification. While this ancient technique came into public controversy when the motivational "expert" James Arthur Ray's infamous sweat lodge in Sedona, Arizona, resulted in three deaths, it is a time-honored tradition with many benefits to the body, much like a sauna. I have been in numerous sweat lodges with no negative affects whatsoever, but they were led and conducted by an experienced Indigenous person.

Craniosacral Therapy: This gentle, noninvasive type of bodywork directly influences the brain and spinal cord. It is used to locate and release tension, and calm overly stressed systems and overstimulated nerves.

Paraffin Poultices: Soft, heated compresses of paraffin wax are applied to areas of the body to relieve soreness and inflammation. This treatment can be exceptionally effective in treating arthritis, joint stiffness, and sports-related injuries when combined with massage therapy.

V. Diet, Sleep, and Meditation

Indeed, if you wish to live a long, healthy, and disease-free life, you'll need to keep the following important concepts in mind. Needless to say, you must also have good Feng Shui and a healthy environment.

Diet and Sleep

Water: We begin our journey into this world in water—our mother's womb—and we float in this life-giving fluid (a saline solution) until the moment of birth. In fact, the human body is more than 70 percent water. Our planet is also approximately 70 percent water; it is one of the most complex elements on Earth and is naturally designed to support life.

If eating provides energy for the body, then water is a more vital source of energy than *anything* we eat. It may be shocking to think of water as a nutrient, but it's true: after more than twenty-four years of research exclusively on dehydration, world-renowned Dr. F. Batmanghelidj made some amazing discovering about water, disease, and the many ways the human body demands it.[10]

---

10. Dr. F. Batmanghelidg is a London-educated Iranian medical doctor who has made revolutionary, even controversial discoveries about the water metabolism of the human body. His astounding breakthrough was made while confined in a Teheran prison. Dr. "Batman" is of aristocratic lineage in his native Iran, and was imprisoned along with more than 3,000 other high-born victims during the Khomeini revolution. After his release, he emigrated to America and continued his amazing research on the numerous effects of dehydration, health, and disease. He is the author of numerous books educating people about the significance of water!

According to Dr. Batmanghelidj, the body needs *no less* than two quarts of water and some salt every day to compensate for its natural losses via urine, respiration, and perspiration. By and large, he says, the average-sized body needs about four quarts a day. If you drink bottled water (usually about 16 ounces), that would mean eight bottles a day. He explains that the lungs alone use more than a quart of water a day evaporated when we breathe. If you have health issues, you may need more.

Here's a rule of thumb for those interested in weight-loss: drink half an ounce of water for every pound of body weight per day. For example: someone weighing 200 pounds will need 100 ounces of water daily (a gallon has 128 ounces). Dr. Batmanghelidj recommends drinking two glasses (sixteen ounces) first thing in the morning to compensate for the water loss during the eight hours of sleep. To support weight loss, drink one or two glasses of water before a meal. Two and half hours after you eat, drink another glass to aid in digestion.

According to Dr. Batmanghelidj's more than two decades of study and thousands of letters from those who've drastically improved their health and weight using his recommendations, he identified the numerous benefits of keeping the body properly hydrated in his numerous papers, presentations, and books. Here are but a few:

- Water generates electrical and magnetic energy inside the cells.
- Water prevents damage to the DNA.
- Water increases the efficiency of the immune system.
- Water energizes food.
- Water clears waste from different parts of the body.
- Water is the main lubricant in the joint spaces and prevents arthritis and back pain.

- Water is used in the spinal discs and acts as shock absorption "cushions."
- Water prevents heart attacks and strokes.
- Water prevents clogging of arteries in the heart and brain.
- Water is essential to manufacture of all neurotransmitters, including serotonin.
- Water prevents attention deficit disorder in children and adults.
- Water prevents stress, anxiety, and depression.
- Water makes the skin smooth and prevents aging.
- Water decreases premenstrual pains and hot flashes.
- The human body has no method of storing water to draw on; it must be drunk throughout the day.
- Water takes away morning sickness of pregnancy.
- Water is the best laxative and prevents constipation.
- Water prevents loss of memory as we age.
- Water reverses additive urges including caffeine, alcohol, and some drugs.

To read more amazing benefits of water and how to prevent many conditions and diseases, or to lose weight naturally, refer to Dr. Batmanghelidj's book *Obesity, Cancer, Depression: Their Common Cause & Natural Cure*. In addition to water, the doctor explains the necessity of salt.

Salt: When people get sick and go to the hospital, one of the first things they are given is a saline drip to hydrate and restore electrolyte levels. Salt is a vital substance for the survival of all living creatures, particularly humans, and it has been used through the ages as medicine. The body regulates its water content using water, salt, and potassium. However, in order to work as a healthy supplement; it needs to be unprocessed sea salt, gray salt, or Himalayan salt (pink). Here are some of Dr. Batmanghelidj's findings concerning salt:

- Salt is a strong natural antihistamine and is good for relieving asthma.
- Salt is a strong anti-stress element for the body.
- Salt is vital for the kidneys.
- Salt is essential in the treatment of emotional disorders; lithium is a salt substitute for treating depression of bipolar disease.
- Salt is very effective in stabilizing irregular heartbeat.
- Salt is vital for sleep regulation, it's a natural hypnotic.
- Salt is vital for the treatment of diabetes.
- Salt is vital to the communication and information processing of nerve cells the entire time that the brain cells work—from conception forward.
- Salt is vital for preventing gout.
- Salt prevents muscle cramps.
- Salt is vital for maintaining sexuality and libido.
- Salt is vital for reducing a double chin.
- Salt is essential in preventing varicose veins.
- Sea salt and unrefined salt contain approximately 80 minerals.
- Salt is vital for maintaining muscle tone and strength.

Aspartame: This toxic, poisonous product also goes by the brand names of NutraSweet or Equal and it has FDA approval; even with the overwhelming amount of negative reporting, it remains on the market.

It is now in more than five thousand American food products. Aspartame is banned in several countries because it has been concluded to be dangerous to health.

Dr. Roberts, the director of the Palm Beach Institute for Medical Research, has done extensive research on this product and has coined the phrase "aspartame disease."

According to his findings, typical health symptoms and complaints from users are headaches, dizziness, confusion, memory loss, Alzheimer's disease, seizures, insomnia, chronic fatigue, hypoglycemia, joint pain, hair loss, and skin rashes. In his article "Aspartame Disease: An FDA-Approved Epidemic," Dr. Roberts says:

> "Diet products containing the chemical sweetener aspartame can have multiple neurotoxic, metabolic, allergenic, fetal and carcinogenic effects. My database of 1,200 aspartame reactors—based on logical diagnostic criteria, including predictable recurrence on rechallenge—is reviewed. The existence of aspartame disease continues to be denied by the FDA and powerful corporate entities. Its magnitude, however, warrants removal of this chemical as an 'imminent public health threat.'"

There are healthier replacements for those who are diabetic or for those who wish to restrict sugar intake, including natural products such as Stevia (a plant native to South America) and Lakanto (made from the monk fruit). These products have zero calories and do not elevate/spike glucose levels.

Fresh Food: If you're interested in living healthy, you'll need to be conscious of eating well and making good choices. While there are endless views on the "best" diet, a good rule of thumb is eating closest to nature, meaning foods that are not too far from their original source or form. Once food is overly processed and preservatives are added, it has lost most of its nutritional value and may even be harmful.[11] And if you nuke it, you lose even more. Fresh vegetables and fruits will keep you healthy, and a certain amount of whole grains, proteins, and good fats are also essential. As covered in the section before, lots of water is required to keep the whole body—including the brain—hydrated. Remember, it is a nutrient! Avoid foods that contain hormones or that have been genetically modified.[12] Equally compromising to your health are hydrogenated oils; the hydrogenation process alters oils in such a way that it makes them almost impossible for the body to break it down. Use cold-pressed oils instead.

If you have serious health concerns, you should consult a physician to create a healthy diet plan tailored to your unique constitution and issues. It's also imperative that your environment both inside and out is *not* supporting sickness. We will discuss numerous scenarios in chapters 3 through 5 that can adversely affect your state of health.

Sleep: It may seem overly obvious that sleep is beneficial. Even without fully grasping what sleep does for us, we know that going without sleep for too long makes us feel terrible and look haggard, and

---

11. "10 American Foods that are Banned in Other Countries" by Dr. Mercola; the 10 foods are either loaded with harmful chemicals or drugs to read the article, go to articles.mercola.com/sites/articles/archive/2013/07/10/banned-foods.aspx?e_cid=DNLWelcome_Art1&et_cid=DM43801&et_rid=499100331

12. *Genetically modified foods* (or *GM foods*) are foods produced from organisms that have had specific changes introduced into their DNA using the methods of genetic engineering.

that getting a good night's sleep can make us feel ready to take on the world. Scientists have gone to great lengths to fully understand sleep's benefits. In studies of humans and other animals, they have discovered that sleep plays a critical role in immune function, metabolism, memory, learning, and other vital functions.

Sleep is a subject that many clients ask about, and while I can adjust the Feng Shui of their homes, I can't see what they are eating or drinking which will also affect sleep patterns. For a more restful sleep and for those suffering from insomnia, here are some important ideas to consider: no caffeine after 4 PM, no blue-screen electronics a few hours before bed, no more than a fifteen-minute power nap, and don't eat heavy foods (hard proteins such as meat or cheese) too close to bedtime.

With that said, here are some considerations in Feng Shui terms that can create an environment for a deep, restorative sleep. The bedroom needs to be very yin (dark and cool), no electronic devices, including digital clocks (computers, televisions, and so forth), close off the windows with drapes or blinds, find a great bed direction, limited amount of fire colors (red, purple, or oranges) close off skylights, and no water fountains or fish tanks. The exception to water is the ocean; if you are blessed enough to live next to the ocean and can hear the waves from your bedroom, this is primordial and reminiscent of being in the womb—a deep sleep is almost assured.

Meditation: This is a great way to calm the body and mind and has many health benefits; I've practiced meditation since my mid twenties. Note that I'm not referring to a religious practice or the once very-popular Transcendental Meditation (TM) that promotes stillness for hours on end. Meditation is simply relaxing the body and clearing the mind; this alone will ease many health issues such as high blood pressure, depression, and anxiety. Meditation has been practiced since antiquity; if you wish to start meditating on a regular basis, here are some ideas:

Setting a time: Morning is often preferred because the mind is often much calmer than it is later in the day. If I don't commit to this time of day, I can get very distracted with other concerns. Also, meditating in the morning sets the tone for the rest of my day. However, the best time is the time that you can realistically commit to on a regular basis.

Finding a space: If possible, dedicate a space exclusively to your daily meditation. Choose a relatively protected and quiet space where you can leave your cushion (or chair) so that it is always there.

Posture: Sit on a chair or cushion and sit as upright, tall and balanced as possible. Around a straight spine, let the rest of your skeleton and muscles hang freely. Let your hands rest comfortably on your knees or lap; allow your eyes to close. When I was first learning to meditate, I lit a candle and would stare at the flame until I was totally relaxed. Taking several deep breaths will help you relax the mind and body; make no attempt to manipulate or control the experience.

Meditation CDs: These are a great way to train the mind to go free. There are numerous CDs with soft tones, sounds, and music designed to induce meditation; in fact, they encourage the brain waves to slow down. CDs that have the "Om" sound are really good, or soft nature sounds such as ocean waves will put you into a meditative state rather quickly.

Summary: Things that Will Kill Your Looks and Health

I will state the obvious here, but because the impact on health is so great, it bears repeating. The things that will *kill* your beauty and health are drugs (even prescription ones), EMFs, aspartame, chemicals in processed foods, and smoking; insufficient exercise, sleep, salt, and water; too much sugar, alcohol, and sun (including and *especially* tanning beds)![13, 14] The lack of or overindulgence in these things will compromise almost every organ in your body; avoid them like the plague and you'll be lightyears ahead regarding the quality of your health, retain your looks, and age gracefully well into your senior years. Be responsible for your own health and you'll not need to rely on crippled, ineffective health care systems to secure it. Vibrant health is naturally attractive; take care of your body and it will take care of you—it's an amazing, biological machine!

---

13. "How Sunbathing is More Dangerous Than Driving: Skin Cancer Kills Thousands More People Than Car Accidents Each Year, Study Finds" by Madlen Davies on July 2015. www.dailymail.co.uk/health/article-3154668/How-sunbathing-dangerous-driving-Skin-cancer-kills-thousands-people-car-accidents-year-study-finds.html.

14. In 2013, there were 43,982 drug overdose deaths in the United States, 51.8% were related to pharmaceuticals. Prescription drug overdose now kills more Americans than traffic accidents. www.cdc.gov/drugoverdose/data/overdose.html

Two

The Science of Classical Feng Shui: Premise and Roots

The greatest wealth is health.

Unknown

Over thousands of years of research and development, eventually a cache of Feng Shui formulas were designed to consider the most important areas of life—health, prosperity, and relationships. These various techniques are derived from the basic principles of this science. Almost every book on Feng Shui introduces the legendary precepts of the Ba Gua, Five Elements, Yin-Yang theory, Luo Shu, and He Tu; this often leaves the reader confused as how to apply them. Think of these tools as ingredients; they are flour, sugar, butter, milk, spices, and eggs. From them an endless variety of goodies can be created; in this case, Feng Shui techniques/formulas in every diverse form.

The tools in this chapter are principles and building blocks, not standalone formulas or methods. For instance, the Ba Gua was never intended to be superimposed over your floor plan and "energize" the south with fire or the north with a fish tank, as many books maintain.

Rather, the Ba Gua is an energy map, which secrets are unlocked when combined with actual Feng Shui formulas. Without question, Feng Shui experts will consider the ideology of the eight Guas and their extensive layers when examining a site or structure's energy.

If you have many books on Feng Shui, you may have never heard them explained in this manner, so at least skim over these basic building blocks of Feng Shui even if you are somewhat familiar.

If this is your very first Feng Shui book, take a few minutes to peruse these important ideas. This section of the book is not for implementation; it is informative.

Feng Shui is part of Chinese metaphysics, a huge body of knowledge comprised of five major categories of study. All five categories (aka the "five arts") start out with the same energy tools—the Ba Gua, five elements, yin-yang, among others—and develop into different branches of study with their specialized focus.

We'll start with the five arts and then briefly discuss, one by one, the fascinating energy tools that create the foundation of Feng Shui.

Classical Feng Shui is just one of the five main art-sciences of Chinese metaphysics. Deeply rooted in the *I Ching* and the Tao, these philosophical tenets—mountain, medicine, divination, destiny, and physiognomy—are the origin of the Chinese culture developed over five thousand years. It is said that a person able to master just one of these studies would have made a significant lifetime accomplishment.

The Five Metaphysical Arts (Wu Shu)

Mountain (Shan or Xian Xue): This category encompasses philosophy, including the teachings of the fourth-century-BCE philosophers

Lao Tzu and Zhuang Zi, Taoism, martial arts, Qi Gong, Tai Chi Chuan, meditation, healing, and diet. This category also includes the study of alchemy—the science of prolonging life through specific rituals and exercises, which are deeply rooted in Taoism.

Medicine (Yi): The Chinese follow an integrated, holistic, and curative approach to medicine: acupuncture, herbal prescriptions, and massage fall into this category.

Divination (Po): The Chinese are acknowledged for creating systems of cultivating intuition as well as symbols to be read and interpreted. The divination techniques of Da Liu Ren, Tai Yi Mystical Numbers, Qi Men, and Mei Hua Xin Yi (Plum Blossom oracle) employ numbers to predict everything from wars to missing persons to the details of one's past and future.

Destiny (Ming): Most forms of Chinese augury seek to interpret fate and determine the timing of life events; the ancient sages devoted much time and research to this study. The most popular methods of Chinese fortune telling include *Zi Wei Dou Shu* (Purple Star Astrology) and *BaZi* (literally means "eight characters" but is also commonly known as the Four Pillars of Destiny), both of which examine a person's destiny and potential based on their date and time of birth. A complimentary form of Ming is the Science of Divination (*Bu Shi*), which is analogous to the mathematics of probability.

Physiognomy (Xiang Xue): Grandmaster Yap Cheng Hai refers to this category as *Sow,* and it involves making predictions based on the image, form, and features of landscape, the human face and palms, architecture, and gravesites. Feng Shui is the fortune telling of a building by rendering an accurate observation of the structure's appearance, shape, direction, and other surrounding environmental features.

The Nature of Chi

The Purpose: Energy (chi) permeates our Universe; Feng Shui evaluates the quality of energy at property sites and in living spaces

Chi simply means energy; the ancient Chinese were one of the first cultures to discover that humans and our entire universe are comprised of pure energy. Modern-day science confirms this. Also spelled "qi" (either spelling is pronounced *chee*), it is the life-force energy of the universe, heaven, earth, and human. Sometimes it is also referred to as the "cosmic breath," present in every living and nonliving entity; it can be auspicious, inauspicious, or benign. Chi is the life-force energy that pervades humanity's existence; it is the unseen force moving through the human body and the environment. It is energy that determines the shape and form of the landscape as well as the vitality of all living things. The famous Tai Chi symbol, which resembles two interlocking fish, demonstrates the polarity of energy—either yin (female) or yang (male).

Figure 1: The famous Tai Chi symbol representing polarity.

While China had this secret knowledge for thousands of years, it was unknown to most of the world, including us in the West. Chi is called the "dragon's cosmic breath" and key to good Feng Shui; in fact, the science implies the presence and accumulation of auspicious chi along with protection against killing chi.

The Eight Guas or Trigrams

The Purpose: Feng Shui uses the Guas (Trigrams) to represent the eight directions

Also known as Trigrams, the concept of the Guas dates back to Chinese antiquity. These important symbols give a macro, inclusive perspective of our universe, energy, and direction. Each of the eight Guas is comprised of three lines either solid or broken. The broken lines indicate yin or female energy while the solid lines represent yang or male energy. The three lines also represent the cosmology of heaven, earth, and humans. The famous Ba Gua includes all eight trigrams: *Ba* means the number eight and *Gua* means "the result of divination."

The eight Guas, in addition to representing the eight directions, have several layers of information that becomes useful in assessing the energy of land, homes, or buildings. This information was related to everyday life such that there is a Gua representing the father, mother, eldest son, eldest daughter, and so forth. In the end, each Gua represents yin or yang energy, relates to a family member, an element, a body part, or possible related illness, a season, a number, human personality types, direction, and a natural and human phenomenon. Additionally, they have numerous interpretations and slight distinctions that can be overwhelming to the Feng Shui novice. All the same, these implications and interpretations have great significance in Feng Shui and other Chinese metaphysical studies. The eight Guas are Kan, Gen, Chen, Xun, Li, Kun, Dui, and Chien representing north, northeast, east, southeast, south, southwest, west, and northwest, respectively.

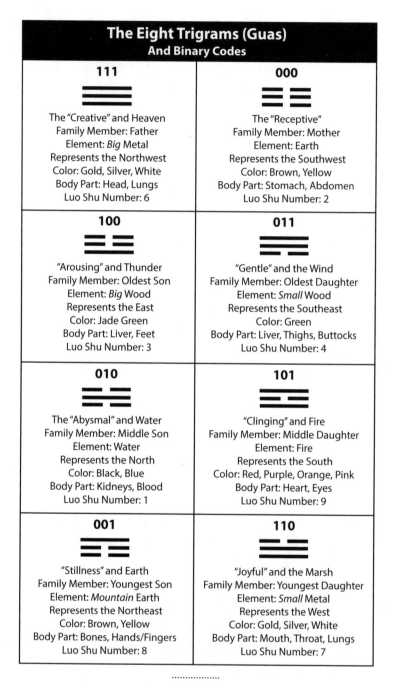

The Eight Trigrams (Guas) **And Binary Codes**	
111 The "Creative" and Heaven Family Member: Father Element: *Big* Metal Represents the Northwest Color: Gold, Silver, White Body Part: Head, Lungs Luo Shu Number: 6	**000** The "Receptive" Family Member: Mother Element: Earth Represents the Southwest Color: Brown, Yellow Body Part: Stomach, Abdomen Luo Shu Number: 2
100 "Arousing" and Thunder Family Member: Oldest Son Element: *Big* Wood Represents the East Color: Jade Green Body Part: Liver, Feet Luo Shu Number: 3	**011** "Gentle" and the Wind Family Member: Oldest Daughter Element: *Small* Wood Represents the Southeast Color: Green Body Part: Liver, Thighs, Buttocks Luo Shu Number: 4
010 The "Abysmal" and Water Family Member: Middle Son Element: Water Represents the North Color: Black, Blue Body Part: Kidneys, Blood Luo Shu Number: 1	**101** "Clinging" and Fire Family Member: Middle Daughter Element: Fire Represents the South Color: Red, Purple, Orange, Pink Body Part: Heart, Eyes Luo Shu Number: 9
001 "Stillness" and Earth Family Member: Youngest Son Element: *Mountain* Earth Represents the Northeast Color: Brown, Yellow Body Part: Bones, Hands/Fingers Luo Shu Number: 8	**110** "Joyful" and the Marsh Family Member: Youngest Daughter Element: *Small* Metal Represents the West Color: Gold, Silver, White Body Part: Mouth, Throat, Lungs Luo Shu Number: 7

Figure 2: The Eight Guas representing the eight directions.

Tien-Di-Ren (The Three Types of Luck/Opportunities)

The Purpose: To understand that excellent Feng Shui covers roughly 65 to 80 percent of your overall luck and opportunities

> "*Heaven Luck* is the boat given to you by God. *Earth Luck* is the wind that fills the sails and the currents of the ocean. *Man Luck* is the way in which you use the wind and the currents to steer your boat."—Grandmaster Yap Cheng Hai

The three types of luck (opportunities), known as Tien-Di-Ren, are Heaven Luck, Earth Luck, and Man Luck. Each one of these categories will visit you in a very different way. This aspect of Feng Shui is called the Cosmic Trinity; in other words, all three areas will influence your life and living space.

"*Heaven Luck* is the boat given to you by God." This category of luck is often referred to as destiny or karma. What goes around comes around; past deeds—for good or evil—will visit you again in this life. They also contend that this area of luck is fixed and may not be influenced; it counts as a third of your overall luck and opportunities in life.

"*Earth Luck* is the wind that fills the sails and the currents of the ocean." This category is the dominion of Feng Shui. If your home site and living space has auspicious and harmonious energy, you will reap the rewards. Additionally, life will support your efforts, goals, relationships, health, and prosperity if this aspect is taken care of. In Earth Luck, you have total control and it can exceed the normal third associated with it if you have superior energy at home and work; Grandmaster Yap purports that it can be raised to two-thirds.

"*Man Luck* is the way in which you use the wind and the currents to steer your boat." This category of luck is another area in which you have total control. You create your own efforts and make your own choices in life. This may include your education, morals, hard work, beliefs, and your ability to seize and exploit good opportunities that might present themselves. This area accounts for approximately a third of your overall luck.

The He Tu and Luo Shu

The Purpose: Feng Shui uses these numerical diagrams to unlock the secrets of universal energy

These two, very distinct mathematical diagrams representing universal energy are so endemic to Chinese culture that its people are often referred to as the "He-Luo culture."

The progenitors of Classical Feng Shui, these famous diagrams are frequently mentioned in ancient Chinese literature, and together they form the foundation of Chinese philosophy.

Comprised of a series of lines connected with black and white dots in both diagrams, most scholars believe the He Tu chronicles the cycle of birth, while the Luo Shu represents the process of death—yang and yin, respectively.

Ancient lore surrounding the He Tu began with the reign of the legendary shaman king Fu Xi, who was supposedly born in 29 BCE. Fu Xi witnessed a mythical dragon-horse bearing strange, unusually patterned markings on its back emerge from the mighty Yellow River.

This design became known as the He Tu (pronounced "hur too"). Fu Xi examined these markings (see figure 3), and they revealed valuable information pertaining to cosmic laws of the universe.

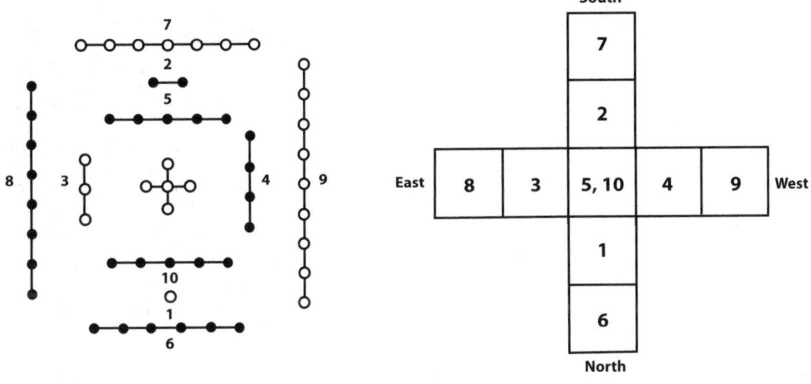

Figure 3: The He Tu diagram pertaining to cosmic energy dating back to the 29th century.

The dots (black are yin and white are yang) of the He Tu illustrate several concepts including direction, the five elements of Feng Shui, and the flow of chi.

Following Fu Xi's life, succeeding scholars meticulously preserved and passed down the mysteries of the He Tu.

Even today, it is found in written texts and ancient scrolls pervading Eastern philosophies and ideologies, including Traditional Chinese Medicine and some of Feng Shui's basic principles.

The Five Element theory—how water, wood, fire, earth, and metal work together—has its basis in the He Tu; these elements identify, interpret, and predict natural phenomena.

Though the Guas (trigrams) would make their formal appearance much later, the theories and principles described in the He Tu gave birth to the first Ba Gua, known as the Early Heaven Ba Gua (Xien Tien Ba Gua).

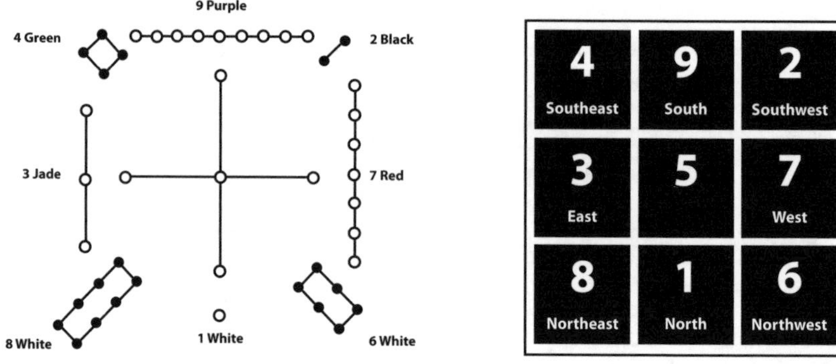

Figure 4: The Luo Shu representing movement of energy dates back to 2100 BCE.

The Luo Shu is also surrounded by legend and myth. One day while sitting beside the River Luo, Emperor Yu of the Xia Dynasty (in or around 2100 BCE) saw a giant turtle emerge from the water; its shell featured a pattern and series of black and white dots on its back. From this, he created the Luo Shu, a nine-square grid containing nine numbers. Each of the nine numbers represents a trigram, body organ, family member, direction, or element and is either male or female energy. Interestingly, no matter which way you add the numbers in the grid they total 15; thus the Luo Shu is often referred to as the "Magic Square of 15." This arrangement of numbers became part of the Later Heaven Ba Gua (LHB). The Luo Shu is used extensively in all methods and applications of Classical Feng Shui.

The Luo Shu and He Tu are coded diagrams that represent the cosmology of heaven and earth; they are energy maps that are included in virtually every Feng Shui formula and system. These ancient oracles are considered the backbone of Chinese metaphysics; unlocking their mysteries takes many years of study, contemplation, and a learned teacher.

The Five Elements: Wu Xing

The Purpose: All energy is placed into five categories

> "If you wish to master Feng Shui, you must master the Five Elements."—Grandmaster Yap Cheng Hai

As with most brilliant discoveries made by man, nature served as the inspiration.

In ancient China, they paid close attention to the predicable cycles of energy—fire burns wood, metal comes from the earth. By associating this information with the human body and everyday life and events, the Five Element theory was created.

They knew energy was part of everything, by placing pervasive energy into five categories, it offered a viable solution in assessing its interaction with one another. These five categories or five phases of energy are known as Wu Xing.

The five elements are metal (jin—literally the word for gold), wood (mu), water (shui), fire (ho), and earth (tu). Each element is a representation of matter and energy as it coalesces from one form to the next.

The Five Element theory simply elucidates the relationship among different types of energy; it is understood as both figurative and literal for Feng Shui applications.

The premise of the Five Elements is used in virtually every study of Chinese metaphysics—Feng Shui, astrology, Traditional Chinese Medicine, and martial arts.

If you wish to master Feng Shui, you must master the Five Elements. The Five Elements have three cycles—productive, weakening, and controlling.

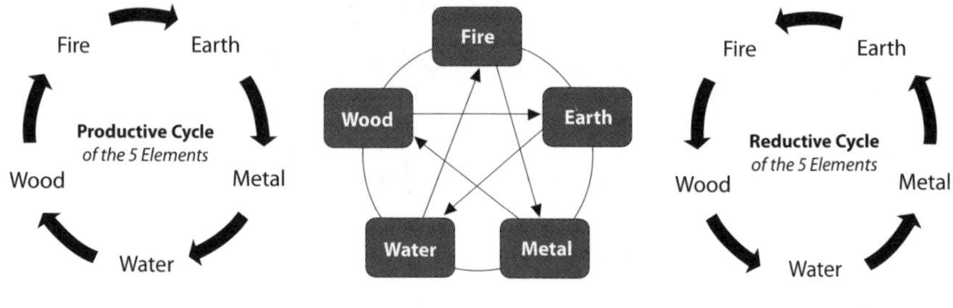

Figure 5: The Three Cycles of the Five Elements: Productive, Controlling, Reductive.

Productive Cycle: This important cycle produces or gives birth to something. Wood feeds fire. Fire produces ash and creates earth. Earth gives birth to metal. Metal melts to a fluid and becomes water, which in turn produces wood.

The Weakening or Reductive Cycle: This process is the reverse of the productive cycle, because what we give birth to weakens us. Wood stokes fire; therefore, fire weakens wood. Fire generates ash and creates earth; therefore, earth weakens fire. Earth produces metal; therefore, metal weakens earth. Metal melts to a fluid and produces water; therefore, water weakens metal. Water produces wood; therefore, wood weakens water.

The Controlling or Destructive Cycle: This process can conquer, control, or destroy. Water extinguishes fire, fire melts metal, and metal cuts wood. Wood, in the form of plants or tree roots, controls the earth by breaking it apart or keeping it together. Earth is big enough to hold water—without earth, water would have no boundary or shape.

Note: Body organs are also placed in one of the five elements' category; see the chart in chapter 5 on Flying Stars.

Element	Color	Shape	Physical Objects	Direction	Properties	Number
Wood	Greens	Tall and rectangular	Trees, plants, furniture, bamboo, tall objects	**East Southeast**	Grows upwards, tall and outwards	**3, 4**
Fire	Red, purple	Pointed and triangular	Stoves, fireplaces, grills, TVs, computers, lamps, electrical towers	**South**	Heat, radiates and spreads in every direction	**9**
Earth	Brown, terra-cotta	Square	Mountains, granite, stone, boulders, rocks	**Southwest Northeast**	Attractive, dense, stable, centered	**2, 5, 8**
Metal	Silver, Gold	Round and spherical	Swords, knives, coins, bronze, gold, silver	**Northwest West**	Piercing, pointed and sharp	**6, 7**
Water	Blue, black	Wavy	Ocean, lakes, ponds, pools, fountains	**North**	Unfettered, free, runs to low ground	**1**

Figure 6: The Five Element chart.

The Two Ba Guas

The Purpose: The Two Ba Guas are the Mother to all Feng Shui Formulas/Techniques

Likely the second most recognizable image after the Tai Chi symbol is the Ba Gua, but most people aren't aware that there are actually two. The Ba Gua appears in all Feng Shui books; it is an octagonal map that depicts the eight trigrams. The two Ba Guas are the Early Heaven Ba Gua, *Fu Xi* or *Xien Tien Ba Gua*, and Later Heaven Ba Gua (*Ho Tien* or *Wen Wang Ba Gua)*. Both are used in the practice of Classical Feng Shui as all formulas, methods, and techniques are born from the two arrangements of the Guas.

The Early Heaven Ba Gua (EHB), which dates back approximately 6,000 years, depicts the polarities in nature. It reflects an ideal world of harmony in which chi is in a constant, perfect state of polarization. The eight Guas, or trigrams, create a conceptual model that marks the changes in energy.

The Early Heaven Ba Gua, representing a "perfect" world, can be commonly seen over doorways to repel negative energy; used extensively in Westernized styles of Feng Shui. It has more profound implications and uses in Classical Feng Shui as it is the basis of complex formulas, primarily water/road formulas.

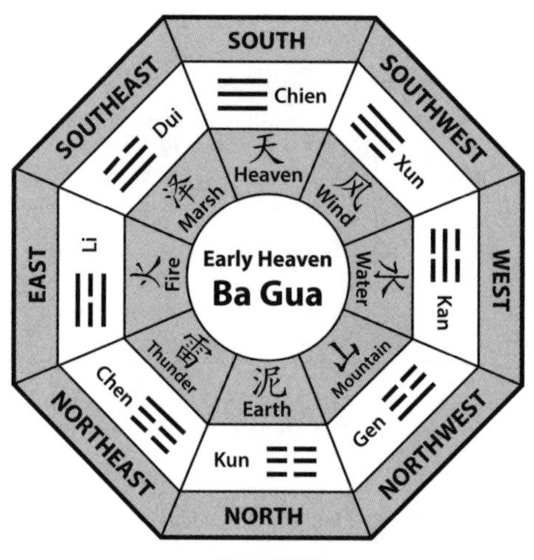

Figure 7: Early Heaven Ba Gua (EHB).

The Later Heaven Ba Gua (*Ho Tien* or *Wen Wang Ba Gua)* was the brilliant work of King Wen, a Chou Dynasty ruler who elaborated on Fu Xi's earlier diagrams. This arrangement was done to represent the cyclical forces of nature. The Later Heaven Ba Gua (LHB) describes the patterns of environmental changes. Unlike Earlier Heaven Ba Gua, the LHB is dynamic, not static; it represents the ever-changing structure of the universe and the circular nature of life. Many Feng Shui applications stem from the understanding of the Later Heaven Ba Gua. For instance, the Luo Shu is the numerical representation of the Later Heaven Ba Gua.

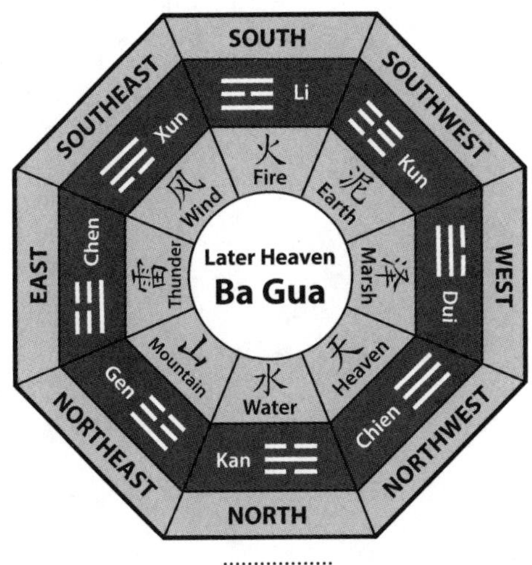

Figure 8: Later Heaven Ba Gua (LHB).

The Chinese Luo Pan

The Purpose: Feng Shui measures directional energy via a compass

A Luo Pan is a professional instrument; you need not purchase one to implement the Feng Shui recommendations found in this book. A simple hiking compass or an app on your smartphone will suffice.

The ancient Chinese were the first to discover the magnetic compass, having this valuable tool hundreds of years before the West. The lore surrounding its discovery sounds like something out of a movie: the Warrior Goddess of the Nine Heavens presented the Yellow Emperor, Huangdi, the first ruler of a united China, with a compass to find his way out of the fog and defeat his enemies. Other stories tell about Huangdi's unique invention, a compass cart that leads to victory.

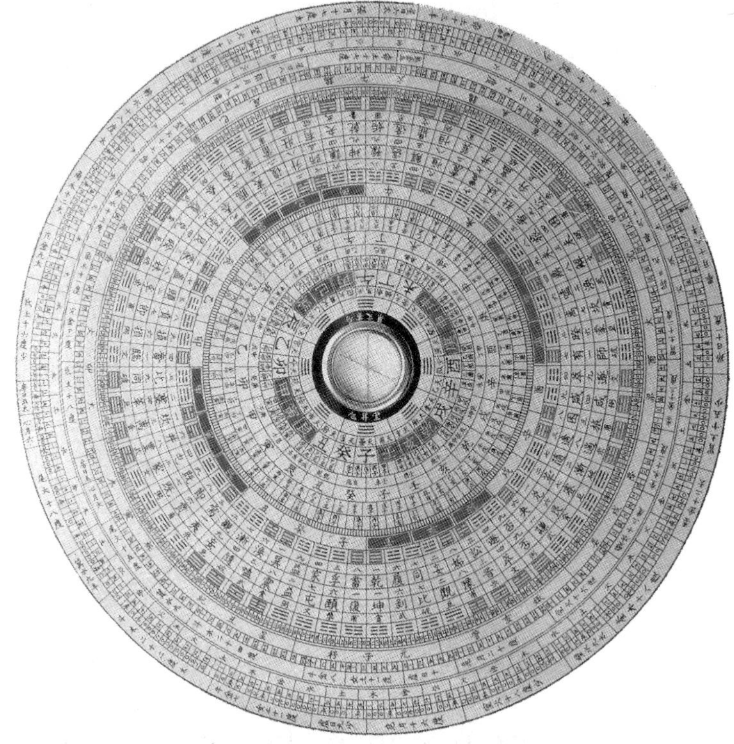

Figure 9: A Chinese Luo Pan (compass).

Throughout its illustrious and long history, the Luo Pan has been redesigned and refined many times over so that it would align with the latest discoveries relating to landforms, techniques, and directional energy. There are two standard types of Luo Pan—San He and San Yuan—designed to include formulas of these two main disciplines of Feng Shui. The third standard Luo Pan is the Chung He, which combines the most important information of the San He and San Yuan Luo Pans.

The purpose of the Luo Pan is the same as a conventional compass—to locate direction. However, the Luo Pan contains some very important differences. A typical compass may display four or eight directions. A Luo Pan divides up the 360 degrees into twenty-four sectors; this is derived by dividing the forty-five degrees of the eight directions into three fifteen-degree increments (3 x 8 = 24). This is very fundamental in Classical Feng Shui, and the ring on the Luo Pan is known as the 24 mountain ring (not actual mountains; only a traditional term). The Luo Pan is an impressive and beautiful instrument, truly a work of art and well worth the several hundred dollars it usually commands. Here are the three types:

San Yuan Luo Pan: Used in the Flying Stars and the Xuan Kong systems, the San Yuan Luo Pan is readily identified by the 64 hexagrams of the I Ching ring. It has only one 24 mountain ring. The first ring of this Luo Pan is always the Later Heaven Ba Gua arrangement of trigrams.

San He Luo Pan: The San He Luo Pan, used for San He formulas and schools, is easily identified by its three 24 mountain rings. These rings are used to measure direction, mountains, and water as each of these elements has distinctly different energy; however, these rings also relate to the three harmonies associated with this school.

Chung He Luo Pan: Also spelled or referred to as Zong He, Zhung He, or Chong He. This Luo Pan is an amalgamation of the San He and San Yuan compasses. This is a great instrument for practitioners who use both systems. Though some rings have been eliminated for size considerations, all essential rings are in place.

Due to the explosive worldwide interest in learning Classical Feng Shui, many modern Luo Pans have some English; personally, I believe learning the Chinese connects you to its ancient and illustrious past. The Luo Pan is often called the "universe on a plate" and it is the quintessential and indispensable instrument of ancient and modern Feng Shui masters. To learn more about the Luo Pan and its history, refer to Stephen Skinner's 2010 book, *Guide to the Feng Shui Compass* (Golden Hoard Press), the most comprehensive book ever written on the subject.

Good Feng Shui ensures that your family and all the residents under your roof are safe, secure, and stable. Living within the protective embrace of excellent energy will help you avert accidents and overcome life's obstacles. In addition, good Feng Shui that comes from well-placed enhancers can bring longevity, good health, success, wealth, and great relationships. Furthermore, the Feng Shui formulas discussed in this book add a stunning dimension to this wonderful practice. No two properties are alike; so let's begin to explore how you may start analyzing your site and living space for better health. In the next chapter, you will learn about landforms and modern products that can seriously harm your body and health; having any of them may require your immediate attention.

Part II
Feng Shui Systems to Enhance Healthy Living

Three

Unhealthy and/or Detrimental Formations, Devices & Environments

The appearance of a disease is swift as an arrow; its disappearance slow, like a thread.
Chinese Proverb

Before we delve into the two most popular systems to enhance longevity and to create a healthy environment, let's discuss some scenarios that can be detrimental and counterproductive to securing vitality. Having some of these situations could compromise the great Feng Shui you may have in the Flying Stars and Eight Mansions.

Feng Shui afflictions and detrimental formations can take different forms as a result of a whole mélange of circumstances. These afflictions can be caused by phenomena in proximity to your property such as physical structures, mountains, landscape, water, the building's door orientation, or simply that the energy has changed over time. Here we'll explore some of those afflictions that will need to be addressed if they have played havoc in your life, particularly with health. Our modern world bears little resemblance to that of ancient China. There are more people who live in cities than in open landscapes when Feng Shui was in its infancy. Although Feng Shui is as viable as ever, it must be practiced with a more expansive, broader view and interpretation. High-rise buildings are like mountains, cell phones and computers are fire, and highways/roads are fast-moving rivers. Unlike our ancestors, we live in a society that incorporates more technology, pollution, toxic waste, smog, adulteration of our food, air, and water—not to mention what the normalized, fast-paced lifestyle and daily stress has done to our health and state of mind.

Even though humankind has done little to consider how we're building and designing our modern-day working and living spaces beyond aesthetics—individually, we must. Feng Shui is all about engendering an atmosphere conducive to securing and achieving a healthy and successful life. With this in mind, Feng Shui as it was developed over time came to include comprehensive techniques to determine what would affect our well-being, create disease, and cause stress in the human body. The following are some of the most pronounced ways in which your health could be compromised in some general Feng Shui categories: 1) Fire, 2) Form and Shape, 3) Water, 4) Mountains, and 5) Other Negative Scenarios.

How Fire Affects Health

In the ancient world, fire referred to actual fire such as candles, fireplaces, torches, wood-burning stoves, and oil-burning lamps. In the modern world, all these things are also fire *in addition to* "virtual fire" such as electrical towers, electric or gas stoves, electric or gas fireplaces, televisions, cell phones, radar devices, GPS satellites, transmission lines, microwave ovens, electrical panels, computers, and radio and TV broadcast systems to name a few; many of which emit ELF emissions (*extremely low frequency),* electromagnetic radiation fields generated by common electrical appliances.

Real Fire in Feng Shui Affecting Health

Electric Stoves, Gas Stoves, Ovens, Kitchens, and Fireplaces

Location of Fire in the House

Indicates heart attacks and high-blood pressure

It is very inauspicious and taboo to place a kitchen, stove, fireplace, or fire pit in the dead center of the home or business. A stove on an island is worst of all; generally, they are located right in the *center of the kitchen*, not necessarily in the center of the house. According to Grandmaster Yap, you will never see kitchen islands in Asia although they are hugely popular in almost all Westernized countries. I have noticed that this scenario will almost always affect the man of the house more than the woman. A client of mine in Phoenix had a fireplace in the center of the house; she contacted me after seeing my interview on a local television station. Her first husband had died of a heart attack a couple of years before, and she was remarried to an old friend who had issues with high blood pressure—I recommended that she rarely (if ever) use the fireplace. While the lovely marble-encased fireplace could not be moved, not lighting the fire would help calm the energy. On a related note, candles are not considered powerful enough to affect you one way or another in the center of the house or other locations.

Kitchen and Stove Locations

If badly placed indicate cancer, high-blood pressure, and heart attacks

The location of your kitchen—more importantly, the stove—will affect your health. A badly placed stove will "burn up" your health or "stoke" illness, disease, and cancer. It can cause infertility or miscarriages. Stoves (fire) will affect your health for better or worse, so pay close attention to the section on the Eight Mansions to find your personal health area known as the Tien Yi (+80). The home's most important fire, the stove, should not be located here. If so, you may suffer from serious health issues.

Virtual Fire in Feng Shui Affecting Health

EMFs, Computers, Microwaves, Cell Phones, Fluorescent Lighting, High Voltage Electrical Towers, Electrical Hubs, Electric Blankets, and Televisions

We are constantly bombarded by electromagnetic fields (EMFs) that can harm us and our health depending on how close we live to them and how we use our in-home devices; walls, of course will insulate us from some of it. Other modern creations that can harm us and our environment are secret projects such as HAARP located near Gakona, Alaska.

This negative technology (concepts from Nikola Tesla) could have been used for good, but in fact is/has been used for ill; it became fully operational in 1998.[15] In 2010, I met one of the scientists who worked on HAARP in the early days, and she thought, and was led to believe, it was being designed to help mankind. It was shut down in 2014; ownership was transferred to the University of Alaska–Fairbanks in 2015.

> "We don't realize that we are exposed to hundreds of thousands times more electromagnetic fields than in past generations. In fact, scientists estimate that your daily exposure to EMF radiation is 100 Million times higher today than it was in your grandparents' time!"[16]

Human beings, and all living creatures for that matter, have their own electromagnetic energy balance. Since our first moments on Earth, we have met with external EMFs as part of the energetic continuum. Planet Earth is naturally webbed with simple EMFs that are interconnected

---

15. The *High Frequency Active Auroral Research Program* (HAARP) was an ionospheric research program jointly funded by the U.S. Air Force, the U.S. Navy, the University of Alaska, and the Defense Advanced Research Projects Agency (DARPA). Read more in the book by Dr. Nick Begich entitled *Angels Don't Play This Haarp—Advances in Tesla Technology.*

16. Reported by EMFNews.org

with astrophysical activities such as solar flares and other atmospheric events such as lightning. Earth itself contains an iron core that generates a halo of electromagnetic energy, reaching far beyond our atmosphere. Life on Earth has adapted to and existed in this natural electromagnetic environment for millions of years. However, in the last century, we have in a most aggressive way, altered our environment. It's now saturated with powerful human-made EMFs, the likes of which have never been seen. The energy fields created by humans have a different resonance, coherence, and frequency from naturally occurring EMFs and the negative effects on human biology is just beginning to be understood. In fact, EMF pollution may be the most significant form of pollution that humans have produced in this century, all the more dangerous because it is invisible.

While it is true that magnetic fields can penetrate biological organisms, the ones of most concern are those that are very strong, near the body, or of high frequency. Strong fields are generated by transformers in electronic equipment, motors and generators, and wires carrying a high current. In the home, the largest fields come from microwave ovens, computers, and televisions. Smaller fields may also be an issue for health such as electric blankets or laptop computers as these directly touch the body. Other products emit high frequency energy such as fluorescent lights and cellular phones; these too will affect your health.

There is much controversy over the effects of electromagnetic fields (EMF) on the human body and health. One thing is certain: the level of electro-pollution is at an all-time high and rising, and coincidentally, so are human diseases. The modern-day "fire" affecting health and longevity are discussed below.

Computers

Indicate headaches and eye strain

The modern convenience known as the PC (personal computer) has quickly become a necessity in our lives. In contrast are the large mainframe computers used by corporations and government organizations in which several people may access or process information, often at the same time. Computers are in almost all businesses around the world, and people are constantly in front of them.

Since computers are here to stay, it's essential that we take precautions to safeguard our health. Research on how prolonged use and viewing of PC monitors and laptop screens can cause headaches is still ongoing. Computers emit electromagnetic radiation; take frequent breaks—it may eventually affect your eyesight and vision.

In a recent, scientific study in Russia using lab rats, it was found that chronic radiation by the video terminal of a personal computer can: lead to the acceleration of sexual maturation and premature termination of the reproductive function; decreases the nocturnal level of melatonin (causing insomnia); alter blood serum in females (but not males); and has a marked biological effect that may affect adversely the health of users.[17]

In an article in the magazine *For Women First,* a woman was reported to suffer from extreme exhaustion and was "barely hanging on"; she was only thirty-nine years old.[18] She reported not being able to sleep, sledgehammer headaches, brain fog, scary heart palpitations, muscle weakness, and impaired immunity. Doctors could not figure out what was wrong with her. One day, she came across an article on the negative effects of blue light (an artificial bandwidth of artificial light emitted by cell phone, laptop, tablet, and e-reader screens). She learned that using these devices in the evening meant that the light frequency they emitted interfered with her sleep-regulating hormones. It also was responsible for all her other symptoms. She says she was stunned to find this out, and once she

17. From a study entitled "Effect of Irradiation from a Personal Computer Video Terminal on Estrus Function, Melatonin Level, and Free Radical Processes in Laboratory Rodents" www.ncbi.nlm.nih.gov/pubmed/9567194. Source: *PubMed*; U.S. National Library of Medicine and National Institute of Health.

18. From the article "I Cured My Fatigue in 3 Days!" by Jessica Drummond in *For Women First* magazine; May 12, 2014.

stopped using these devices after 8 PM, her energy returned and she started feeling like herself again after only three days.

Microwaves

Compromise health and affect the heart

Another modern convenience introduced almost forty years ago, using the microwave on a daily basis has the ability to really compromise our health; we are ingesting food cooked by electromagnetic radiation. Microwaves heat food by causing water molecules in it to resonate at very high frequencies and eventually turn to steam, which heats your food.

While this rapidly heats food, what most people fail to understand is that it also alters foods' chemical structure. We've all experienced some foods coming out rubbery from being "nuked."

Microwaving distorts and deforms the molecules of whatever food or other substances are subjected to it. An example of this is blood products. Blood is normally warmed before being transfused into a person. Research now proves that microwaving blood products damages the blood components. In fact, one woman died after receiving a transfusion of microwaved blood in 1989, the result of which was a well-publicized lawsuit.[19]

Another problem with microwave ovens is that carcinogenic agents can leach out of your plastic and paper containers/covers, and into your food. The January/February 1990 issue of *Nutrition Action Newsletter* reported the leakage of numerous toxic chemicals from the packaging of common microwavable foods, including pizzas, French fries, and popcorn. Chemicals included polyethylene terephthalate (PET), benzene, toluene, and xylene. Microwaving fatty foods in plastic containers leads to the release of dioxins (known carcinogens) and other toxins into your food.

---

19. Source from the *Wyoming State Law Library*; the case of Norma Levitt, who died on November 8, 1989.

A new study confirms that microwaves affect the heart: Dr. Magda Havas of Trent University led a study that discovered *immediate and dramatic changes in both heart rate and heart rate variability caused by approved devices that generate microwaves at levels well below federal guidelines (0.3 percent) in both Canada and the United States.*[20]

Some excellent scientific data has been gathered regarding the detrimental effects of microwaves on the nutrients in our food.[21] As far as common health issues associated with microwave use, it has been documented that people who have been exposed to high levels of microwave radiation may experience a variety of conditions and symptoms such as insomnia, night sweats, various sleep disturbances, headaches dizziness, swollen lymph nodes, weakened immune system, impaired cognition, depression, irritability, nausea, appetite loss, vision and eye problems, frequent urination, and extreme thirst.

There has been almost twenty years of research into the safety health concerns regarding microwaves, primarily in Russia, but in-depth studies have been conducted in Germany (they invented it during WWII to heat food for soldiers) and Japan as well. The Russians first banned the microwave only to release it again with dire warnings concerning its use. Powerwatch was able to summarize the findings from that research as follows: [22]

- Russian investigators found that carcinogens were formed from the microwaving of nearly all foods tested.
- The microwaving of milk and grains converted some of the amino acids into carcinogenic substances.

---

20. Studies done by Dr. Magda Havas of Trent University.

21. From an article entitled "Why Did the Russians Ban an Appliance Found in 90% of American Homes?" By Dr. Joseph Mercola. A study published in the November 2003 issue of *The Journal of the Science of Food and Agriculture.*

22. *Powerwatch* has been researching the links between electromagnetic fields (EMFs) and health risks for about 20 years, and is completely independent of government and industry. They were formed in the UK in 1988.

- Microwaving prepared meats caused d-Nitrosodienthanolamines (a well-known carcinogen).
- Thawing frozen fruits by microwave converted their glucoside and galactoside fractions into carcinogenic substances.
- Extremely short exposure of raw, cooked or frozen vegetables converted their plant alkaloids into carcinogens.
- Carcinogenic free radicals were formed in microwaved plants, especially root vegetables.
- Structural degradation leading to decreased food value was found to be 60 to 90 percent overall for all foods tested, with significant decreases in bioavailability of B complex vitamins, vitamins C and E, essential minerals, and lipotropics.

Clearly, as the evidence shows, it is time to wean ourselves off cooking with this convenient appliance altogether; our health may be seriously compromised. Going back to using a traditional oven, crockpot, toaster oven, or pan heating are worth the time and effort. Nutrition expert, author, and owner of True Food Kitchen, Dr. Andrew Weil, also expresses concerns for the effect of microwaving and wrote: "There may be dangers associated with microwaving food . . . there is a question as to whether microwaving alters protein."[23]

Cell Phones

Indicate stress on the organs and bones; possible cancer

As of 2014, there are over 7 billion cell phone users in the world and they are increasing every day. Not just for making phone calls, these devices are

---

23. Source: awescience.com/2013/12/11/why-we-decided-to-stop-using-the-microwave/#sthash.rrbEuvBD.dpuf

more akin to small, handheld computers. People are very much attached to their smartphones, never leaving home without them. It's now quite normal to see people in public holding them in their hands, storing them in their pockets, or clipping them somewhere on their bodies for quick access.

There is much controversy as to whether these devices harm our health; cell phones do emit a form of radiation; electromagnetic radiation in the microwave range. Other digital wireless systems such as data communication networks produce similar radiation. Cell phone providers are not likely to ever admit or support such research; the industry is valued at $100 billion, and *if they admit the harm, they will be responsible.* Nevertheless, there is research that suggests mobile phones can harm body cells and even damage DNA.

In 2011, International Agency for Research on Cancer (IARC) classified mobile phone radiation as Group 2B: "possibly carcinogenic." That means there "could be some risk" of carcinogenicity, so additional research into long-term, heavy use of mobile phones needs to be conducted. Extensive research into the possible health risks of cell phone usage have been conducted in Germany and China; a German company called G-Hanz introduced a new type of mobile phone claimed to have no harmful radiation as a result of shortening the radio signal bursts.

Until research uncovers definitive results, it's best to take some precautions when using your cellular phone:

- Don't wear a cell phone *anywhere* on your body; not on a chain around your neck, in your pockets, or clipped on your belt.
- For lengthy calls, use the speaker phone feature or a headset. I personally always use the speaker phone feature, and never put my phone near my head or ear except in a public space.
- Place an EMF protector or other anti-electromagnetic products on the back of your phone. I have used EMF protection products for more than twenty years.

- Pregnant women should keep cell phones away from their abdomens, and men who wish to become fathers should never keep activated phones in their pockets.
- Don't allow babies or small children to play with or use your cell phone. Older children should use a headset or speakerphone when talking on a cell phone. Children are more at risk from long usage as the bone marrow of a child's head absorbs ten times more radiation than an adult.
- Do not text and drive, and use specially adapted antennas for cars to avoid absorbing maximum power as the phone moves from one cell system to another.

Fluorescent Lighting

Indicates a host of health issues

Fluorescent lights are a common light source in office building and shopping markets, noted for their characteristic humming sound. With the advent of compact fluorescent lights, they are becoming commonplace in most homes as well. Fluorescent lights are cheap to buy compared to how long they last (about thirteen times longer than regular incandescent bulbs) and cheap to operate requiring a fraction of the energy incandescent bulbs do. But they can be incredibly bad for you.

There are a number of negative health effects that have been linked to working under fluorescent lights that are theorized to be caused by this body chemistry mechanism such as:

- Migraines
- Eye strain
- Problems sleeping due to melatonin suppression
- Symptoms of Seasonal Affective Disorder (SAD) or depression

- Endocrine disruption and poor immune systems
- Hormonal/menstrual cycle disruption in women
- Increases in breast cancer rates and tumor formation
- Stress/anxiety due to cortisol suppression
- Sexual development/maturation disruption
- Obesity
- Agoraphobia (anxiety disorder)

If you are forced to work for prolonged hours under these lights, take frequent breaks outdoors in natural sunlight. Also consider specialized lighting or lightboxes for SAD (Seasonal Affective Disorder).

High Voltage Electrical Towers

Indicate an increased chance of cancer

A high voltage electrical tower, cell tower, electricity pylon, or hydro tower is a tall (15 to 55 meters or 49 to 180 ft), steel structure used to support overhead power lines—and they can be found in all landscapes of the world. They are used in high-voltage AC and DC systems to bring electricity to homes and businesses. Transmission towers and their overhead power lines are often considered to be a form of visual pollution; methods to reduce the visual effect include undergrounding.

Prior to 1920, we lived in relative harmony with the earth without electricity; there was only the natural background of Earth's EMFs. However, since the 1920s, America and almost the entire industrialized world became electrified. Most of us were conceived and born into this human-made, EMF environment and have been exposed to it our entire lives.

It has been proposed and studied by many scientists that the naturally generated EMFs from Mother Earth may actually correlate to the timing of bodily functions. However, such is not the case with human-created AC electrical systems that produce a sort of electrical barrier of chaotic pulsing electrical currents (approximately sixty times per second) that disconnects us from the information stored in the earth for optimal functioning.

Power transmission lines, radio/microwave transmissions, and the electricity in our dwellings create constant stress on our immune systems that can degrade and compromise it over time. A wide range of studies have documented and confirmed the debilitating effects of electropollution-induced stress on the immune system. Human-made EMFs can also interfere with the body's electrical-based healing system.

Scientists are concluding that power line electromagnetic fields should probably be classified as a "probable human carcinogen." While a direct link has not been made connecting EMF radiation as the cause of health issues such as brain tumors, the outcome is likely due to the blood-brain barrier being opened. By exposing this barrier, toxins and pathogens can be carried by the blood to the brain. Due to the comparative low level of immune activity in the brain, regular exposure to the toxins and pathogens being transported in the blood could be one of the causes of cell dysfunction and deterioration causing tumors, leukemia, brain cancer, and other health problems; some epidemiological studies have suggested this is ongoing. If you live near an electrical tower, the danger can be compounded if you also have a Robbery Mountain Sha formation (this is described later in the chapter).

MASTER'S TIP

Never choose to live next to a power transmission tower, high-voltage lines or worse, a substation with multiple transmission towers. High-voltage towers can seriously compromise your health and other areas of your life; it is best to relocate. If you are unable to move, plant a fast-growing tree that will get at least 16 to 30 feet tall, as it will absorb a great deal of the energy the tower emits and protect your health.

The Hub

Indicates nervous conditions, heart and brain issues

In most places of business is usually a type of room I call the "hub," designated to house the phone system, servers for computers, the main power box/electrical panel or circuit breaker, and other things needed to run a modern-day office. All of these necessary items *combined* are so powerful that if an office/s or desk is too near them, it can cause a host of health issues. If you have an office next to or near the hub, it will cause brain-fog, concentration issues, confusion, nervous conditions, and headaches; with prolonged exposure, cancer is likely as this energy is too intense and emits EMF radiation. Many clients have reported an abnormally fast heartbeat. I've been in offices where they will also place a fax machine or copy machine in such a room; this is not a good idea because it means people will need to use it from time to time and be directly exposed to this energy.

MASTER'S TIP

Do not place any work stations, desks, or offices near the "hub"; install extra barriers/walls and place anti-EMF technology such as Earth Calm or QuWave. Money loss may also be indicated for businesses if this room is located in certain Flying Star combinations (2, 5). See more on Flying Stars in chapter 5.

Electric Blankets

Indicates brain tumors and cancer

In 1990, *The American Journal of Epidemiology* reported two studies regarding the use of electric blankets. One revealed a "quadrupling in the risk of brain tumors among children whose mothers slept under electric blankets during the first trimester of pregnancy." The other indicated that children who used electric blankets were more likely to develop cancer. The findings also demonstrated that cancer is not the only ailment that can disrupt immune system function, modify brain waves, and cause other serious abnormalities in physical function and formation.

> "When electricity passes through a wire, it creates an electromagnetic field that exerts force on nearby objects, including animals and humans. At one time, it was believed that low-level magnetic fields were not harmful, but scientists now agree that EMF fields are indeed hazardous to human health. They are now considered probable carcinogens, and have been linked to cases of childhood leukemia, lymphoma, and other health conditions. The exact mechanism by which exposure leads to cancer has not been established. One potential mechanism may be due to EMF ability to alter the expression of certain genes, turning them on and off at inappropriate times, which may cause them to initiate cell proliferation."[24]

In response to EMF concerns, U. S. electric blanket manufacturers are now offering blankets with "zero magnetic fields" to reduce or eliminate the harm, but they may still generate electric fields. One way to use your electric blanket is to turn it on to warm the bed, then turn it off and *unplug* it (this is the only way to ensure that you are eliminating the EMFs) before you retire for the night.

Televisions and Computers in the Bedroom

Indicates insomnia and illness

As we have discussed previously, televisions and computers emit EMFs that can harm your health and body; they will also affect your ability to get into a deep, restful sleep. Take care not to locate them in bedrooms. Remove televisions, routers, and computers from the master bedroom.

---

24. From the article entitled "Is Your Electric Blanket Safe" by Dr. Joseph Mercola at articles.mercola.com/sites/articles/archive/2009/02/24/is-your-electric-blanket-safe.aspx

If you house the television in an armoire with doors to close it off from view and unplug it before sleeping, you will not be affected negatively. Flat-screen televisions that hang on the wall are slightly less harmful (they don't contain the cathode ray tube in analogue televisions), but locate them at least ten feet from your bed and place an anti-EMF device on the back as it will eliminate the need to unplug it.

2. How Form and Shape Affect Health

Anything that has an extreme shape or design in Feng Shui is basically taboo and is likely to spell disaster; this is particularly true for a house or building. The shapes that best support health, wealth and relationships are, in general, square or rectangular—referred to as the "four point gold." It would be impossible to list every type of extreme design that may affect you; however, here are some of the worst and most common seen in cities, communities, and neighborhoods around the world; but don't worry, we can still work with what you have.

Shapes/Designs in Feng Shui Affecting Health

- Triangular-shaped homes or office buildings
- U-shaped buildings
- L-shaped homes or structures
- Half-circle designs
- Space-ship designs
- Huge missing sectors, especially in the center such as an atrium
- Designs with heavy tops and small "legs" or foundation
- Designs with irregular angles
- Homes or office buildings with "leaning" designs

- Offices or homes that look like a jail or garrison
- Extreme metal and glass designs that appear unstable
- Office or homes with knife-like attached objects or designs
- Split or multilevel homes that go in several direction
- Homes or offices that appear they may be falling or the design elements are asymmetrical or disproportional
- Any design that would make the building appear to be unstable, odd, or weird-shaped, sharp or with pointed edges, terraced designs or a harsh, intimidating appearance

These designs will bring disease, money loss, and harm to the householders'/workers' health, and disharmony to the home and workplace. For example, buildings with excessive, sharp metal designs indicate that the occupants could experience violence with knives or lots of surgery involving "cutting" the body. It is best not to office in such buildings or select these types of designs for your living space.

MASTER'S TIP

Avoid setting up an office/business or purchasing/renting a home in any structure with an extreme design, as there is no true cure. If you are unable to move your office or home, make sure you activate the recommendations in chapters 6 and 7; this will insulate you from disasters and bad luck. When practical or possible, select a more stable home or office building.

Land Sites/Lot Shapes

Indicates bankruptcy and spirits haunting the land

Land plots that have odd shapes will usually indicate loss of money, poor health; with triangular corner/s, the plot may be haunted. The best lot shapes and where the energy is distributed most evenly are square or rectangular; both are "golden" according to Feng Shui.

Split-level Homes

Indicates headaches, confusion

This is not the same as a regular two-story or three-story home; no indeed, this is where the home design splits off in several different direction and levels. One of the worst I've seen was in Salt Lake City where the home had seven different levels splintering off in several directions starting with the main entrance.

Sickle-shaped Driveways

Indicates rare and unusual diseases

This shape is like an extreme arch; regular, circular driveways are not necessarily bad. The arch must be an extreme design like a short U shape to bring harm to the occupant's health.

Exposed Overhead Beams

Indicates cutting body organs or heart

If the overhead beams run horizontal, they will cut across the heart, reproductive organs, or the stomach; they can cause heart issues, lung/breathing problems, serious digestive problems such as Crohn's disease, and sexual or reproductive problems. Beams located over the bed that run vertical can cause the couple to split, and depending where you sleep they may cause health issues as well. The lower the ceiling and the closer they are, the more serious the negative results may be.

MASTER'S TIP

The only real remedy for this is to completely cover the beams with plaster or sheetrock. Classical Feng Shui does not rely on bamboo flutes in these scenarios as a "cure." The beams are still there and can cause great harm. Make them disappear by covering them up if you are under them no matter where you place the bed. If you do not own the home, try covering the area where you bed is located with fabric and thumb tacks.

How Water Affects Health

The importance of correctly located water in Classical Feng Shui cannot be overstated. Water must be properly placed and *pristine*; it should never be out of control, flowing, or crashing wildly—this will cause a host of money and health issues. Where you live in proximity to natural or constructed water features is also paramount. In modern times, roads are considered "virtual water" and are also extremely important to the Feng Shui of your home or business. Here are some types of water (both virtual and real) that will greatly affect your health, money, and relationships: canals (clean or dirty), ponds, swimming pools, streams, rivers, lakes, waterfalls, property near the ocean, roads, highways, toilets, huge storm drains, and sewer treatment plants.

Depending on where they are in relationship to your home, these features can cause drug abuse, affairs, bankruptcy, scandals, reputation loss, divorce, gambling, diseases, cancer, alcoholism, and blood-related accidents. The correct placement of water for your home or office is clearly described in chapters 6 and 7 so as *not* to activate these undesirable conditions. Discussed below are some circumstances in which real and virtual water can harm us on many levels, for certain our health and the body.

As with other cultures the world over, water has long been held to have mystical power in China. In 1994, Dr. Masaru Emoto, a Japanese scientist, conceived the idea to seriously observe frozen water crystals.[25] Using high-speed photography, he discovered that crystals formed in frozen water reveal changes when specific, concentrated thoughts are

25. The movie *What the Bleep Do We Know*, produced in 2004 introduced Dr. Emoto's work. The movie features a scene with actress Marlee Matlin where she is speaking negatively to herself in the mirror; since the body is 70% water, it gets the message!

directed toward them. He found that water from clear springs and water that has been exposed to loving words shows brilliant, complex, and colorful snowflake patterns. In contrast, polluted water, or water exposed to negative thoughts formed incomplete, asymmetrical patterns with dull colors. The implications of this research create a new awareness of how we can positively affect the earth and our personal health.

Even in the human body, water can be mystical and wondrous; in 2013 Rose-Lynn Fisher wanted to find out about human tears, and launched a project she called "the Topography of Tears"(www.rose-lynnfisher.com/tears.html). Ms. Fisher wanted to know whether tears would look different under a microscope depending on their source (tears of joy, relief, grief/sadness, laughter, or peeling an onion).[26] Indeed they were, with very *distinctive* shapes and forms much like Dr. Emoto's water depending on the emotion.

Virtual Water in Feng Shui Affecting Health

Eight Roads of Destruction, T-roads, surrounded by too many roads

Eight Roads of Destruction

Indicating disease, divorce, and money loss

This is one of the worst formations involving a door direction and water exits. Remember that "water" could apply to real or virtual water—specifically a road. This formation is also known as "Eight Roads to Hell," an apt description of what it can bring to the householders. It only involves 15-degree increments for the door direction and the water /road. The real danger is how the chi or energy exits the site; certain degrees can result in disaster. One example of an Eight Roads of Destruction is when a door is northeast (between 37.6 to 52.5 degrees) and the road or water coming from or exiting the east (between 67.6 to 82.5 degrees).

26. Read the full article at www.lifebuzz.com/tears/#!Mo01e

MASTER'S TIP

The door, the road, or the water needs to be changed; these formations can wreck a family. This formula only involves specific 15-degree increments for both the road and the door; there are eight such possible formations in total. Tilting the door a few degrees is usually the way a Feng Shui expert will take care of it. Re-angling the door a few degrees forces the door to receive energy differently, thus eliminating the Eight Roads formation. In chapters 6 and 7, you will be alerted to any possible Eight Roads of Destruction for your home.

T-Juncture or T-Road formations

Indicates discord and sickness

A T-juncture or T-road formation is when there is a road directly aligned with your front door or perhaps even the garage door. In Feng Shui, this is considered one of the most toxic formations, as it will cause a host of negative events for the householders. While energy is good, too much will have the opposite desired effect. This intense, direct energy is called *sha* or "killing" chi; in almost all cases, it will lead to discord, money loss, divorce, illness, accidents, and other mishaps depending on how fast and close the road is to your property.

MASTER'S TIP

Block off a T-juncture with a stucco wall, a solid gate near the front door, boulders, or dense landscaping. Whatever you choose should be enough to stop a car. If you are shopping for a new home, pass on these residences; even when cured they can cause issues.

Homes Surrounded by Too Many Roads

Accidents with the body, alcoholism, and drugs

Roads are fast-moving purveyors of energy, much like raging rivers. It is extremely inauspicious to be too close or have too many roads surrounding your site. Numerous roads near a home can make it vulnerable and unstable. Think about stories in the news where someone is describing a car crashing into their bedroom or living room where they barely escaped with their life!

Roads near the back of the property can be the worst. Consider, too, virtual roads such as ditches or huge, open drains located in cities where monsoons and frequent rains cause flooding. These sites can be so unstable they will activate affairs, divorce, illness, and all types of misfortune.

MASTER'S TIP

Create a strong backing at the rear of the property. Also, insulate the site on the left- and right-hand sides from the roads. Consider moving if you have experienced very bad events in your life such as disease, loss of money, affairs, or lots of sickness.

Real Water in Feng Shui Affecting Health

Water in the center of the house, natural streams under foundations, and fluoridated water

Water in the Center of the House

Indicates problems with the kidney, blood, and the lymphatic system

Water should not be located directly in the dead center of the house—this could be a toilet, fountain like in an atrium, laundry room, pool, or waterfall. These possible health issues do not immediately take effect as soon as you move into the home, rather about eighteen months or longer. Disconnect a fountain or water feature in the center of the house, particularly if you have been experiencing any of the common concerns. Use a different toilet if possible; not activating these features will protect you from the health issues.

Natural Streams Running Under the Foundation

Indicates sickness, disease, bankruptcy

A home or business should never be built on top of or over a natural stream; it causes instability for the occupants as well as sickness, disease, and money loss. In the Phoenix area, there's a multi-million dollar home that has been built directly over a natural stream, the center of the house acting as an internal bridge. This is taboo in Feng Shui as it creates extreme instability for the occupants, who will suffer ill health, money loss, and problems in all their relationships.

The famous Fallingwater house in Pennsylvania designed by Frank Lloyd Wright is unfortunately another example of an extremely inauspicious design and placement. This home is built directly on top of a natural waterfall. It's fortunate that the home only served as a vacation getaway and not the main residence; however, it is still considered unstable. These properties are good for tours but not occupancy. In May 2008, *Phoenix Home & Garden* magazine featured a unique home that installed a large, straight indoor stream; the architect aligned it to the Summer Solstice. The stream cut across much of the living space and ran under a glass wall, where it continued its path connecting to the outdoor swimming pool. Such features create an unstable environment for the occupants, and will over time accumulate negative outcomes such as health issues, financial problems, and a split within the family or couple. Special attention must be paid when incorporating water into the design of a home; it will absolutely affect the occupants for good or ill.

Water Treated with Fluoride

Fluoride is a poison—more so than lead and slightly less than arsenic. In 1991, the Akron (Ohio) Regional Poison Center reported that "death has been reported following ingestion of 16mg/kg of fluoride."

That means that 1/100th of an ounce of fluoride could kill a 10 lb child or 1/10th of an ounce could kill a 100 lb adult.

The prolific and pervasive use of fluoride became one of the most controversial issues of the twentieth century, and continues to be so. It was first placed in tap water in the 1950s as an anti-cavity product; in fact, it is the strongest free radical known.[27]

This poison, once it has accumulated in the body, can cause genetic damage, cancer, diabetes, thyroid and neurological disorders, hormonal imbalances, heart disease, arthritis, severe/premature aging, and osteoporosis; even death where there is heavy or chronic fluoride ingestion.

In chronic doses, fluoride (like arsenic and lead), will accumulate in the body causing a blockage in the way cells breathe and leads to the malformation of collagen.

Currently we are over exposed to fluoride in everyday products such as toothpaste, rinses, water, food, medicines, showering, bathing, and even the air that we breathe; our environment has become a literal fluoride dumping ground.

The use of fluoride is now banned in China, Austria, Belgium, Sweden, the Netherlands, Japan, Finland, Germany, Denmark, Norway, and Hungary; its use is not banned in the United States, however.

Filter your tap water with a device that will specifically get rid of fluoride and other harmful chemicals. Avoid products containing fluoride (such as toothpaste).

When you shower, open a window to release the fluoride gases that may be present in the water. It is best to purify the water at its source, from the tap.

---

27. Free radicals are atoms or groups of atoms with an odd (unpaired) number of electrons and can be formed when oxygen interacts with certain molecules. Once formed, these highly reactive radicals can start a chain reaction, like dominoes. Their chief danger comes from the damage they can do when they react with important cellular components such as DNA, or the cell membrane. Cells may function poorly or die if this occurs.

How Mountains Affect Health

Real Mountains in Feng Shui Affecting Health

Broken Mountains, Robbery Mountain Sha, Eight Killing Mountain Forces, 60 and 72 Dragons, and Boulders

Broken Mountains

Hurts the Human Body

The term "broken mountain" refers to a mountain that has been scarred, tunneled, excavated, or mined. There are a variety of words in Chinese for mountains—shan, sar, and lung, which means "dragon." Feng Shui most commonly references them as dragons. Mountains rate very high in Classical Feng Shui, as important as water. To the Chinese, "mountains" represent humans or humankind. Therefore, mountains are closely associated with the human body, and everything about the mountain tells a tale: its shape (pointed, rounded, square, and so forth), the height and main peak, the color, where it is located in proximity to the site, and its condition—mined, scarred, or excavated.

Because they affect the body, they will have a great influence on health. Mining mountains is common everywhere in the world—everything from coal, metals, precious stones, or gold; if you live close to or in view of a scarred, broken mountain due to mining—it will greatly affect your health. Generally, a beautiful mountain at the back of the property is considered very auspicious; however, if it is tampered with and made ugly it will bring incredibly bad events. As far as yin and yang are concerned, mountains are yin energy—unmovable, quiet, and even haunting.

On March 22, 2014, in the tiny town of Oso (about fifty miles from Seattle), a mountain side about one square mile in area gave way and sadly claimed the lives of more than forty-three souls. Heavy rains and naturally loose soil were blamed, but evidently mountain mudslides are common in Washington state and this particular mountain had a slide nine years previous; surviving homeowners stated in interviews that they had no idea that the mountains could be dangerous. This mudslide is said to be the most dramatic and disastrous in Washington's recorded or recent memory. While not technically a broken or excavated mountain—building on it or near it is clearly not recommended due to its nature; to force the issue is out of harmony with nature and will bring negative results.

It is never recommended to build directly on top of a mountain—it will adversely affect every category of Feng Shui—money, relationships, and most assuredly your health and body. It is not advised to cut into a mountain and create a building site—it is totally disharmonious and will not bring good results—you have also scarred the mountain. Humans have been awed by the majesty of mountains since the beginning of time; even in modern times conquering a mountain by climbing its highest peak risking life and limb is considered a celebrated accomplishment.

The greatest care should be undertaken in selecting a home or a building site where mountains and hills are located. Some of the most detrimental Feng Shui I've ever seen were badly placed homes on or near a mountain where people's health, money, and relationships were compromised. Much respect to the natural inclination of a mountain must be considered before locating a home there. It is best to locate a mountain-home with the mountain supporting the back of the house.

Robbery Mountain Sha

Indicates an unusual disease or getting hurt by knives

The Robbery Mountain Sha formation (*Chor San Kibb Sart*) is harmful to the household if in certain areas there are negative features such as high-tension electrical towers, an excavated or scarred mountain nearby, a quarry, a jagged cliff, or huge dead tree. An example is if the home faces southwest (meaning it "sits" northeast; this is the back of the property), and there is one of the above mentioned anomalies in the southeast—you may have a Robbery Mountain Sha affecting the home or building. This is cured by blocking off from view the sha (killing) energy. In chapters 6 and 7, you will be alerted to any possible Robbery Mountain Sha for your home.

Eight Killing Mountain Forces

Death and Blood-related accidents

The Eight Killing Mountain Forces *(Pa Sha Hwang Chuen)* is a very serious formation; the energy of the mountain and door are in conflict, causing a host of negative events for the householders, including loss of life and blood-related accidents. These formations involve specific 15-degree increments for both the door direction and the mountain. If you live in an area of the world without mountains, tall buildings must be considered as well. Here is an example of the formation: if your door faces northeast (52.6–67.5) and you have a real mountain or tall building also in the northeast (37.6–52.5), you may have an Eight Killings.

MASTER'S TIP

It takes a great deal of practice and skill to determine whether you have this formation because it hinges on such small increments and involves any exterior door. Since it is impossible to move a mountain or a building, a Feng Shui master or practitioner will usually change the degree of the door in question to avoid the "crush of the dragon."[28] *In chapters 6 and 7 you will be alerted to any possible Eight Killing Forces for your home.*

The 60 Earth-Penetrating Dragons Method

Evaluates Mountain Energy to be Auspicious/Inauspicious

The 60 Earth-Penetrating Dragons take into consideration the energy of a hillside or mountain immediately behind the house or building, basically evaluating its quality. The "dragons" cover only six degrees, but all sixty dragons are assessed by one of five types of energy being either auspicious or inauspicious. The 60 Dragons method was most likely invented by Ts'ai Shin Yu in the tenth century. The energy of the mountain may be likened

---

28. In Feng Shui, the term *Dragon* is used to indicate a mountain.

to an electricity cable that supplies power to a light; the energy fed to the site will "light" it up.

Remember that mountains in Feng Shui are closely related to the human body; therefore, the energy and quality of a mountain or hill can affect and influence the health. An example would be a mountain or hillside at the rear of the property—with its highest peak between 337.6 and 343.5 degrees; this six-degree increment may indicate "yellow fever, swelling, insanity, and an ill female in the household."

As ominous as that sounds, even with such a mountain, these inauspicious events may never happen. There are many good "dragons" as well supporting health, wealth, longevity, and good relationships.

The 72 Piercing Dragons Method

Evaluates Mountain Energy to be Auspicious/Inauspicious

The 72 Piercing Dragons are similar to the 60 Dragons; they are also used to examine the energy of a mountain; it covers 5-degree increments. However, the 72 Piercing Dragons is mainly concerned with evaluating the *largest* or main mountain at the back of the property, whereas the 60 Dragons measure closer, more specific energy fed immediately behind the site. The method for the 72 Dragons is attributed to the famous Master Yang Yun Sung who lived during the Tang Dynasty (618–907 CE). He also created the "Secret Verses" to accompany the seventy-two possible mountain measurements. These describe what the occupants may expect in the way of fortune and health depending on the mountain's degree.

The 72 Dragons also calculates the quality of the mountain into one of five types of energy. Some have seriously negative implications with descriptions like "fire pits."

An example of this would be a main mountain measuring between 97° and 102° and the Secret Verses explains this 5-degree increment as "lonely, death, hunchbacks, bow-legged, and a short life-span." However, many mountain directions are very auspicious; for example, if the largest mountain at the back of your property is between 352° and 357°, then the Secret Verse describes it as "very auspicious, good children, real estate holdings, very rich and a noble government position."

Massive Boulders Inside the Home

Indicates sickness, accidents, broken bones

Building a home where large boulders are part of the house is harmful for the occupants. A very upscale community in Scottsdale called Troon has gorgeous, massive natural boulders in the landscape; the area is hauntingly beautiful. Some of the homes have been built directly around these massive rocks including them as part of the interior.

While this may look cool and edgy and an interesting conversation piece, the practice is taboo in Feng Shui; it can cause great harm to the body. Such homes can expect lots of sickness, accidents involving harming/breaking the bones, and extreme anxiety disorder/attacks.

Virtual Mountains in Feng Shui Impacting Health

Interior staircase location

Interior Mountains (Staircases)

Indicates scoliosis, skeletal and joint issues

It is taboo, in Feng Shui, to have a staircase in the dead center of the house indicating back problems, pressure on bones/joints (osteoporosis) and other diseases such as scoliosis (curvature of the spine).

A huge floor to ceiling fireplace made of stone, granite, or marble is also considered an internal mountain; these are often placed dead center of a home. The only real cure is to relocate the staircase.

If this is not possible and you are experiencing poor health, consider moving to another residence.

Other Negative Scenarios in Feng Shui Affecting Health

Void Lines, Vortexes, Hoarding, and Toxic Sites

Death and Empty Lines (DEL) or Void Lines

Indicates illness and ghosts

A longtime secret of Feng Shui masters was that the facing direction of doors and entrances should never lie exactly on the cardinal lines. These are referred to as Kong Wang or Kun Mang; "Death and Empty Lines" (DEL) or Void Lines. It's worth noting that "death" in this context does not mean dying; rather it means that the property is devoid of energy and will bring all sorts of extreme misfortune and loss such as sickness, bankruptcy, and other forms of bad luck.

These degrees may also explain why some buildings don't sell and languish on the market. There are lesser DELs where, for example, west changes to northwest (292.5) or south ends and southwest begins (202.5). All DELs are inauspicious degrees that attract ghosts and spirits, which are never appropriate for homes or businesses. Benevolent spirits belong in churches and holy places. Listed below are the most serious void/empty lines:

Major Void Lines
90° (East), 180° (South), 270° (West), and 360/0° (North)

Emptiness Lines
202.5°, 247.5°, 292.5°, 337.5°, 22.5°, 67.5°, 112.5°, and 157.5°

If you've had a run of bad luck, remove the door from its hinges and leave it off for an hour or so, then re-hang the door. This will take a door out of the DEL, at least for a while. A more permanent cure is to re-angle the door within its frame, but doing so will require carpenter skills. Metal on or near the door may also help, but give it some time and then take another compass direction in a month or so. Since compass degrees are based on the earth's magnetic energies, metal can reduce the affliction of this negative scenario.

Energy Vortexes and Ley Lines

Indicates nervousness, dizziness, and ghosts

Energy vortexes and ley lines are quite mysterious; the source of much speculation among New Age and supernatural enthusiasts. In 1921 an Englishman named Alfred Watkins noticed that ancient sites/ruins such as Stonehenge were built on straight lines; he began to call them "ley lines." He also noted that hilltops, churches, standing stones, castles, and burial mounds seemed to be connected to these lines. His study of Ordinance survey maps convinced him that these places were built intentionally along straight lines. He wrote about his findings in a book entitled *The Old Straight Track*, but his theories and ley lines in general were relegated to pseudoscientific phenomena and not taken seriously.

On January 25, 1987, Research Director Joe Parr conducted a field survey for Bethe Hagens, professor of Anthropology at Governors State University, Illinois.[29] He was the first to bring scientific verification that ley lines do exist and can be quantified using scientific equipment. The results of the study were fascinating: they discovered that ley lines could be like magnetic fields but they don't work until they are crossed! For example, a ley line may never indicate its location unless you cross it fast enough to induce a voltage into a large enough coil. Dr. Hagens herself indicated that some of the lines could be miles across.

My first experience with ley lines was in the late 1990s in San Antonio while working with a client on a new-home build site. The house was 75 percent complete when I first visited; my client felt something was wrong with the energy, as a series of very negative events had happened during construction. The first thing I noticed was a large, very

29. See more about the study in *"Comments on Lei Lines"* by Joe Parr, J.D. at www.gizapyramid.com/parr/lei-lines.htm

odd-growing tree in the front garden; the tree trunk was growing parallel to the ground!

After standing near the front door (which was aligned with this tree), I became very dizzy and nauseated. The property had a ley line going right through the middle of the house. It was dormant if left alone, but once construction started it released negative energy. My client said the builder went bankrupt within a couple of months of construction and had to be replaced, there were constant delays, and a worker was seriously injured with an electric saw. The house also "felt" haunted; the overall feeling was very eerie. When it came down to it, I recommended my client opt out of the house. At the time, she had four days left to leave, and she did. Ley lines are not harmful until you build on them and disrupt their energy. Regarding ancient sites such as Stonehenge, these lines could intensify the energy, but these sites were used for special occasions and events—not everyday living!

My second experience with ley lines was another home built over where two ley lines intersected, creating a vortex of energy. This home is in the Fountain Hills area of Arizona, in a mountainous setting. When I took a compass direction at the front door, it was a major DEL at 180°; the back door was at 0°. The lines crossed and intersected in the master bedroom area. The client told me after moving in, for the first three months, she was dizzy all the time. Her two small sons (seven and nine years old at the time) were too afraid to sleep in their beds; they said they saw ghosts. Her husband would wake up every night without fail at some weird time like 2:22 AM.

Unfortunately, these issues could not be fully cured; I recommended that they sell the property. I explained that their issues would be aggravated due to the new construction next door, where they were jackhammering the very rocky land to prepare it for development. Doing so "shook up" the ley lines, setting off a chain reaction of negative events that lasted three years—the woman became an alcoholic, they went bankrupt, and finally, the couple divorced. They didn't want to leave their house because her husband had personally designed it—it was gorgeous. After the house was built, they were very attached to it. However, this house was built *out of harmony* with the natural environment and would never support the occupants, no matter who lived there.

Building a business or home over the lines of energy will wreck havoc in every area of your life; the energy is just too intense. Trust your instincts when considering building, buying, or renting on such sites; I find most people will have accurate gut feelings when exposed to ley lines and vortexes—but they just choose to ignore them!

Hoarding and Cleanliness

Indicates serious health issues

The energy of your home or workplaces should flow freely and evenly throughout the space. Doing so ensures that it will support the occupants in important areas of life such as health, money, and relationships. Your living space should be clean, in good repair (no broken windows, water leaks, or things falling apart), and kept neat and organized. A little bit of clutter is not a real issue but mountains of clutter in every room definitely is; excessive clutter constricts the flow of energy. If you live with animals, special care needs to be taken to maintain cleanliness; this will affect yours and their health. For example, don't place litter boxes for your felines near the kitchen or where you prepare or eat your meals.

Hoarding seems to be a new mental disease or disorder where people cannot give up things—even garbage; there are popular television shows telling people's sad stories. It's a good idea to schedule a deep cleaning at least twice a year, to de-clutter and donate to the less fortunate in your community. Doing so will keep the energy fresh in your home or workplace; health will improve as well. Americans in particular have too much stuff! While Feng Shui is not strictly about clearing your clutter, it is a practical aspect of fostering good energy.

Living Next to Negative or Toxic Sites

Compromises health and well-being

Here are other extremely negative sites not to live near or worst, *next to*; they will most assuredly affect and harm your health and well-being:

Radio towers, satellite stations, broadcast antennas, military and aviation radars, or electrical towers (*harmful radiation emissions*); graveyards and alleyways (*causes depression, attracts ghosts and spirits*); sewer treatment plants, pig farms, slaughterhouses, meat-packing plants, landfills, and garbage dumps *(bacteria, viruses, and animal violence)*; oil refineries, chemical plants, gas stations, crematories, living too close to highways and funeral homes *(harmful chemicals and fumes in the air that will harm the lungs);* and hospitals *(bacteria, viruses, diseases, staph germs, and death).*

The Los Angeles Times published an article about the manufacture of Sriracha, a very popular Chinese hot sauce that was reported causing headaches for those living nearby. The city of Irwindale is asking a judge to stop production of the hot sauce, saying it's making residents' eyes water and throats burn. The city filed suit against Sriracha as of 2013; they produce in excess of 200,000 bottles per day.

The article states:

> "Now the city is demanding that the factory shut down until the problem is solved. Irwindale filed suit in Los Angeles County Superior against the sauce's company, Huy Fong Foods, alleging that the odor was a public nuisance and asking a judge to stop production. A business- and industrial-heavy city, Irwindale is no stranger to smells, including some emanating from a dog food manufacturer—especially on an overcast day, said Lisa Bailey, the president of the Irwindale Chamber of Commerce. Also in Irwindale is the MillerCoors Brewery."[30]

---

30. From an article entitled "Some Neighbors Say Sriracha Factory's Smell is Creating Headaches" by Frank Shyong, Hector Becerra and Jessica Garrison; October 29, 2013. Read more about this at: www.latimes.com/local/la-me-1030-sriracha-smell-20131030,0,4852984.story#ixzz2wX2p6uVs.

Who could ever forget the famous PG & E (Pacific Gas & Electric) lawsuit for poisoning the water with toxic wastes in Hinkley, California, made public by the law firm of Edward L. Masry in which his assistant, Erin Brockovich, initiated the investigation; she and the firm exposed years of abusing the environment and destroying the health of hundreds of residents living near the plant. More recently, in the city of Charleston, West Virginia, the water has also been seriously compromised making people sick due to Freedom Industries releasing 75 thousand gallons of toxic waste from coal processing that seeped into the ground.[31]

The article states:

> "By now, it's been thoroughly reported that Charleston-based Freedom Industries—a small, two-week old company that stored and distributed coal-processing chemicals from eleven huge, 48,000-gallon containment units on the shores of the Elk River—accidentally allowed 7,500 gallons of the chemical 4-methylcyclohexane methanol (MCHM) to seep into the region's main water source. The Elk supplies drinking water to some 300,000 residents through the publicly traded West Virginia American water company. And because not much is known about MHCM, the state's Department of Environmental Protection (DEP) was forced to order last Thursday that no one use the water flowing into homes and businesses in a nine-county region surrounding Charleston."

Clearly, living next to toxic sites is not in our best interest, as places like these will invariably affect our health in one way or another—either ingesting or breathing harmful toxins. There are some things that are not in our control; however, those things that are, be diligent in avoiding or mitigating them. Reduce or eliminate the use of a microwave, protect

---

31. From "Poisoned: Why West Virginia's Water Crisis is Everyone's Problem" by Matt Stroud on January 14, 2014, www.theverge.com/2014/1/14/5307842/poisoned-why-west-virginias-water-crisis-is-everyones-problem.

yourself from harmful radiation, move if you live next to one of the aforementioned harmful sites, keep your home clean and orderly so that energy flows freely, and if possible, correct some of the negative scenarios described in this chapter. These actions will go a long way in improving or securing your health and longevity.

There are numerous modern-day products that will help reduce or eliminate EMFs, vortexes, and the effects of radiation in our environment from cell phones, televisions, computers, and so forth. Make use of what you can, where you can.

Let's begin with learning some important ideas and methods that can significantly improve and support our health. We'll start with a more personalized type of Feng Shui, the Eight Mansions system—simple and profound. In the next chapter, you'll discover your personal health direction and important ways in which to activate it.

Four

Using Eight Mansions for Health & Vitality

To keep the body in good health is a duty, for otherwise we shall not be able to trim the lamp of wisdom, and keep our mind strong and clear.

Buddha

Feng Shui's popularity has encompassed the globe and the most sought-after techniques are the Eight Mansions (*Ba Zhai*) and Flying Stars (*Xuan Kong Fei Xing*); we'll go into great detail about Flying Stars in the next chapter. The Eight Mansions system is also known as Eight House Feng Shui and the East/West System. No matter what you call it, it is simple and can yield dramatic results when applied correctly. It also has many aspects and layers that make it rich and versatile. Eight Mansions is a more personalized technique based on the horoscope (birthday) of the occupants. Once you have discovered your unique Life Gua Number using the tables provided in this chapter, you will be able to arrange your home, rooms, and office to create advantageous Feng Shui. Moreover, based on your Life Gua Number, you will have distinctive personality traits and characteristics; it is always helpful to gain insights in our own and others' energy.

There are several styles of Eight Mansions, eight in fact, all developed during the Tang Dynasty. However, two immerged as the most popular and favored styles: the Eight House Bright Mirror featured in *The Complete Idiots Guide to Feng Shui* by Elizabeth Moran, Master Joseph Yu, and Master Val Biktashev; and the Golden Star Classic taught in this book. I learned this style directly from my teacher, Grandmaster Yap Cheng Hai. He was made famous when he collaborated with author Lillian Too in writing *Applied Pa-Kua and Luo Shu Feng Shui* published in 1993; this was the first modern book to introduce the Eight Mansions system in English.

Like all Feng Shui systems, the objective is to determine how auspicious the structure is and then extract the energy in such a way so that it supports the occupants. It's also used to determine how compatible you are with those in your sphere—spouses, siblings, children, co-workers, clients, and employees; this is where the Life Gua Personalities comes into play. While Flying Stars primarily deals with structures and timing, Eight Mansions' focus is on *people*. In chapters 6 and 7, Flying Stars and Eight Mansions are combined to give you optimal results. Until then, we'll fully explore all the aspects of Eight Mansions as a stand-alone body of knowledge.

Implementing Eight Mansions correctly activates positive energy that brings dazzling prospects for excellent health, romance, longevity, business opportunities, promotions at work, flourishing investments, and wealth-luck. On the other hand, harmful energy will be obvious when the occupants suffer from disease, poor health, a crippling divorce, bad relationships, accidents, disastrous events, and bankruptcy.

Please note that there are several important aspects of the Eight Mansions system: 1) Finding the Life Gua Number and Life Group; 2) All Life Guas have four good and four bad directions, good ones will enhance health, prosperity, and relationships. We'll discuss how to put this into action; 3) Advanced Eight Mansions is an aspect using specific 15-degree increments in the eight directions, this is important for certain couples who may be in different Life Groups; and 4) Depending on your personal Life Gua, you are assigned certain energies that shape your personality, career preferences, and possible health issues which is similar to astrology. This is called the Life Gua Personality.

How to Find Your Life Gua Number and Life Group

This is how the system works: according to your Life Gua Number you will be influenced in positive and negative ways by the eight directions: four will support you and four won't. The lucky directions will augment wealth and money-luck, health, good relationships, and stability; the other four can ignite divorce, bankruptcy, betrayals, lawsuits, cancer, and so forth. The idea of course is to use and *set in motion* your good directions and bear down on and suppress the negative ones. Before you can begin using this impressive technique, you will need to determine your *personal* Life Gua Number.

To find your Life Gua Number, refer to figure 10, the Eight Mansions chart; make sure you are in the right column as there is one for males and one for females. There is a specific calculation to arrive at this number, but I've included the quick reference chart for ease.[32] If you were born prior to February 4 in any given year, use the previous year to get your Life Gua Number as the new year begins on that date 99.9 percent of the time, according to the solar calendar. For example, if you were born January 8, 1986, use the year 1985 to get your correct number. If you were born on February 3, 4, or 5, please refer to the appendix (figure 53) to find when the new year actually began in the year of your birth.

32. For the Eight Mansions formula, refer to *Classical Feng Shui for Wealth and Abundance.*

1933–1960				1961–1988				1989–2016			
Animal	Year	Male ♂	Female ♀	Animal	Year	Male ♂	Female ♀	Animal	Year	Male ♂	Female ♀
Rooster	1933	4	2	*Ox*	1961	3	3	*Snake*	1989	2	4
Dog	1934	3	3	*Tiger*	1962	2	4	*Horse*	1990	1	8
Pig	1935	2	4	*Rabbit*	1963	1	8	*Goat*	1991	9	6
Rat	1936	1	8	*Dragon*	1964	9	6	*Monkey*	1992	8	7
Ox	1937	9	6	*Snake*	1965	8	7	*Rooster*	1993	7	8
Tiger	1938	8	7	*Horse*	1966	7	8	*Dog*	1994	6	9
Rabbit	1939	7	8	*Goat*	1967	6	9	*Pig*	1995	2	1
Dragon	1940	6	9	*Monkey*	1968	2	1	*Rat*	1996	4	2
Snake	1941	2	1	*Rooster*	1969	4	2	*Ox*	1997	3	3
Horse	1942	4	2	*Dog*	1970	3	3	*Tiger*	1998	2	4
Goat	1943	3	3	*Pig*	1971	2	4	*Rabbit*	1999	1	8
Monkey	1944	2	4	*Rat*	1972	1	8	*Dragon*	2000	9	6
Rooster	1945	1	8	*Ox*	1973	9	6	*Snake*	2001	8	7
Dog	1946	9	6	*Tiger*	1974	8	7	*Horse*	2002	7	8
Pig	1947	8	7	*Rabbit*	1975	7	8	*Goat*	2003	6	9
Rat	1948	7	8	*Dragon*	1976	6	9	*Monkey*	2004	2	1
Ox	1949	6	9	*Snake*	1977	2	1	*Rooster*	2005	4	2
Tiger	1950	2	1	*Horse*	1978	4	2	*Dog*	2006	3	3
Rabbit	1951	4	2	*Goat*	1979	3	3	*Pig*	2007	2	4
Dragon	1952	3	3	*Monkey*	1980	2	4	*Rat*	2008	1	8
Snake	1953	2	4	*Rooster*	1981	1	8	*Ox*	2009	9	6
Horse	1954	1	8	*Dog*	1982	9	6	*Tiger*	2010	8	7
Goat	1955	9	6	*Pig*	1983	8	7	*Rabbit*	2011	7	8
Monkey	1956	8	7	*Rat*	1984	7	8	*Dragon*	2012	6	9
Rooster	1957	7	8	*Ox*	1985	6	9	*Snake*	2013	2	1
Dog	1958	6	9	*Tiger*	1986	2	1	*Horse*	2014	4	2
Pig	1959	2	1	*Rabbit*	1987	4	2	*Goat*	2015	3	3
Rat	1960	4	2	*Dragon*	1988	3	3	*Monkey*	2016	2	4

Note: If you were born *before* February 4th in any given year—use the *previous* year.

Figure 10: The Eight Mansion Chart.

Now that you have your personal Life Gua Number, figure 11 will give you all the pertinent information to start improving your Feng Shui.

Let's examine the chart; it has a good deal of information on it. First, based on your Life Gua number, you will be part of the East Life Group or the West Life Group. Those who are a 1, 3, 4 or 9 Guas are part of the East group, and those who are a 2, 6, 7, or 8 belong to the West group. In the Eight Mansions system, the number 5 is not used. In other systems such as the Flying Stars, it is quite important.

		East Life Group				West Life Group			
		1	3	4	9	2	6	7	8
GMY Code:	**Outcomes/ Indications:**								
+90	Wealth	SE	S	N	E	NE	W	NW	SW
+80	Health	E	N	S	SE	W	NE	SW	NW
+70	Relationships	S	SE	E	N	NW	SW	NE	W
+60	Stability	N	E	SE	S	SW	NW	W	NE
-60	Setbacks	W	SW	NW	NE	E	SE	N	S
-70	Lawsuits/Affairs	NE	NW	SW	W	SE	E	S	N
-80	Bad Health	NW	NE	W	SW	S	N	SE	E
-90	Total Disaster	SW	W	NE	NW	N	S	E	SE

Figure 11: The Eight Mansions Directions.

Next, notice the GMY Code column; this is the clever creation of Grandmaster Yap to refer to your good and bad directions without using the Chinese words associated with them. For example, your best direction will be +90, which indicates prosperity or wealth-luck. The +80 will help you to secure vital health. The +70 direction is your personal direction to enhance romance, relationships, and harmony and so forth. Once you have located your personal Life Gua Number on the chart, just follow down that column to see all good and bad directions and a brief description of what they'll indicate if you use them.

The Gua number is highly significant: not only can you derive the directions that support you, it will also give you important clues about your personality (more about this in the next chapter) and key relationships. Now let's discuss what the good and bad directions actually indicate and mean; these eight types of energies are given with their proper Chinese names and with GMY's Code.

Your Good and Bad Directions

Collectively, the following eight types of energy/chi below are known as "the Eight Wandering Stars" (or, Big or Greater Wandering Sky). They are also closely related to the Tan Lang Nine Stars, known as the "Small Wandering Stars" (or, Small or Lesser Wandering Sky), you can find out more about these in the Glossary of Terms.

While your four good and the four bad directions (North, South, Northwest, and so forth) are easily located in Figures 11 and 12, I've listed them below for quick reference.

The Four Good Directions:

Wealth (Sheng Chi) +90: Sheng Chi means "generating breath" or energy that gives life. This is the number one direction for stimulating wealth. Often referred to as "millionaire chi," this direction is good for business opportunities, timing, promotions at work, descendants, and wealth-luck. Your Sheng Chi direction will also establish positions of authority and powerful connections. If you wish to increase money-luck, this is the direction to use for your bed direction, desk direction or use a door facing to this direction.

The +90 direction is ***SE*** for 1 Guas, ***NE*** for 2 Guas, ***South*** for 3 Guas, ***North*** for 4 Guas, ***West*** for 6 Guas, ***NW*** for 7 Guas, ***SW*** for 8 Guas, and ***East*** for 9 Guas.

Health (Tien Yi) +80: Tien Yi means "heavenly doctor" and it is the best direction to ensure good health. This direction also has been known to bring unexpected wealth, as if from the heavens. Using this direction can bring a long life, close friends, excellent social standing, and the power of speech. Activating this direction can assist in overcoming a prolonged or inexplicable illness/disease, particularly if the bed or stove faces this direction.

The +80 direction is ***East*** for 1 Guas, ***West*** for 2 Guas, ***North*** for 3 Guas, ***South*** for 4 Guas, ***NE*** for 6 Guas, ***SW*** for 7 Guas, ***NW*** for 8 Guas, and ***SE*** for 9 Guas.

Relationships and Longevity (Yen Nien) +70: This direction is all about personal relationships, love of family, romantic partners, networking, longevity, and family harmony. If this direction is used, it can bring well-off, famous, and rich descendants. If you want to have children quickly, place your bed to this direction. The Yen Nien direction also connotes health and longevity; it is often misspelled "Nien Yen." Activate with a door, bed, or stove facing this direction; harmony and longevity are stimulated.

The +70 direction is ***South*** for 1 Guas, ***NW*** for 2 Guas, ***SE*** for 3 Guas, ***East*** for 4 Guas, ***SW*** for 6 Guas, ***NE*** for 7 Guas, ***West*** for 8 Guas, and ***North*** for 9 Guas.

Stability (Fu Wei) +60: This direction is a mirror of your own energy and can bring stability. It indicates moderate wealth and happiness; it is a good alternative if you cannot use your best directions. The Fu Wei direction suggests a middle-class family with good harmony. If you want older children to move out of the house, place their headboards to this direction.

The +60 direction is ***North*** for 1 Guas, ***SW*** for 2 Guas, ***East*** for 3 Guas, ***SE*** for 4 Guas, ***NW*** for 6 Guas, ***West*** for 7 Guas, ***NE*** for 8 Guas, and ***South*** for 9 Guas.

The Four Worst Directions:

Setbacks (Wo Hai) -60: If this direction is used, it will attract all sorts of aggravating obstacles, persistent setbacks, and losing money in investments. It can bring small disasters but not overwhelming ones; nothing goes smoothly. For example, you may win your court case but not receive the monetary settlement. Locate or use a toilet in this area.

The -60 direction is ***West*** for 1 Guas, ***East*** for 2 Guas, ***SW*** for 3 Guas, ***NW*** for 4 Guas, ***SE*** for 6 Guas, ***North*** for 7 Guas, ***South*** for 8 Guas, and ***NE*** for 9 Guas.

Lawsuits, Affairs, and Betrayals (Wu Gwei) -70: This direction is referred to as the "five ghosts," and it primarily indicates lawsuits and litigation. Using this direction can bring lots of trouble in romance, rebellious children, drug use, petty people, robberies, illicit affairs, hot-tempered people, betrayals, lack of support by employees, gossip, and being undermined. This would be a good area for a stove or toilet.

The -70 direction is ***NE*** for 1 Guas, ***SE*** for 2 Guas, ***NW*** for 3 Guas, ***SW*** for 4 Guas, ***East*** for 6 Guas, ***South*** for 7 Guas, ***North*** for 8 Guas, and ***West*** for 9 Guas.

Backstabbing, Accidents, and Bad Health (Liu Sha) -80: Known as the "six killing" direction; utilizing this direction can attract six types of disasters such as injury, loss of wealth, backstabbing, affairs, harm to you and the family, betrayals in business, accidents of all sorts, and serious illness such as cancer. The Liu Sha direction can render you unrecognized in the world. This is a good location for a toilet or stove, health will improve greatly.

The -80 direction is ***NW*** for 1 Guas, ***South*** for 2 Guas, ***NE*** for 3 Guas, ***West*** for 4 Guas, ***North*** for 6 Guas, ***SE*** for 7 Guas, ***East*** for 8 Guas, and ***SW*** for 9 Guas.

Total Disaster and Major Losses (Cheuh Ming) -90: Activating this direction can bring grievous harm that may include bankruptcy, a death in the family, divorce, horrific failure in business, accidents, and no descendants. It brings total disaster and major losses and should be avoided. This is a good location for a toilet or stove.

The -90 direction is ***SW*** for 1 Guas, ***North*** for 2 Guas, ***West*** for 3 Guas, ***NE*** for 4 Guas, ***South*** for 6 Guas, ***East*** for 7 Guas, ***SE*** for 8 Guas, and ***NW*** for 9 Guas.

Putting the Life Gua to Work

Using direction in important areas of the home

Now that you have your Life Gua Number and have located your best/worst directions, you will be able to improve the Feng Shui of your home and business environments considerably, thereby maximizing the potential of the rooms in which you live and work. The following recommendations concern features such as doors, toilets, stoves/knobs, bedroom locations, and bed directions. The stove knob direction is important because they ignite fire; stoves are the most important fire feature in the house.

The following is great information but need not be committed to memory; the Eight Mansions' principles are automatically factored in for you in chapters 6 and 7's recommendations for your home. Here are some important ways in which to use Eight Mansions in your living space in order to enhance health-luck and to give you an idea why the recommendations in chapters 6 and 7 were formulated as they are.

Doors. You must have a good door that brings you great health-luck. If you have a door facing one of your four good directions, use it. Doors are so important in Feng Shui: they get the highest priority, no matter the system used. Your house and front door ideally would face and receive energy from your +80. The door you enter from 90 percent of the time must be one of your four good directions. If not, use another door to enter from. For example, if your front door is excellent, and your interior garage door is not, mix it up. Use your garage door only 20 percent of the time and your front door 80 percent of the time or vice versa. This one change alone will immediately alter your luck; that's how powerful doors are!

Bedrooms and bed direction. Bedrooms are such an important part of our life; the energy must be conducive for harmonious and healthy living. Since the master bedroom is crucial, particular attention should be paid to it as it will determine the luck of the owner/s or heads of household. This room governs the finances, harmony, and well-being of the family. Feng Shui places great emphasis on not only the location of the bedroom but the bed direction as well. The sleeping direction is of vital significance for both married and single people. This area of the house is an opportunity not to be missed to enhance your life.

If your master bedroom is located in a good sector of the house for you, this is a good start to excellent health. Since direction is more powerful than location, make sure your bed is in a good direction. To activate the correct bed direction, you will need to place your headboard to that direction. Move your bed to the health direction (Tien Yi or +80); even if it means you have to angle it to do so. Your bedroom should ideally be located in the +80 sector of the house. The bed direction/headboard would be to your +80 direction as well if your goal is better health.

As an added note, bedrooms should not be located in the basement; this is considered overly yin or "cold" chi. Everyday use of a basement bedroom will affect the health adversely. Other general sleeping taboos are mirrors in the bedroom, sleeping under architectural beams, toilets over your head, and water features in the room. Refer to *Classical Feng Shui for Romance, Sex & Relationships* for ideas on how to cure these situations.

Toilet placement. The toilets of the house *should not* be located in any of your good sectors; if so, use one located in another area of the house if possible. Toilets are best placed in your -90, -80, -70, or -60 locations. You should NOT have a toilet located in your +80 sector of the house; health will suffer. Many have the mistaken idea that the toilet will "flush away" something—money, health or relationships. This is not accurate; the reason toilets should not be located in your good sectors is the *nature* and *use* of the toilet.

The stove. A good location of the stove is another powerful way to use the Eight Mansions system. It is said that "fire" has the ability to burn up your bad luck. So it should be located in any of your negative areas, especially on your -70 or -80 if you want to increase health-luck, by doing this, you'll be "burning up" your bad luck. However, you will not have a good result if your stove is located on your +80, health may be seriously compromised. The knobs of the stove should be to one of your good directions, particularly your +80 to secure vibrant health. Knobs are typically located in the front or right-hand side. The stove knobs, controls, or buttons are referred to as the "firemouth."

The office and desk. The location of a home office becomes really important if you have a home-based business or if you spend a great deal of time there. At minimum, you will need to face, while sitting at your desk, a good direction (+60, +70, +80 or +90). Face your +80 direction if possible; this will support health and longevity. If you face your -80, you will activate bad health, illness, and disease.

The "Nachos" of Feng Shui *(The door, bed, stove)*

There are three things that you must *absolutely* have supporting you: the door, bed, and stove—and this means in *both* Eight Mansions and Flying Stars! While there is much more to Feng Shui, if these three areas are *not* good, you will likely suffer in your relationships, money, and health. Why are these three areas so important?

Let's start with the way you come and go from your space, the door. There is a famous Chinese saying: "If your door is worth a thousand pieces of gold, your house is worth four," indicating the significance of a good door; indeed, a good door is golden! The reason is simple: doors breathe in the energy from the outside *and* you activate it with your own powerful energy with every use. When a door opens and closes, it "flaps the chi," another way of saying that it activates it and stimulates the energy. Therefore, the door must be excellent for you personally. In a single-family dwelling or even an office building, you may have several doors to choose from. In most apartments, condos, or high-rise buildings, however, the door to your home/unit has only one way in and out. So it must be in one of your good directions, otherwise you will be constantly activating negative energy that does not support you.

Next is the bed direction. Because we spend approximately a third of our lives in the sleep state, it's very important that our bed is placed to support us. This is how we rejuvenate, and it too should be in one of our four best directions.

The stove/kitchen is also very important in Classical Feng Shui; it is the most important "fire" in the house. The range or stovetop is where food is prepared and how we nourish our bodies; it rates higher than ovens. The stove knobs, buttons, or controls (how the fire is ignited) must face one of our good directions. Additionally, the stove *cannot* be located on one of your good sectors/directions or it will "burn up" your good luck.

So my students would remember the great importance of these three areas *and* to always examine them first, I started calling them the "nachos"—just an appetizer, not the whole enchilada or whole meal. (I'm from Texas and we love our Mexican food.) My analogy is very humorous to them, and humor is a great way to remember a point.

Even when my students have me review one of their clients' homes—the first thing I ask is, "How are the nachos?"

These three things sound really simple but it is often very challenging to implement them effectively as there are often obstacles to overcome.

Make an effort to examine how you're using your space in these three extremely important areas and implement small changes, and they'll make a huge difference.

Advanced Eight Mansions

Opposites Attract

The Eight Mansions system has two levels: Basic Eight Mansions and Advanced Eight Mansions (AEM). Basic Eight Mansions is used to determine your Life Gua Number, good/bad directions, and personality type.

Advanced Eight Mansions allow certain 15-degree increments of your bad directions to be used and activated. This becomes really important when a couple belongs to different Life groups—often, opposites attract.

In general, this is how it works: the South is a bad direction for anyone who is West Life Group (2, 6, 7, or 8), but in AEM the first and third 15-degree of South can be used.

That means you can face your bed direction or desk, or use doors facing these specific increments. If you are part of the East Life Group (1, 3, 4, or 9), West is one of your bad directions.

However, in AEM you can use the first and third 15 degree increments. Now having said that, the entire 45 degrees of North cannot be used by anyone who is part of the West Life Group (2, 6, 7, or 8), unfortunately, not one single degree.

Advanced Eight Mansions			
East Life Group (1, 3, 4, or 9 Guas) **North, South, East & SE plus:**		*West Life Group* (2, 6, 7, or 8 Guas) **SW, West, NW & NE plus:**	
Direction	Degrees	Direction	Degrees
Southwest 1	202.6° to 217.5°	South 1	157.6° to 172.5°
Southwest 3	232.6° to 247.5°	South 3	187.6° to 202.5°
West 1	247.6° to 262.5°	North	none
West 3	277.6° to 292.5°	East 1	67.6° to 82.5°
Northwest 1	292.6° to 307.5°	East 3	97.6° to 112.5°
Northwest 3	322.6° to 337.5°	Southeast 3	142.6° to 157.5°
Northeast 3	52.6° to 67.5°		

Figure 12: Advanced Eight Mansions.

Couples who are part of different Life groups need special considerations to make it work for both of them. These differences have been factored in the recommendations located in chapters 6 and 7, so pay close attention to suggested directions according to your Life Gua. This is really important where you may share the same space—the marital bed. In this case, choose a direction that states it is good for all Guas. Don't worry if you see I'm recommending a "bad" direction; remember in Advanced Eight Mansions certain 15-degree increments can be used. Figure 12 shows which directions and increments are usable:

Eight Mansions Life Gua Personalities

This aspect is similar to astrology

Now let's explore another aspect of Eight Mansions, the Life Gua Personalities. Since you know your personal Life Gua Number, you now have information on which directions support you and those that can bring trouble. Also, based on your Life Gua, you're assigned certain personality traits, energy, and characteristics. Do keep in mind that they are general and not meant to be definitive; however, I find after consulting with several thousand clients, that they are very accurate. The personality narratives work very similar to astrology; each Life Gua will have an element (water, wood, fire, earth, or metal) and this energy will influence the person's behavior, habits, physical looks, health issues, attraction to specific occupations, thinking process, and sexual desires—both negative and positive in all these areas. I call these portrayals the Life Gua Personalities and I'm the originator of this particular extraction from the Eight Mansions system; they were first introduced in *Classical Feng Shui for Wealth and Abundance.*

Although the Life Gua Personalities cannot be found in ancient classic texts, the information on the Guas can, which is where I derived the information. The idea started in 2000, when in class one day, Master Yap gave us quick, three- or four-word verbal descriptions of each of the Life Guas' propensities. We found it greatly entertaining, and I began sharing the descriptions when consulting with my clients giving them key information about their spouses, children, coworkers, business partners, bosses, and family members. I also started including it in my training classes and public lectures; people loved it! It gives some very interesting insights into personalities, and it is very accurate.

After many years of doing this verbally and informally, I decided to expand on Master Yap's three- or four-word descriptions of the Life Guas and pen it; this was based on the extensive information available on the eight Guas themselves (see chapter 2 under the Eight Guas/Trigrams), the five element theory, and the Tan Lang Stars (the 9 Stars). Throughout history, masters have developed formulas based on the basic principles/energy tools and the Life Gua Personalities are an example of that; Classical Feng Shui is a living science.

In the following descriptions you will see good and bad; please keep in mind that everyone is capable of exhibiting negative, dark aspects of them at any given time. All energy, including humans, has a yin and yang aspect—this is our nature. Our level of self-awareness will largely determine which of the qualities we primarily show to the world. We all have times we are not "on" and may slip into the negative aspects of ourselves. Do not be offended or focus on the negative aspects of your personality descriptions; you may already have grown past most of it.

The 1 Life Gua Personality

Gua Name: Kan

The Element influencing this personality: Water

Life Group: East

Key Words: Secretive, Emotional, Scholarly

Personality: The 1 Guas are highly intellectual and can be studious or even scholarly. To the outside world, they appear calm and cool; however, inside they have a rich emotional makeup. As a result, at times they can be overly emotional, moody, anxious, and high strung. They are full of brilliant ideas and concepts, and are usually very good at making and holding onto money. The 1 Guas are skilled at sizing up people using their natural, intuitive abilities. Since their element is water, they can be hard to pin down. They are sensual and can be highly sexual. Tending to keep secrets below the surface, 1 Guas are known to have secret and arcane lives.

The Best Occupations/Industries: Philosopher, irrigation, finance, freight, shipping, spa and pool industry, communications, bars/pubs, tourism, firefighting, law enforcement, maritime, sex industry (therapy or tantric), diplomacy, counselors, artist, consultants, sales, teachers, viticulture, scholars, and designers.

Health Issues: Kidney, blood disease, blood pressure, blocked blood vessels, heart/stomach vessel blockage, kidney stress, water retention, dehydration, food poisoning, ovarian problems, nerve sickness, circulation problems, urinary problems, incontinence, weak sperm, premature ejaculation, alcoholism, sickness and problems related to childbirth, problems associated with sex organs, tinnitus, and dry throat.

The 2 Life Gua Personality

Gua Name: Kun

The Element influencing this personality: Earth

Life Group: West

Key Words: Persistent, Reclusive, Dependable

Personality: 2 Guas exhibit persistence, dependability, and a calm demeanor. They can also be nurturing and supportive to their inner circle. With their calm, relaxed demeanors, 2 Guas are dependable and tend to have developed psychic abilities. They make excellent doctors or practitioners of alternate healing arts such as chiropractry, massage therapy, and acupuncture. Since the 2 Guas have the most yin energy of the Guas, they enjoy and feel comfortable in dark spaces, but have a tendency toward depression or dark moodiness. Good spelunkers, these grounded people relish activities that focus on the earth—gardening, farming, construction, and agriculture.

The Best Occupations/Industries: Property, real estate, construction, earthenware, consultancy, hotel, insurance, architecture, interior design, cave explorers, pottery, recruitment, quarry, human resource, handyman, farmer, gynecology and obstetrics, and clergy.

Health Issues: Fatigue, sickness, contracting a chronic disease, mental confusion, too much coldness in the organs, weakness in body, cancer, esophagus, depression, intestines, digestive issues, no appetite, indigestion, dropping of stomach, constipation, toothache, skin disease, always feeling cold, spleen problems, typhoid, stomach infection, and muscle pain.

The 3 Life Gua Personality

Gua Name: Chen

The Element influencing this personality: Wood

Life Group: East

Key Words: Enterprising, Impatient, Self-Confident

Personality: The 3 Guas are extremely enterprising and have progressive ideas. They tend to be outspoken, direct, and organized. The 3 Gua's nature is one of nervousness punctuated by lots of energy and steam. Constantly crafting new inventions, new ventures, or the latest thing, they love new beginnings and start-ups. When in a negative energy, 3 Guas tend to self-punish, spread their energy too thin leading to collapse, and can be abrasive. However, they are full of surprises, 3 Guas have a sense of vitality and vigor that can overwhelm people.

The Best Occupations/Industries: Education, philosophy, social services, medicine, pharmaceuticals, print media, publishing, bookstores, gardening, farming, agriculture, textiles, fashion, telegraph operator, technician, musician, broadcast announcer, and transportation.

Health Issues: Liver disease, problems with the feet (especially the left foot), vocal chords, gall bladder, nerve disease, too much heat/fire in stomach/body, very dry throat, teeth, ovary problems, nervous system issues lead to weight issues, face and head problems, a general feeling of disease and painful, head/hand injuries, obesity, headaches, and leg problems.

The 4 Life Gua Personality

Gua Name: Xun

The Element influencing this personality: Wood

Life Group: East

Key Words: Honest, Malleable, Progressive

Personality: Malleable, flexible, indecisive, the 4 Guas may "blow with the wind" if not grounded, finding it hard to take a stand. In general, they usually are attractive people or may have movie-star qualities. The 4 Guas are more prone to be sexually controlled by their partners than other Guas. They have progressive ideas and can become famous in writing or rich in the publishing business. The un-evolved 4s may self-destruct by refusing good advice. The 4 Guas can be somewhat remote and private, but they are also gentle people with an innocent purity.

The Best Occupations/Industries: Education, philosophy, social services, medicine, pharmaceuticals, print media, publishing, bookstores, gardening, farming, agriculture, textiles, fashion, telegraph operator, technician, musician, broadcast announcer, and transportation.

Health Issues: Liver issues, too much exercise causes problems, sickness, weak body, children undernourished, breathless, bald head, rheumatism, cold sickness, shivering, dizziness, coughing, and snakebites.

The 6 Life Gua Personality

Gua Name: Chien
The Element influencing this personality: Metal
Life Group: West
Key Words: Leaders, Solitary, Creative

Personality: The 6 Guas can easily step into positions of power and authority as they are natural leaders who seem to be blessed by the heavens. They make excellent lawyers, judges, and CEOs as their energy commands respect. The 6 Guas have a regal, royal air about them that is naturally unpretentious. Clear thinkers, lots of courage, possessing foresight, extremely creative, and they can hold their own in a debate. They need time alone as they often get caught up in over-thinking, which can lead to being sleep-deprived. Oozing with creativity, 6 Guas are filled with ideas that involve large groups of people, a community, or an organization.

The Best Occupations/Industries: Emperor, ruler, president, sovereign, dictator, leader, monarch, sage, founder of a religion, pope, church elder, prime minister, board chairman, military commander, director, governor, teacher, banker, statesman, CEO, chief, leader, head of government office, engineering, computers, gold, hardware, heavy machinery, lawyers, judges, sports equipment, clocks, and lecturers.

Health Issues: Bone fractures, strokes, insanity, neurosis, skin disease, baldness, head injury, Parkinson's disease, coughs, dry and/or sore throat, breathlessness, influenza, panting, arthritis, pain of bones, head and nose problems, and easily-caught colds.

The 7 Life Gua Personality

Gua Name: Dui
The Element influencing this personality: Metal
Life Group: West
Key Words: Charming, Excessive, Talkative

Personality: 7 Guas tend to be youthful in behavior or appearance. They are very attracted to metaphysical studies and arts; they can be talkative, lively, and nervous. 7 Gua women are often blessed with very good looks, and sensuous beauty. Comfortable with the stage, the 7 Guas are good at acting and speaking in front of the camera or on the radio. With a strong tendency to overindulge in life's pleasures, they must keep a balanced life. They can be a fast-talker, a smooth talker, or have a razor-sharp tongue. The 7 Guas are very social, charming, and charismatic; they create stimulating, informative conversation wherever they go.

The Best Occupations: Actors, celebrities, singers, Internet-related businesses, engineering, computers, gold, hardware, heavy machinery, lawyers, judges, sports equipment, clocks, artist, soldiers, and lecturers.

Health Issues: Catches colds easily, inflammation of the lungs, shortness of breath, hurt by knives, toothaches, mouth cancer, face and leg scars, cancer, miscarriage, difficulty giving birth, STDs, and suicide by hanging.

The 8 Life Gua Personality

Gua Name: Gen
The Element influencing this personality: Earth
Life Group: West
Key Words: Successful, Hoarders, Dependable

Personality: The 8 Guas have a stubborn, dependable, and steadfast nature. They tend to have a great deal of integrity and are vey attracted to all things spiritual. They can become spiritual seekers, trekking and scaling mountains in search of "answers" and to find themselves. Hardworking and loving things of the earth, the 8s are talented in construction, real estate, and landscaping. They also have a little "save the world" energy. While the 8 Guas tend to resist change, they can deftly handle trouble without falling apart. Undeveloped 8 Guas can become hoarders, self-righteous, and short-tempered. They are geared for success and often become very rich with worldly honors, recognition, and status.

The Best Occupations/Industries: Property, real estate, construction, earthenware, consultancy, hotel, landscape architect, insurance, architecture, interior design, pottery, recruitment, quarry, human resources, handyman, farmer, gynecology and obstetrics, clergy, restaurateur, Taoist spirituality, and celebrity.

Health Issues: Backbone, shoulder, hand, leg, stomach, feeling haggard and tired, coccyx pain, bone fractures, injury by twisting, gallstones, problems with the left leg, pain in the ribs, spinal problems, weak looking, hip problems, chronic illness, and back pain.

The 9 Life Gua Personality

Gua Name: Li
The Element influencing this personality: Fire
Life Group: East
Key Words: Adventurous, Rash, Brilliance

Personality: 9 Guas have a sharp, brilliant intellect; they can also be wise, loyal, and sentimental. Blessed with a fiery spirit and energy, these Guas have a decided adventurous streak. 9 Gua women are usually beautiful, like divas or goddesses but can be argumentative, aggressive, and rash. With concentrated and focused effort, they can reach great height of achievements and standing in the world. Un-evolved and imbalanced 9 Guas will exhibit mental illness such as paranoia and psychotic, unstable behavior. When grounded and well developed, 9s can light up a room with their radiant energy!

The Best Occupations/Industries: Acting, show business, public speaking, fuel, oil, chemicals, optical, cosmetics, advertising, television, restaurants, lighting, beauty, writers, war correspondence, soldiers, barbers, hairdressers, or welders.

Health Issues: Heart, eyes, eyesight, stroke, irritated mind, breast pain, high blood pressure, bleeding, electrical shock, gas poisoning, eye disease, heart failure, heart sickness, burning, and frequent illness.

Deeper Into the Life Gua Personalities

Even though the Life Gua gives great insights into our personalities, I noticed that not all Life Guas were created equal. While in general, for example, 1 Life Guas are very intelligent, secretive, love their freedom and are very sensuous, they can be very different depending on the animal year in which they were born. For example a 1 Gua born in the year of the Rat is very different from the 1 Gua born in the year of the Horse.

With that in mind, I created an expanded version of the personality types combining them with the animal years of birth; this is more specific to your energy and personality traits. I've dubbed the more expanded version of the Life Guas the Life Gua Zodiac Personalities. You will find the complete descriptions of the Life Guas matched up with all the twelve animals of the Chinese Zodiac in *Classical Feng Shui for Romance, Sex & Relationships*; it is very detailed and will give you important clues into your energy and others in your sphere.[33]

Now let's explore how health may be enhanced or compromised using the famous Flying Star System (*Xuan Kong Fei Xing*); a formula that's essential in altering your Feng Shui to be advantageous. Flying Stars is a method of computation, and the interpretation of the "stars" (numbers) and their meanings will indicate the potential for immense luck and good health, but these benefits will not materialize unless activated. Learning a little about Flying Stars Feng Shui places the potential for tremendous good fortune in the palm of your hand!

---

33. This book was released by Llewellyn on January 8, 2015, under the full title of *Classical Feng Shui for Romance, Sex & Relationships: Design Your Living Space for Love, Harmony and Prosperity.*

Five

Flying Stars: The Vital Link in Identifying Disease

When you are sick of sickness, you are no longer sick.
Old Chinese Proverb

On February 4, 2004, we experienced a capital change worldwide and hit a major milestone in energy. There will be another significant change in 2024. These milestones have a tremendous effect on the luck transformations of all homes and buildings and will continue to affect them for twenty-year periods. We will discuss all the possible ways in which to take advantage of these major shifts in energy. Many interesting things will happen on the world stage during these times; the idea is to use Flying Stars to safeguard the energy of your homes and workplaces to not just survive but thrive.

Flying Stars Feng Shui is in fact the most *mathematical* system in the endless variety of techniques used in the practice of Feng Shui. Unlike Eight Mansions, where the focus is on people, Flying Stars provides an energy map for all structures whether it is a home, shopping mall, office building, or anywhere. It is an advanced method of investigating the potential luck of any building at any time. However, our focus in the book is on homes. As with all systems of Feng Shui, it involves direction or orientation. Once the correct Natal Star chart is located, you will be able to do an analysis as to the meaning of the stars and star combinations. This powerful technique has an emphasis on the aspect of time and cycles of time, and is sometimes referred to as "Time Dimension Feng Shui."

At first blush, Flying Stars may appear daunting; indeed, it takes some time to master. However, having knowledge of this method makes arranging, building, or remodeling a home very worthwhile. What you will learn here works fast and can bring an easier life of abundance and good health; although, you must also participate in life and make efforts in tandem with great Feng Shui.

When done right, Flying Stars ensures there are fewer obstacles in your life. There's an explicit method to this system, which creates an environment conducive for better health, and to attract greater harmony that leads to success. It can also create energy that can magnetize a higher income and improve your wealth-luck. Using Flying Stars leaves less room for mistakes, as the techniques are specific and precise.

Xuan Kong Fei Xing

The Flying Stars system is also surrounded by mystery. While Masters will readily acknowledge that it is one of the *best* systems, it has had an interesting journey into modern-day Feng Shui practice. It has been around for more than 1,500 years, but many of the ancients followed the "secrets of Heaven should not be revealed" mandate, which unfortunately increased the secrecy surrounding the transmission of the art. Flying Stars Feng Shui's popularity faded until the middle of the Qing Dynasty (1644–1911 CE); it was later during the prominence of the Song culture when interest was revived.

Another major turning point for this system occurred around 1927 in Hong Kong; the modern-day Masters there were responsible for its great popularity and use today around the world. The famous text *Shen Shi Xuan Kong* ("Shen's Study of the Mysterious Void") by Shen Zhao-Min and Jiang Yu-Sheng was published in 1927 and became extremely popular. It was further edited by Master Shen's sons and republished under the title of *The Expanded Shen Shi Xuan Kong Xue*; it remains a favorite in China, Hong Kong, and southeast Asia.

Flying Stars is part of a foremost branch of Classical Feng Shui and has been around and used by Feng Shui masters since the first major revival without interruption for over 400 years (Song era). The full name for this method is *Xuan Kong Fei Xing* (pronounced Shoon Kong Fay Sing). *Xuan Kong* means the "subtle mysteries of time and space" and *Fei Xing* means Flying Stars. It is also referred to as "time dimension Feng Shui" as it so accurately predicts the energy/events of a structure in the past, present, and the future.

While there have been several books on Flying Stars in recent years, most Americans haven't heard of the practice as they are more familiar with the simplistic, Westernized styles of Feng Shui. Flying Stars is a system that explains why no structure would forever enjoy good or bad Feng Shui as it cycles through time. Natal Star charts are calculated according to the facing direction and the move-in date of the structure under examination. It's very similar to an astrological chart for a person, but it's for buildings. Due to the fact that Flying Stars is an advanced system and "flying the stars" is one of the more challenging aspects, I will not be teaching the technique here; it really deserves an entire book to do it justice.[34]

34. To fly the stars, numbers move around the Luo Shu grid in pre-set sequences that set the "flight path" for how all other numerals should "fly." Refer to chapter 2 to refresh your memory on the 9-celled Luo Shu grid (aka the magic square).

There is more than enough information in the book to design excellent Feng Shui for your interiors, the kind that will activate good fortune in the health, wealth, and relationship areas of life. So let's get right to the good stuff: I've provided all the Natal Star charts for every possible facing direction which is the actual purpose of "flying the stars" in the first place.

Natal Star Charts

Remember, contingent upon the specific compass direction that a structure faces, it will have a unique Natal Flying Star chart; this is like an astrological chart as it identifies strong and weak aspects. Except in this case, it identifies the building's potential and energy map. Once you have identified your Natal Star chart, you will know how to correctly activate the different sectors with auspicious energy.

The "stars" are not actual stars in the night sky; rather they are numbers (1 through 9) that represent different types of energy relating to life's conditions and situations. That said, the nine stars do have an earthly correlation to the seven real stars of the Big Dipper (aka Ursa Major or "the Northern Ladle") with two additional imaginary ones.

Each "star" has unique qualities and energy that can influence behavior and events; I'll cover this in more detail later. Flying Stars is based on huge and small time cycles and planetary alignments. These cycles of time are energy patterns of the environment that influence the welfare of all living beings, and they ebb and flow with the passage of time. You can find these energy patterns in Flying Star charts; they are recognized as the *winds of chi* that bring either blessings or afflictions, good fortune or misfortune.

Time Cycles of Flying Stars Feng Shui

As we discussed earlier, Flying Stars has a time dimension aspect in addition to several key areas regarding the cycles of time; understanding them brings a practice forward to modern-day Feng Shui. Basically, there are three important blocks of time: the 180 Great Cycle, three sixty-year cycles, and finally nine twenty-year increments known as periods (see Figure 13). We will put most of the focus on periods in this book, although all are important in the system.

Cycle	Period	Years	Trigram/Gua
Upper	1	1864-1884	Kan
	2	1884-1904	Kun
	3	1904-1924	Chen
Middle	4	1924-1944	Xun/Sun
	5	1944-1964	No Trigram
	6	1964-1984	Chien/Qian
Lower	7	1984-2004	Dui/Tui
	8	2004-2024	Gen/Ken
	9	2024-2044	Li

Figure 13: The San Yuan 180-year Cycle of Time.

Regarding the Great Cycle, according to the ancient Chinese scholars, the planets in our Solar System align in a straight line once every ~180 years. It is believed that the first observation of this phenomenon was around 2500 BCE. Modern-day scientists have named this the "Jupiter effect." Next, the 180-year cycle is divided into three sixty-year cycles called Upper, Middle, and Lower.

The sixty-year cycles were once more divided into twenty-year increments called periods or ages. Each period is assigned a number (1 through 9) and a trigram (except 5, which has no trigram) that has a unique energy it exhibits for twenty years that affects the world. Why periods of twenty years? It is interesting that Chinese astronomers also noted that the Milky Way shifted every twenty years, thus affecting the luck of a building/home and people as well. Figure 13 gives an example of the nine twenty-year periods comprising the 180-year Great/Mega cycle of time that covers the years of 1864 to 2044.

As you can see, we are currently in Period 8 (aka Age of 8) and will be until February 3, 2024. In fact we are more than midway through it; homes that have not been transformed into Period 8 may be described as declining in vitality and perhaps, even stagnant. We will discuss how to bring your house's energy back and reenergize it if you moved in between February 4, 1984, and February 3, 2004, or Period 7.

The next period, 9, will start February 4, 2024. The ruling energy or influence is always the number and associated trigram of the Period. For example, 8 is the king for Period 8! The number eight—even when we are not in Period 8—has always been venerated in Chinese culture as it is believed to have noble energy, and it is a homophone for "getting rich." In chapters 6 and 7 you will find all the Flying Stars Charts from 1984 to 2024.

This covers two twenty-year Periods, and we will be only discussing Period 8 and Period 7 as most homes fall into these two time periods. Period 6 charts are not covered in this book, as it would be extremely rare that someone moved into a home between 1964 and 1984 and did not remodel or update it. With renovations, it would have changed to a Period 7 home or if remodeled *after* 2004, it would have become a Period 8 residence.

Components of a Flying Star Chart

So what does a Flying Star chart look like anyway? Remember, the Flying Star chart of a property is simply the building's energy map. Feng Shui Masters use this chart to make accurate predictions on relationships, the potential for prosperity, success in a career, health, and diseases, when a promotion or marriage may take place, lawsuits—anything that may happen in the human experience.

A Flying Star chart is made up of three numbers in a nine-square grid; these individual squares are also referred to as sectors, palaces, locations, or directions. Figure 14 shows the components.

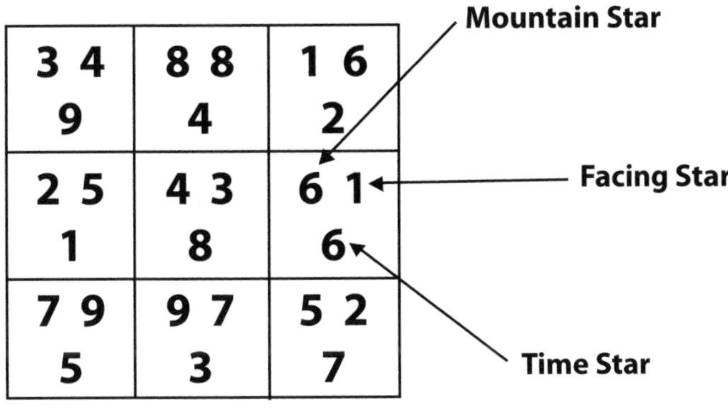

Figure 14: Components of a Flying Star chart.

Facing Star. Also known as "water stars," these numbers are located in the upper right-hand corner in all nine palaces of the chart. The "facing stars" bring luck associated with the accumulation of wealth. The good stars indicate prosperity and financial status, while the bad stars denote money loss and even bankruptcy. The Chinese name is *Siang Sin.*

Mountain Star. Also known as *sitting stars*, these numbers are located in the upper left-hand corner in all nine palaces of the chart. The *mountain star* is associated with health- and relationship-luck. The good stars indicate vibrant health and great relationships, while the bad stars denote disease, bad romance, reproductive issues, affairs, and bad behavior. The Chinese name is *Chor Sin.*

Time Star. Also known as the *base star*, this number indicates the period to which the chart belongs. It is the single star below the facing and mountain stars.

To keep things simple and consistent throughout the book, I will use the terms "facing star" and "mountain star"; these are the two most important stars in the chart in terms of influencing the energy. The facing star reveals the potential for wealth, finances, or loss of wealth, while the mountain star is associated with health, relationships, romance, family, authority and mental attitudes. Masters will immediately focus their attention on the facing and mountain stars of the current period, at present this is the 8 star.

In order to fully understand the soul of Flying Stars, you must be familiar with what each star portends. In this system, the auspicious stars with the most benevolent energy are 1, 6, 8, and 9, facing or mountain stars. Since we're currently in Period 8, the 8 Star is the most fortunate of all stars and is in its peak in strength and vigor. The 4 Star is good for romance, writing, scholarly pursuits, publishing, fame, and public persona. The unlucky and inauspicious stars are 2, 3, 5, and 7—that can deliver sickness, lawsuits, disasters, and robbery—respectively.

The 5 Star is the most pernicious star and is considered evil because it has no assigned direction, remember it is in the center of the Luo Shu (aka Magic Square). It does, however, possess immense power. The unlucky stars are only good in their period; otherwise, they are considered inauspicious and harmful. In other words, the 5 Star is only advantageous in Period 5, and the same follows for the 2, 3, and 7 stars in their respective periods. When a Flying Star chart is analyzed, there are several important factors—the nature of the star (good or bad), the landforms in your immediate environment, and the interior layout of your living space and how you're using it.

In Feng Shui, water and mountain are two important icons of good fortune. Thus, water and mountain must always be placed in a way where they complement each other. This concept applies to the exterior with landforms/topography and in the Flying Star system with mountain and facing/water stars.

If the external formations support the energy of the chart, you will get a positive result. An auspicious formation can bring good fortune, while landforms that do not support the chart can attract misfortune. The chart can only come *alive* and bestow benevolent energy when the interior living space and external landforms support it.

How to Locate the Right Star Chart

Before you can locate your home's unique chart, you will need the following information before getting started. You will also need this information before implementing all the recommendations in either chapter 6 or 7.

There are two important factors that must be determined in order to locate (or fly) the correct chart for your house: the move-in date and the house facing. The move-in date will tell us which period the structure belongs to; this is where those time cycles come into consideration. The house facing is how the structure receives energy from a specific direction.

1. Move-in Date

Homes will be either Period 7 or Period 8

Even in Classical Feng Shui, there are various opinions about the approach to some systems; Flying Stars is one of those. The discussions of whether to use the construction date or the move-in date is a perfect example of such controversy. According to Grandmaster Yap, these debates can get very passionate—everyone thinks they're right! For the most part, masters in Hong Kong prefer the construction date, while those in Malaysia, Singapore, and Taiwan use the move-in date. Personally, I think it is ridiculous to believe a home built in the 1800s or even fifty years ago will maintain the same energy today; people moving in and out essentially change the chi. At the end of the day, I'm in the lineage of Master Yap Chen Hai, so I use the move-in date as he does; I find it extremely reliable and far more accurate than the construction date.

Use the following information to determine what period your home belongs to:

- Your home is a ***Period** 7*, if you moved in between ***February 4, 1984,*** and ***February 3, 2004.***
- Your home is a ***Period 8*** if you moved in between ***February 4, 2004,*** and ***February 3, 2024.***
- Exceptions for Period 7 homes are if major renovations took place after February 4, 2004.

What constitutes a major renovation? Removing the entire roof—with some small percentage exposed to the open sky at least for a few hours, major interior remodeling, renovating the front entrance and door, painting the entire inside and outside at the same time, remodeling kitchen or bathrooms, installing a skylight/s, changing all the floors at the same time, adding on a room or adding an attached garage. All of these things will cause a major shift in energy, and therefore your Flying Star chart will change.

So if you did any of these things or a combination of them (*after* February 4, 2004) and you moved in Period 7, your home will now be a Period 8 chart. If you moved into your house after 2004 and have done or are currently doing some renovations, your home is still a Period 8. So, finding out which period your home belongs to is the first part of locating the correct Natal Star chart. The second part is to determine the actual facing direction; you'll need to measure this with a smartphone app or a simple outdoor compass.

Therefore, based on your home's unique facing (the compass direction) and move-in date, you will find the most hands-on part of the book by referring to either chapter 6 or 7; Period 8 charts can be found in chapter 6, while the Period 7 charts can be found in chapter 7. Until you're ready to actually start implementing the recommendations found there by moving your bed, desk, and so forth, let's explore some more fascinating aspects of the Flying Star system. As the scope of Flying Star Feng Shui is so remarkable, further study will no doubt deepen your appreciation before you start making changes to your living space.

2. House Facing

Taking the Compass Direction

You will need a fairly accurate compass or use a good app on your smartphone; remember the phone will not have an actual magnetic in it. So if you are unsure, get a good hiking compass to confirm it.

Take your compass measurement/degree from the front door if it *faces* the road. More than 80 percent of homes have the door facing the road and is located approximately in the center of the house. In these homes, taking your compass direction will be fairly straightforward. If the door does not face the road, stand in the middle of your front yard/garden to determine how your house faces. Any side doors or angled doors—even if they seems to face the road—*cannot* be used to measure from to determine the facing in this system. The general rule for determining the facing is where the most yang energy is; the truth is almost nothing competes with the energy of a street except the ocean.

For those who live in apartment buildings, use the main door/entrance to the structure as the facing direction; superimpose the correct chart/direction over your floor plan. In Figure 15, the arrows show the correct facing direction of these structures. House 2 is the only one that you can take the compass direction at the door itself; all others you must stand in front of the building to get the facing degree in order to find the correct Natal Star chart.

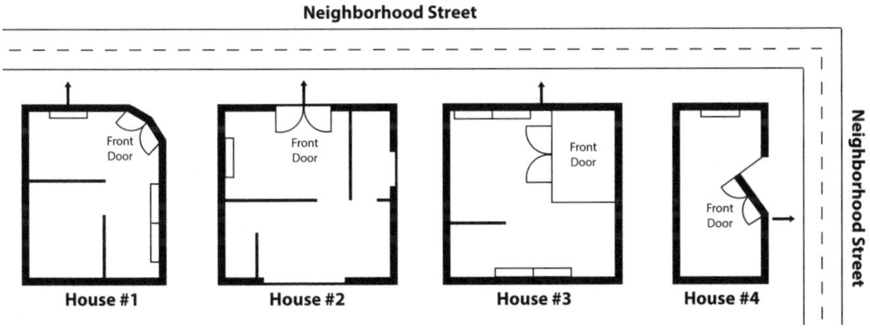

Figure 15: Determining the facing. The arrows point to the correct facing direction which is toward the road; measure this direction with a compass to find your Flying Star chart. In houses 1, 3, and 4, the front door cannot be used to determine facing.

Even though there are twenty-four possible facing directions there are only sixteen Flying Star charts for each period, because the last two sub-divided sectors share the same natal chart. In other words, South 2 or South 3 will have the exact same chart in any given period. It will be simple to locate your chart once you have the facing degree; all the charts are clearly indicated by the degrees and will tell you which charts are South 1, East 2, Southwest 1, and so forth. Make sure you have taken an accurate compass direction of your house so you have the correct Flying Star chart; you will be setting new energy into motion.

The 24 Mountains

In Classical Feng Shui and in Flying Stars, the 360 degrees of the compass is divided into 24 sections/directions (each comprised of 15 degrees). This famous division is referred to as the "24 Mountains" (not real mountains, just a term). According to this understanding, all abodes, buildings, and homes can only face one of these twenty-four directions. These twenty-four 15-degree increments are also referred to as subsectors of a main direction. For example, terms such as South 1, South 2, and South 3 indicate the entire 45 degrees of South, but for Feng Shui purposes, are divided neatly into three subsectors.

The Subsectors

Once you have the exact compass degree, you can easily find the right subsector in the 24 Mountains chart. For example, you have measured the facing direction of your property and get a compass reading of 123 degrees. You can see that by referring to the 24 Mountains chart that the structure faces Southeast 1. Or your compass reading may be 110 degrees; according to the chart, this is East 3. Remember, this information is needed whether you're simply locating the correct Natal Star chart or if you wish to fly a Star chart.

The 24 Mountains Chart

The 24 Mountains chart in Figure 16 indicates the general *direction* (North, South, East, etc.), the *subsector* with exact degrees (S1, E2, NW1, etc.), the ***Chinese name*** (Bing, Wei, Xun, etc.) for the direction, and the

12 Animals (Horse, Rat, Goat, etc.) associated with twelve of the directions. I have used the most common spellings for the directions' Chinese names.

The 24 "Mountain" Facing Directions				
General Direction	**Exact Direction**	**Facing Name**	**Energy or Animal**	**Compass Degrees**
South	S1	Bing	Yang Fire	157.6–172.5
	S2	Wu	**HORSE**	172.6–187.5
	S3	Ting	Yin Fire	187.6–202.5
Southwest	SW1	Wei	**GOAT**	202.6–217.5
	SW2	Kun	Earth	217.6–232.5
	SW3	Shen	**MONKEY**	232.6–247.5
West	W1	Geng	Yang Metal	247.6–262.5
	W2	You	**ROOSTER**	262.6–277.5
	W3	Xin	Yin Metal	277.6–292.5
Northwest	NW1	Xu	**DOG**	292.6–307.5
	NW2	Chien	Metal	307.6–322.5
	NW3	Hai	**PIG**	322.6–337.5
North	N1	Ren	Yang Water	337.6–352.5
	N2	Tzi	**RAT**	352.6–7.5
	N3	Kwei	Yin Water	7.6–22.5
Northeast	NE1	Chou	**OX**	22.6–37.5
	NE2	Gen	Earth	37.6–52.5
	NE3	Yin	**TIGER**	52.6–67.5
East	E1	Jia	Yang Wood	67.6–82.5
	E2	Mao	**RABBIT**	82.6–97.5
	E3	Yi	Yin Wood	97.6–112.5
Southeast	SE1	Chen	**DRAGON**	112.6–127.5
	SE2	Xun	Wood	127.6–142.5
	SE3	Su	**SNAKE**	142.6–157.5

Figure 16: The 24 Possible Facing Directions.

Feng Shui masters and professional consultants use a Chinese compass (Luo Pan) that has the twenty-four divisions/directions (known as the 24 Mountain Ring).

The Luo Pan can have up to 36 rings of information; however, the 24 Mountain ring is one of the most used and important. Many modern-day Luo Pans now have English on them right next to this ring (as seen in Figure 17).

The 24 Mountain ring is used to measure the direction of a door or the facing; it is also referred to as the "Earth Plate/Ring" as we are measuring Earth's magnetic energy. The ***San Yuan Luo Pan*** (used in Flying Stars) has one 24 Mountain ring while the ***San He Luo Pan*** has three 24 Mountain rings.[35]

Notice the beautiful Chinese symbols and names associated with the twenty-four directions. While it is possible to practice Flying Stars without recognizing them, learning them is definitely time well spent. You do not need a Luo Pan to learn Flying Stars, but you will if you go professional; meanwhile, a good compass or app will suffice.

The Nature of the Nine Stars

Affecting health, behavior, prosperity, and relationships

The explanations below provide the positive and negative influences of each star, along with a one- or two-word description of its general indication, good or bad.

The stars will have these same attributes whether they are in the mountain or water position in your chart; the secret name for the stars is also revealed.

---

35. The *San He* Luo Pan's three 24 Mountain rings are used to measure the door, mountains, and water; known as the *Earth Plate*/Ring, Human/*Man Plate*/Ring and the Water/*Heaven Plate*/Ring, respectively. The *San Yuan* Luo Pan has one 24 Mountain ring used to measure the door or facing direction; this Luo Pan is used for the Flying Star system.

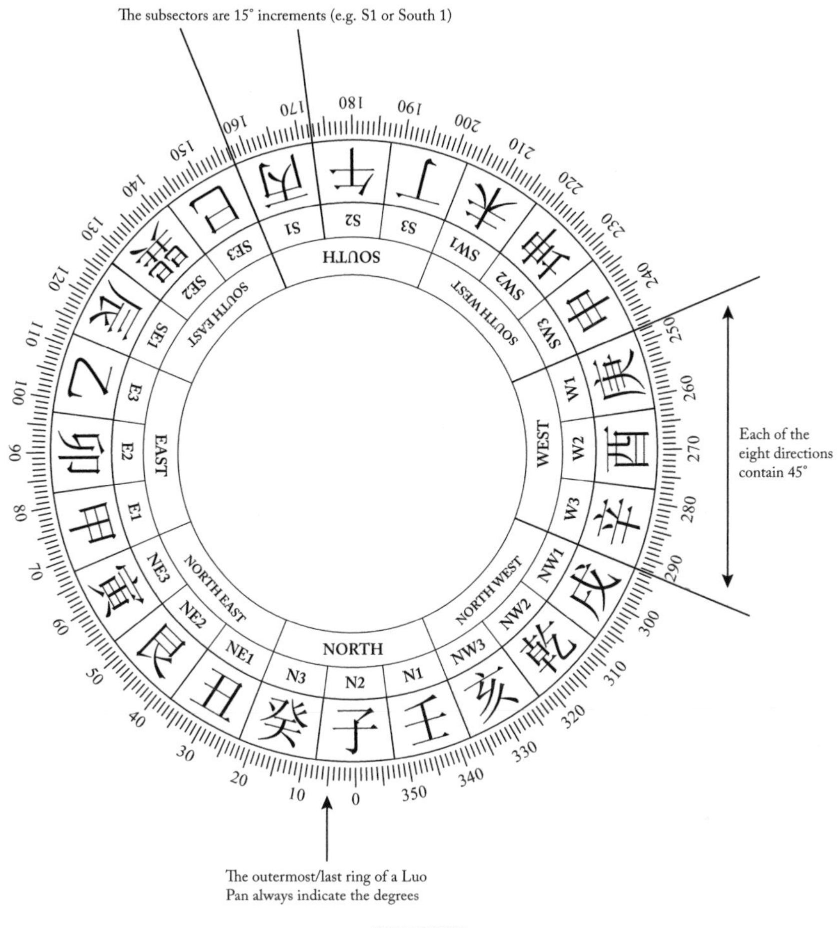

Figure 17: The 24 Mountain Ring.

1 Star

Element: Water

Colour: White

Body Part: Blood, kidney

Good Star: Wealth and Knowledge

Positive Aspects: Research/thinking, knowledge, intelligence, examination, the Scholar, good government positions, promotion and studies, distinction and abundance.

Negative Aspects: The wife dies early, blindness, wandering, divorce, detachment, moving away and disconnecting from people and things.

Secret Name: Greedy Wolf (Tan Lang)

2 Star

Element: Earth
Colour: Black
Body Part: Reproductive organs, stomach
Bad Star: Sickness

Positive Aspects: Wellness and well-being; success at work, money, riches, lots of children, military officers, women in authority, vibrant health, effectiveness, fertility, and productiveness.

Negative Aspects: Difficulties in childbirth, dying young, bad illness, sickness in the stomach, abdominal problems, abortion, and miscarriages.

Secret Name: Huge Door/Gate (Jue Men)

3 Star

Element: Big Wood
Colour: Jade
Body Part: Thighs, feet
Bad Star: Lawsuits and Conflict

Positive Aspects: Power of speech, talented linguist, bright future, good reputation, good scholar, and success in the first business. Food stores and other accumulations of wealth are full.

Negative Aspects: Insanity, asthma, hurting the wife, lawsuits, gossip, slander, arguments, and theft.

Secret Name: Rewards/Salary (Lu Chun)

4 Star

Element: Wood
Colour: Green
Body Part: Liver
Good Star: Romance, Knowledge, Fame

Positive Aspects: Knowledge, passion/romance, wisdom, harmony, success in exams, honesty, authority, beautiful children, high officials, and great wealth.

Negative Aspects: Suicide by hanging, madness, children display bad sexual conduct, scandals/extramarital affairs, adultery, and the family breaks up.

Secret Name: Literary Arts (Wen Qu)

5 Star

Element: Universal Earth
Colour: Yellow
Body Part: Brain
Bad Star: Bankruptcy, Devastation, Cancer

Positive Aspects: Accomplishments, prosperity, high authority, power, a good family, honest, sincere, and good girls in the family.

Negative Aspects: Lawsuits by the government, people in the house die, disaster, calamity, catastrophe, lawsuits, setbacks, disease, grave misfortune.

Secret Name: Chastity (Lien Zheng)

6 Star

Element: Metal
Colour: White
Body Part: Head
Good Star: Power and Authority

Positive Aspects: Authority, government, power, nobility, distinction, respect, fame, honors, activity, fame, success, good money decisions, and a world-famous son.

Negative Aspects: Hurts the wife and sons; very poor, very mean, solitary, lonely, self-centered, robberies.

Secret Name: Military Arts/Career (Wu Chu)

7 Star

Element: Metal
Colour: Red
Body Part: Mouth, throat, lungs
Bad Star: Robbery and Theft

Positive Aspects: Spirituality, metaphysics, good authority and control, lots of money, many children, famous actors, military officers, wealth and mysticism, and productivity.

Negative Aspects: Robbery, theft, government lawsuits, jailed, indictment, fires. *Secret Name:* Broken Solider (Tien Kong).

8 Star

Element: Earth
Colour: White
Body Part: Bones
Good Star: Wealth and Nobility

Positive Aspects: Currently, we are in Period 8 and this star is king (2004–2024)! Riches, wealth, finance, good reserves, excellent investments, gentle people, loyalty, and cultivation.

Negative Aspects: The youngest son dies at very early age; bad diseases in the family, young children get hurt, and tendon problems.

Secret Name: Left Assistant, the Sun (Tso Fu)

9 Star

Element: Fire
Colour: Purple
Body Part: Heart, eyes
Good Star: Promotions and Celebrations

Positive Aspects: Advancement and graduation, reputation, emotion, very smart, good scores on exams, middle son gets very rich, great achievements, promotions, accomplishments, and status.

Negative Aspects: Disease of the blood (e.g., leukemia), blindness, shot by the government, fires, legal litigation, paranoia, psychotic, heart and eye problems.

Secret Name: Right Assistant, the Moon (Fu Pi)

Annual Stars

In addition to the permanent, Natal Star chart of the house, there are stars that migrate to all eight directions/sectors of your property for the year or month.

There are also daily and hourly stars; however, their visit is really too brief to give any serious consideration. Master Yap's personal take on daily and hourly stars was to "get a life"—by the time you've analyzed them, they're already old news. However, it's important to note that visiting annual stars can trigger or set off the energy of certain stars—for good or bad.

In chapters 6 and 7 you'll notice I have alerted you when additional negative energy is visiting for the year that can be harmful to your health. The annual stars are *only* combined with the facing stars in the sector you wish to examine; you'll find these predictions under the "Health Alerts of the Chart" heading and how to cure them. I have selected locations to watch out for; listing all eight directions would be unnecessary.

The Nine Stars and Body Organs

The chart in Figure 18 shows how body organs/systems are allocated certain energy depending on which of the five elements and the Star it is associated with; this is used to determine how occupants may be affected regarding health. This information is fascinating and very accurate as it describes main illness, symptoms, and prognoses.

Star	Element	Body Part	Main Sickness	Symptoms & Problems
1	Water	kidney, ear, blood	blood, nerves	Water sickness, water retention, weak kidneys, easily catches colds, water and food poisons, ovary disease, circulatory system, ringing in the ears, feeling tired, loss of energy, no stamina, back pain, and rheumatism.
2	Earth	abdominal stomach, spleen, skin	stomach, pancreas, digestion	Swollen, purging, infected intestines, trouble with the coccyx or duodenum. Feels cold, ghosts in the house, cancer sickness, throat, stomach problems, constipation, excessive thinness, and skin disease.
3	Wood	feet, liver, voice, hair	hot sickness, obesity	Mobility issues, sickness of the meridians, twisted or pinched nerves, liver problems, drinks too much, gallbladder, hands and feet. Feels cold/hot and head, face and hand injuries.
4	Wood	thigh, upper arm, flatulence	cold sickness	Meridian issues, back pain, twisted waist, sciatica, loss of limb use; muscles and nerves shrink, becomes shorter with age, veins, arteries, and sickness while traveling. Snake bite, under-nourished, bald head, rheumatism, panting, and shortness of breath.
5	Earth	Brain	mouth nerves	Accidental death, falls from the stairs or bathroom, split personality, headaches, poisoning, insomnia, depression, tumors, dizzy, and numbness.
6	Metal	head, bone, lungs	head, nose	Brain tumor, poor brain function, migraine headaches, lung and breathing problems, loss of control, Alzheimer's, incontinence, and Parkinson's disease. Strokes, always coughing—dry throat, panting, colds, bone pain, rheumatism, and arthritis.
7	Metal	tongue, mouth, throat, lungs, salvia	T.B., lung, bone, teeth, under/over sexed	Skin disease, thyroid, lung, catches cold or flu, short of breath, asthma, operations with knives, and the face. Difficulty in childbirth, suicide by hanging, AIDS, sex disease, infection in lungs, face scars, sex business, and mouth cancer.

Figure 18: Body Organs Chart (ctd. next page).

Star	Element	Body Part	Main Sickness	Symptoms & Problems
8	Earth	finger, bones, nose, backbone	spinal cord sickness	Hand and feet deformities, all bone diseases, flu, and osteoporosis. Ghosts haunting the house, tired looking face, back bone, lymphatic system, back pain, bone fractures. Gall and kidney stones.
9	Fire	heart, eyes, shang jiao (from tongue to stomach)	strokes	Blockage of heart arteries or heart problems, blood cancer, strokes, all types of blood disease, circulatory problems, too much heat, and hot tempered. No peace of mind, breast pain, blood discharge, bleeding, high blood pressure, fires, disasters, gas poison, eye disease, nightmares, and burns. Could be killed by lightning.

....

Figure 18: Body Organs Chart (ctd. from previous page).

Star Combinations that Involve Disease and Cancer

The "Nature of the Nine Stars" descriptions explain the stars individually, but when the stars come together or combine, they create a whole other indication. The famous 81 Combinations intermingle the energy of all nine stars with each other (9 x 9 = 81), but I've only included those that apply to health, not all eighty-one combinations. The combinations come from various distinctive texts such as Purple White Scripts (*Tzi Bai Jue*), Ode of Time and Space (*Xuan Kong Mi Zi*), Heavenly Jade Classics (*Tien Yue Jing*), and Time Space Mysticism (*Xuan Kong Jie*).

The predictions below are very interesting and are accurate for Periods 7 and 8. Don't panic if you see that you have one or more of these star combinations in your star chart; there's nothing to worry about if you implement the tips in chapters 7 or 8 as you are energizing auspicious energy and are protected from such grim outcomes as a result.

The star combinations and predictions below can be a combination of the mountain and facing star or the facing star with the visiting yearly star. The cures for these harmful combinations involve the use of high-quality metals (chiming clocks and metal wind chimes are effective as well), small water or fire; however, don't run around "curing" everything, it may have no real effect on your Feng Shui. Pernicious stars that need to be cured are all identified in chapters 6 and 7; keep in mind that sometimes I may recommend you avoid them altogether.

1, 2: This combination indicates no support, rebelliousness, murderers, auto accidents, disputes, and divorce. Illness involving abdominal problems, swollen body, bleeding and an ugly appearance; women activating this energy will suffer from water retention and appear overweight as a result. Males will get cheated and may develop stomach, intestinal, and digestion problems. Women may develop stomach and gynecological problems. *Cure:* Lots of high-quality metal such as bronze, brass, copper, stainless steel, and pewter.

1, 5: The indications here are water-related danger, bankruptcy, and being bloated by water. This combination brings a host of health issues such as hearing problems, kidney problems, sex-related diseases, genital disease, boils on private parts, inability to conceive, and tubular pregnancies. The negative aspects of the 5 Yellow are highlighted here bringing cancer, toxemia, poison by drinking, illnesses, food poisoning, and diarrhea. Women may have a miscarriage, uremia, or womb cancer. *Cure:* Use lots of high-quality metals such as brass, copper, or bronze. No doors in this direction!

2, 1: These stars indicate marital disharmony, premature births, untimely deliveries, abortions, bloating, diabetics, gastric-related problems, upset bowels, and swollen bumps. Males may experience stomach, intestinal, and digestive problems; impotence, and other problems with their sex lives.

2, 2: The 2 star, unless timely, will always bring illness such as skin problems, muscle pain, boils, childbirth problems, abdominal cramps, chronically ill children, stomach, and intestinal and digestive problems. This energy indicates an overly aggressive female, greediness, widowhood, despair, the family losing their good reputation, attracting female ghosts due to excess yin energy, and feelings of exhaustion or depression. *Cure:* Lots of high-quality metal such as bronze, brass, copper, stainless steel, and pewter.

2, 5: This combination of stars brings great misfortune and all types of calamites and catastrophes; it also indicates lots of illness, death, disease, cancer, bankruptcy, unwanted abortions, appendicitis, divorce, and widowhood. This is an extremely bad combination that harms the occupants every way. Bad spirits can haunt the house; they will especially target middle-aged women. During bad periods, it can cause older or middle-aged women to fall sick or die of cancerous diseases. *Cure:* Use lots of high-quality metals such as brass, copper, or bronze. No doors to this direction!

2, 7: This combination indicates no sons, bad daughters, stomach illness, fire hazards, diarrhea, abortions, illicit affairs, money loss, and robberies, especially for those who became wealthy in Period 7. There could be affairs that lead to divorce; possible fire hazards when the 9 star flies in. Likewise, this combination is more dangerous if it is located in the South. This energy signifies difficulty in producing children; epidemics and incurable diseases, bleeding wounds, and knife injuries. *Cure:* Small, still water features.

3, 5: This combination of stars indicate all types of illness such as cancer, madness, heart disease, infectious disease, strange afflictions of the liver, gall bladder, hands, or feet. It supports delinquency, negligence, and gambling; fortunes can be lost when the 3 and 5 combine primarily through gambling. Also, accidents leading to broken limbs may be very prominent with this combination. There will be antagonism in the family and from outsiders. In Period 8, it brings rebellion, quarrels, and harmful aggravation; death or being jailed is indicated caused by money or corruption. The residents can succumb to and be vulnerable to epidemics and/or curses. *Cure:* Use lots of high-quality metals such as brass, copper, or bronze. No doors to this direction!

4, 2: This combination indicates lots of illness such as stomach and gastric problems as well as the spleen and pancreas. It also signifies that the women in the household fight and argue; this energy hurts the mother. Mothers-in-law and daughters-in-law are at odds; it is really bad and threatening for older women so caution needs to be exercised. *Cure*: Lots of high-quality metal such as bronze, brass, copper, pewter, or stainless steel.

4, 5: These stars are dangerous and will bring numerous health issues such as breast cancer, pus and bleeding from sores, sex-related problems, infectious diseases, leukemia, and liver cancer. There could be bankruptcy due to failure in the stock market or shareholdings. The effects also include gang-related problems as well as a nasty gambling habit for the occupants. *Cure:* Use lots of high-quality metals such as brass, copper, or bronze. No doors in this direction!

5, 5: These stars indicate complete and total disaster, traumatic and violent deaths, cancer, idiot sons, bankruptcy, natural calamities, ill fortune, freaky accidents, aggressive and abusive behavior, brain-related injuries/comas, bone cancer, and impotence. This combination also encourages wars, poisoning, lung cancer, and lawsuits accompanied by scandals. This combination cannot be left unattended. *Cure:* Use lots of high-quality metals such as brass, copper, or bronze. No doors in this direction!

6, 2: These stars support mental disturbance, hot/cold sickness, one-sided love, greed, miserly tendencies, celibacy, and expect lots of gastrointestinal problems. With this combination, women should be extra cautious as they may find themselves faced with a host of problems relating to their reproductive system. When a 5 visiting star comes in, it could bring apparitions, spirits, or ghosts; bad spirits can cause disharmony in the family. The man of the house may be sick all the time, especially if he smokes. The mother may experience breathing problems. *Cure:* Lots of high-quality metal such as bronze, brass, copper, stainless steel, and pewter.

6, 3: This combination fosters government lawsuits, fathers and sons fighting, being jailed, and a hard and poor life. Headaches are prevalent as are accidental injuries, especially from sharp metal objects, which must be guarded against. Money does come in, but you may have a limp; getting shot in the leg or the leg is cut. A person's health is compromised when these two stars combine; a fall from a horse could happen. *Cure:* Fire or metal or both.

6, 5: These stars support headaches, migraines, lung cancer, too much pride, being stubborn, bone cancer, brain infections, anxiety, mental pressure, disloyalty at work, mental illness, misfortune, and collapse of a business or power. In waning periods, it can cause impotence, and in extremes cases, going into a coma. Men may find their career paths difficult and may even be retrenched. *Cure:* Use lots of high-quality metals such as brass, copper, or bronze. No doors in this direction!

7, 2: These stars support abortions, miscarriages, fire hazards, women fighting in the family, vomiting blood, difficulties in conceiving, and a young wife prematurely becoming a widow. Mothers-in-law and daughters-in-law may also find themselves at loggerheads all the time. This area should have no fire! *Cure:* High-quality metals such as bronze, brass, or copper.

7, 3: This combination signifies bad health, internal injuries and bleeding that requires surgery, hot tempers, fraud, financial troubles due to lawsuits, stealing, burglaries, and eye-related injuries or illness.

The 7 and 3 are both robbery stars; expect trouble in this area when they are activated. *Cure:* Fire or metal or both.

7, 5: This combination of stars indicates communication breakdowns, bad eating habits, drug addiction, mouth or throat cancer, and aggressive or impatient behavior. Other health issues are venereal disease, mental illness leading to madness, death by a drug overdose, no peace of mind, and heart disease. The 7-5 combination worsens in Period 8; this energy must be addressed if activated. *Cure:* Lots of high-quality metals such as brass, copper, or bronze. No doors in this direction!

8, 5: These stars indicate accidents involving bones, nerve and bone disease, dislocation of bones, nose and stomach cancer, humpbacks, dwarfism, sweet-talkers, paralysis, idiots, and being childless. Cure: Lots of high quality metals such as brass, copper, or bronze. No doors in this direction!

9, 2: This combination of stars indicate widowhood, foolish people, gynecological problems, fires, and cerebral impediments. *Cure:* Lots of high-quality metals such as brass, copper, or bronze.

9, 5: This combination signifies stress, mental pressure, a religious fanatic, cancer, money loss, and lawsuits. The 9 star accentuates the negative aspects of the 5; drug overdoses, poisons, injuries, death, accidents, inflammatory situations, sex diseases, leukemia, fire disasters, eye disease and, when the annual 7 visits, suicide by drugs or poison. This is a very inauspicious combination that could leave anyone in the immediate area with a fiery feeling. These stars lead a person to develop some very hard-headed and stubborn characteristics. *Cure:* Use lots of high-quality metals such as brass, copper, or bronze. No doors to this direction!

9, 7: These stars promote women trouble, being over-sexed, fire hazards and related accidents, AIDS, bad reputations, tuberculosis, fights in a relationship, too many parties with wine, women, and song; and heart issues. *Cure:* Small, still water feature.

Renovation and Ground-Digging Taboos

Each year, it is taboo to renovate, dig, or disturb the ground in certain directions/sectors of your home site. This would include installing a pool, adding on a room, remodeling bathrooms/kitchens, removing huge trees/stumps, adding a detached garage, digging a koi pond or installing a sprinkler system; all involve shaking/digging into the earth or the house (i.e., hammering or demolition). Replacing annual flowers, normal tree trimming, house painting, or locating a fountain will *not* disturb the energy.

There are four *shas* or "afflictions" that visit each year: the most serious are the Three Killings, Grand Duke Jupiter, and Five Yellow (the 5 Star).[36] Please refer to the "Taboo" chart (Figure 19) if you plan to renovate in these areas or to excavate for a large water feature or move the ground; all proper placement of water can be found in chapters 6 or 7 depending on your home's facing direction and move-in date. When there are two or more afflictions visiting in one sector, it is best to wait to renovate or dig until the next year; for example, notice that in 2018 that the Three Killings and the Five Yellow visit the North. Disturbing the North this year may bring money loss, divorce, blood-related accidents, illness, bankruptcy, violence, or severe injuries.

If you must renovate or dig in the area of the Three Killings or the annual 5 Star, bury some metal (copper, brass, or bronze) into the earth near the location of concern. This will counter the affliction and protect you from harm. The chart has terms such as "SW 1," "East 2," "NW 3,"

36. The four annual *shas* or afflictions are the Three Killings (*Sam Sart*), the Five Yellow, Grand Duke Jupiter (*Tai Sui*), and the Year Breaker (*Sui Po*). For more detailed information, refer to *Classical Feng Shui for Wealth and Abundance*. If you must renovate or have already paid for the construction of a pool, Feng Shui Masters will use the Great Sun formula, dates to begin construction to protect you from harm.

and so forth. To find the exact direction the chart is referring to, go to the 24 Mountain Directions chart (Figure 16). For example, NW 3 is between 322.6 and 337.5 degrees; this is the Grand Duke Jupiter area for 2019 and this location should not be renovated or have deep digging such as a pool installation.

Renovation Taboo Chart: Do Not Renovate or Dig in these Sectors/Directions				
Year	Animal Year	Grand Duke Jupiter covers 15°	Three Killings covers 75°	The 5 Yellow covers 45°
2016	Monkey	Southwest 3	South 1, 2, 3 plus SE 3 and SW 1	Northeast
2017	Rooster	West 2	East 1, 2, 3 plus NE 3 and SE 1	South
2018	Dog	Northwest 1	North 1, 2, 3 plus NE 1 and NW 3	North
2019	Pig	Northwest 3	West 1, 2, 3 plus NW 1 and SW 3	Southwest
2020	Rat	North 2	South 1, 2, 3 plus SE 3 and SW 1	East
2021	Ox	Northeast 1	East 1, 2, 3 plus NE 3 and SE 1	Southeast
2022	Tiger	Northeast 3	North 1, 2, 3 plus NE 1 and NW 3	Center
2023	Rabbit	East 2	West 1, 2, 3 plus NW 1 and SW 3	Northwest
2024	Dragon	Southeast 1	South 1, 2, 3 plus SE 3 and SW 1	West
2025	Snake	Southeast 3	East 1, 2, 3 plus NE 3 and SE 1	Northeast
2026	Horse	South 2	North 1, 2, 3 plus NE 1 and NW 3	South
2027	Goat	Southwest 1	West 1, 2, 3 plus NW 1 and SW 3	North

Figure 19: Renovation Taboo Chart.

Part III
Design & Arrange Your Space for Vibrant Health

Six

Period 8 Charts: How to Extract Health, Wealth & Longevity

Healing is a matter of time, but it is sometimes also a matter of opportunity.
Hippocrates

How to Use Chapters 6 and 7

Before you proceed, you'll need to have the following information ready:

- The house facing (South 1, East 3, Northwest 2, and so forth)
- The Period of the house (Period 7 or Period 8)
- Floor Plan divided up (see Figure 20)
- Overlay the Eight Mansions codes (See Figure 20)
- Overlay the Flying Stars

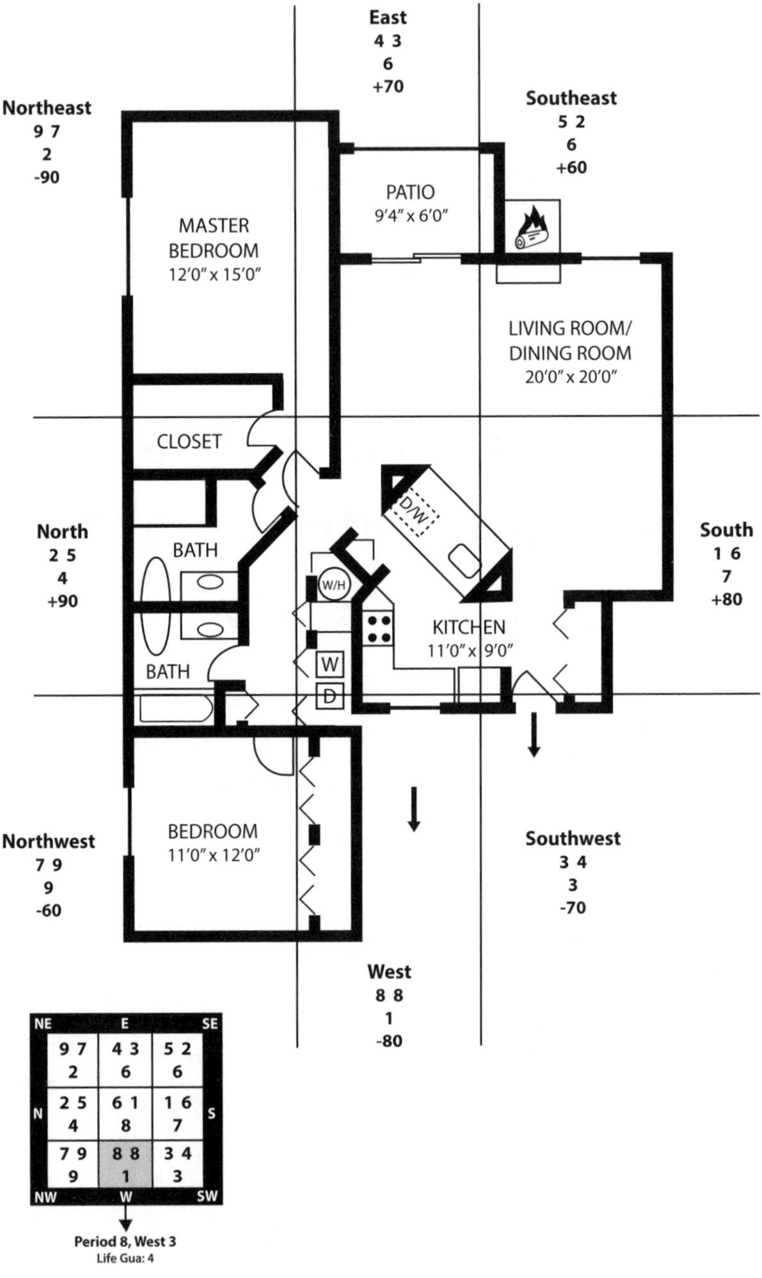

Figure 20: Example Floor Plan for Period 8.

Refer to the 24 Mountains chart to find the house facing, based on the compass degree. Your move-in date determines which period your house falls into. Draw a floor plan of your home. Divide it up into nine cells and overlay the directions, Eight Mansions codes and Star chart. Place this information *outside* the floor plan so you can sketch in possible bed locations, desks, water, and so forth as you read the recommendations. If you are unsure which directions go where, you will find them in the Natal Star charts in the little black area outside the numbers. Only one chart applies to your home and its unique energy; the rest of the charts serve as great reference material assisting your friends, family, coworkers, or yourself if you move into another home. You'll be able to arrange everything perfectly—again!

This chapter and the next will give you recommendations to extract the best energy from your home; this is where all systems of Feng Shui are brought together for a comprehensive assessment and experience. In chapter 5, we discussed the stars, both good and those that bring an assortment of undesirable events, including sickness and disease. Basically, the two stars that support ill health are the 2 and 5 stars. These stars are the most harmful, and when they combine together in the same sector/direction, the energy will denote widowhood, cancer, bankruptcy, ghosts, spinsterhood, disease, reproductive issues, chronic illness, disasters, and abortions or miscarriages.

None of the recommendations include using these directions for sleeping, desks, stoves, doors, and so forth. What's great about Flying Stars Feng Shui is that it will alert you to non-physical, invisible, and inauspicious energies. Unless they are dealt with or cured with appropriate remedial measures, this energy, when aggressive, can cause serious misfortune befalling the householders. Hardships may show up as financial loss, accidents, tragedies, or illness. However, with good Feng Shui information, you can reduce misfortunes in your life. When you energize the auspicious forces, they can bring unexpected opportunities, good health, and a promotion at work or financial windfalls. Keep in mind that attracting the feel-good energies into your living space are a result of correctly activating the Feng Shui!

We are currently in Period 8, which is extremely auspicious; however, your Flying Star chart must be properly activated to materialize the potential. The following information will guide you how to activate the exterior and interior to do just that. If you moved between February 4, 2004, and February 3, 2024, here are all the Natal Star charts for Period 8.

PERIOD 8

South 1 (157.6° to 172.5°)

Facing Name: ***Bing***

Chart: ***Double Stars Meet at Back*** (*Shuang Xing Dao Zuo*)

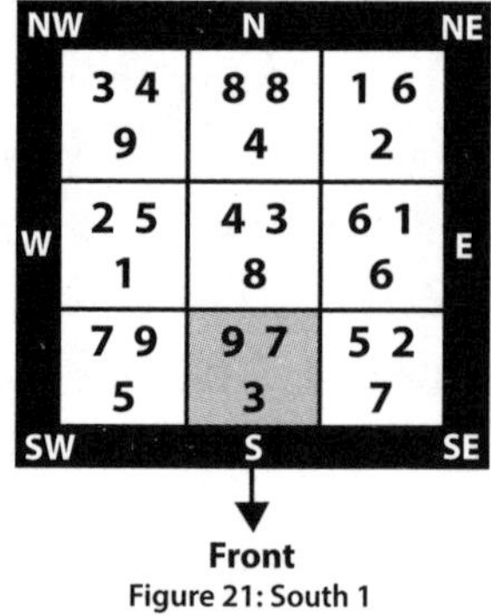

Figure 21: South 1

Health Alerts of the Chart

This chart has two negative areas to pay attention to regarding health; in certain years they become more dangerous. They are the ***West*** (2, 5) and the ***Southeast*** (5, 2). The Southeast brings more illness/bankruptcy in the years of 2015, 2017, and 2021. The West will bring more sickness in the years of 2015, 2018, and 2020. No water (pools, fountains, etc.) or fire (stoves, fireplace/pits, or grills) should be placed in either area no matter the year; it will activate the negative energy in these areas.

Activating the External Environment

Needs Water and Mountain in the North

This chart has the double 8s at the rear of the site known as ***Double Stars Meet at the Sitting***. South-facing structures support people of authority who are charismatic; the family can accumulate lots of property. It can also bring descendants who will achieve high-ranking positions in politics. To fully capture the most benevolent energy and activate health, wealth, and harmony, place big water and solid backing at the rear of the property (North). The water could be a pool, pond, waterfall, huge fountain, or lake. Placing water at the back will magnify the most benevolent and prosperous energy of this chart.

For those living in an apartment, high-rise building, townhome, condominium, or a rented space and who are not able to install a water feature outdoors, place one indoors in the recommended area. To activate the mountain in the recommended area, use a tall armoire, heavy bookcases or stone statues; any of these items will sufficiently activate the energy.

There is a potential *Eight Roads of Destruction* if there is a road or real water coming from/exiting the Southeast direction; they are notorious for bringing bankruptcy, disease, and divorce. This house also has a potential *Robbery Mountain Sha* formation if there is a jagged cliff, electrical tower, huge dead tree, lamppost, or a broken mountain in the Southwest that indicates injury by knives, and unusual diseases and disasters.

Activating the Interior Environment

Master Bedroom + Family

There are two ways to enhance health, harmony, and prosperity in the bedroom—location and direction; the *direction* of the bed will give you the most powerful results. Locate the master bedroom in the *North, South* (second floor), *Northeast,* or *East* as they have good mountain stars. ***Bed Directions:*** Place your headboard/bed to the North (1, 3, 4, or 9 Guas only), Northeast (2, 6, 7, or 8 Guas only), or East (all Guas). These bed directions have a good mountain *and* facing star combination with excellent energy.

Remember, the West and Southeast have the worst energy for this house; do not use if at all possible. If the master bedroom is already located there, make sure that the *bed direction* is also not either West or Southeast.

If so, reposition immediately; activating this direction indicates cancer, bankruptcy, leukemia, divorce, death, and all types of mishaps and disasters. Place high-quality metal in the room such as wall art or statues made of bronze, brass, copper, pewter, or stainless steel. Additionally, use a soft neutral color palette such as whites, creams, taupes, and metal colors like silver and bronze.

Do not use fire colors (reds, pinks, purple, or oranges) in the artwork, rugs, bedding, or wall color. These precautions will ensure that you are extracting the best energy possible and keep the 5s and 2s calm. Use the above directions when placing the bed for other family members; find their Life Gua using the Eight Mansions chart in chapter 4.

Home Office + Study

Face your desk/body to the North (1, 3, 4, or 9 Guas only), Northeast (2, 6, 7, or 8 Guas only), or East, Northwest, and Southwest directions (all Guas). Choose one of the above facing directions coupled with your +80 to enhance health, +70 for relationships, or +90 for wealth if possible.

For example, the 6 Guas can face the NE, it has great energy and it's their +80; the 1 Guas can face the East, it has prosperous energy and it's their +80. For students, use the above directions to energize learning and success in exams.

Stoves and Toilets

The best directions for the stove knobs, buttons, or controls are North, East, or Southwest. You will struggle with money, health, and relationships if there is a stove or toilet located in your +90, +80, or +70 sector of the house.

Select and use a toilet located in one of your negative sectors of the house (-90, -80, -70, or -60). This section applies to the head(s) of household or breadwinner.

Excellent Doors

Always use and activate good doors; the best ones for this chart face North, Northeast, East, Northwest, and Southwest; this applies to all exterior doors as well as an interior garage door used to enter the house. In modern homes, an interior garage door is often the main entry into the house, making it extremely important. If one of these directions is also your +80, you will be very fortunate with your health! In this chart, West-facing doors are the worst of the worst; avoid if at all possible. It has the evil 5 facing star and it can attract all types of disasters. If this is your only door in and out, you will need to cure it with lots of metal next to or directly on the door. Brass, bronze, copper, pewter, and stainless steel are some high-vibrating metals, or you can use large metal wind chimes. However, these doors can never be fully cured, only weakened, as the movement/use of it will always keep it activated. Review the years it becomes particularly pernicious in the Health Alerts of the Chart section.

PERIOD 8

South 2 (172.6° to 187.5°)
Facing name: *Wu* and the *Horse*

South 3 (187.6° to 202.5°)
Facing name: *Ting*

Chart: ***Double Stars Meet at Front***
(*Shuang Xing Dao Xiang*)

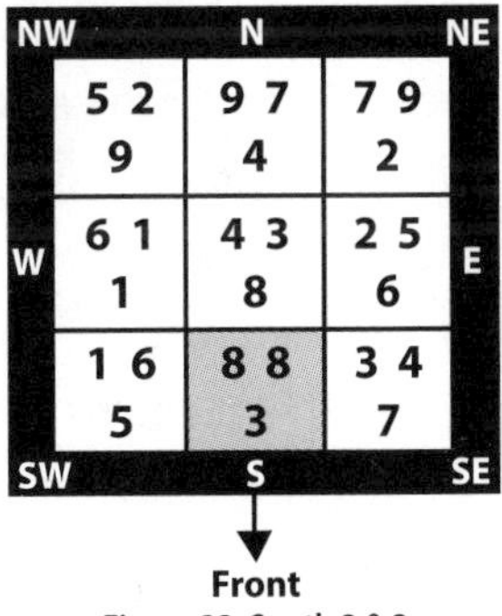

Figure 22: South 2 & 3

Health Alerts of the Chart

This chart has two negative areas to pay attention to regarding health; in certain years they become more dangerous. They are the ***East*** (2, 5) and the ***Northwest*** (5, 2); these sectors have very negative energy. The East becomes more serious for illness in the years of 2016, 2020, and 2023. The Northwest can bring more sickness in the years of 2017, 2019, and 2023. No water (pools, fountains, etc.) or fire (stoves, fireplace/pits, or grills) should be placed in either area no matter the year; it will activate the negative energy in these areas.

Activating the External Environment

Needs Mountain and Water in the Front

The excellent energy of the double 8s are located in the front of the property known as ***Double Stars Meet*** at the Facing and can bring great health, relationships, and money. It is important to activate this chart by installing a mountain and water. The "mountain" can be higher ground, courtyard walls, landscape mounds, boulders (no sharp or jagged edges), or any combination of these—the mountain should be 3 feet or taller. A water fountain, pond, or stream may be placed in the front. If you live in a home where you are not able to place an outdoor water feature, place one inside in the recommended area; consider a wall fountain.

For those living in an apartment, high-rise building, townhome, condominium, or a rented space and who are unable to install a water feature outdoors, place one indoors in the recommended area. To activate the mountain in the recommended area, use a tall armoire, heavy bookcases, or stone statues; these will sufficiently activate the energy.

South 2 and 3 properties usually produce wealthy, intelligent, and skillful entrepreneurs. It also has the potential to produce wealthy leaders who can achieve great heights. However, this facing may not bring the same benefits to the 6 or 7 Life Guas particularly if they were born in the Year of the Snake, Rooster, or Ox.

For homes that face ***South 2***, there is a possible *Eight Killing Forces* if a mountain is located in the Northwest; these formations can bring the loss of life, blood-related accidents, loss of money, and failure in romance and marriage. These homes also may have a *Robbery Mountain Sha* formation if there is a jagged cliff, electrical tower, huge dead tree, lamppost, or a broken mountain in the Southeast; they indicate everyone in household getting an unusual disease, injury by knives, and disasters. For homes that face to ***South 3***, there is a possible *Eight Roads of Destruction* if there is a road or water coming from/exiting the Southwest, it is common for them to bring bankruptcy, disease, and divorce.

Activating the Interior Environment

Master Bedroom + Family

There are two ways to activate great energy in the bedroom—location and direction; the direction of the bed will give you the most powerful results. Locate the master bedroom in the South (second floor), North, West, or Southwest as these sectors have good mountain stars. ***Bed Directions:***

For homes that face South 2, place your headboard/bed to the South and Southeast (1, 3, 4, or 9 Guas only) or the West or Southwest (2, 6, 7, or 8 Guas only). If the home faces South 3, place your headboard/bed to the West, South, and Southwest (all Guas). These bed directions have a good mountain *and* facing star combination with excellent energy.

Take special caution regarding the East and Northwest; do not use either if at all possible. If the master bedroom is already located there, make sure that the bed direction is not also East or Northwest. If so, reposition immediately; activating this direction indicates cancer, bankruptcy, leukemia, divorce, death, and all types of mishaps and disasters. Place high-quality metal in the room such as wall art or statues made of bronze, brass, copper, pewter, or stainless steel.

Additionally, use a soft neutral color palette such as whites, creams, taupes, and metal colors like silver and bronze. Do not use fire colors (reds, pinks, purple, or oranges) in the artwork, rugs, bedding, or wall color. These precautions will ensure that you are extracting the best energy possible and keep the 5s and 2s calm. Use the above directions when placing the bed for other family members; find their Life Gua using the Eight Mansions chart in chapter 4.

Home Office + Study

For the ***South 2*** homes, face your desk/body to the South and Southeast (1, 3, 4, or 9 Guas only) or the West, Northeast, and Southwest (2, 6, 7, or 8 Guas only). For the ***South 3*** homes, place your desk/face to the Northeast, West, South, Southeast, and Southwest (all Guas). Choose one of these facing directions coupled with your +80 to enhance health, +70 for relationships, or +90 for wealth if possible. For example, if you are a 7 Gua, choose Southwest as it is your +80 and supports health and money. For students, use the above directions to energize learning and success in exams.

Stoves and Toilets

The best directions for the stove knobs, buttons, or controls are South, West, or Northeast. If there is a stove or toilet located in your +90, +80, or +70 sector of the house, health, and money loss are at a high risk. This also makes it difficult to conceive children. Select and use a toilet located in one of your negative sectors of the house (-90, -80, -70, or -60). This section applies to the head(s) of household or breadwinner.

Excellent Doors

Always use and activate good doors; the best ones for this chart are facing to the South, Southeast, West, Northeast, and Southwest. This applies to all exterior doors as well as an interior garage door used to enter the house. In modern homes, an interior garage door is often the main entry into the house; therefore, it is extremely important. If one of these directions is also your +80, you will be very lucky with your health. In this chart, an East-facing door is the worst of the worst; avoid if at all possible. It has the evil 5 facing star and its energy can attract all types of disasters. If this is a well-used door or your only door in and out, you will need to cure it with lots of metal next to or directly on the door. Brass, bronze, copper, pewter, and stainless steel are some high-vibrating metals to use, or large metal wind chimes. Keep in mind that these doors can never be fully cured—only weakened—as the movement/use of it will always keep it activated. Review the years it becomes a health threat in the Health Alerts of the Chart section.

PERIOD 8

Southwest 1 (202.6° to 217.5°)

Facing name: *Wei* and the *Goat*

Very Special Chart: ***Combination of Ten*** (*He Shih Chu*) and ***Prosperous Sitting, Prosperous Facing*** (*Wang Shan Wang Shui*)

N	NE			E
	6 9 4	8 2 2	4 7 6	
NW	1 4 9	2 5 8	3 6 7	SE
	9 3 1	5 8 5	7 1 3	
W		SW		S

Front

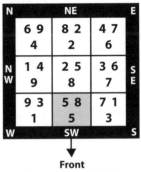

Figure 23: Southwest 1

Health Alerts of the Chart

This chart has one negative area to pay attention to regarding health; in certain years it becomes more dangerous. The *Northeast* (2 facing star) will become double trouble in 2016, 2019, and 2021. No water (pools, fountains, etc.) or fire (stoves, fireplace/pits, or grills) should be placed in this area no matter the year—it will activate the negative energy.

Activating the External Environment

Needs Water in Front, Solid Wall or Mountain at the Back

This property is one of the most auspicious charts of Period 8 with two special aspects known as a ***Combination of Ten*** and ***Prosperous Sitting, Prosperous Facing***. The energy is extremely lucky for all categories of Feng Shui: prosperity, health, and harmony. The Southwest-facing properties are also known for turning bad fortunes into lucrative opportunities and may also denote the birth of an intelligent, wealthy, and prosperous person.

A Combination of Ten chart is where either the mountain star or facing star adds to ten with the time star. The time star is the single number below the mountain star and facing star. When they add to ten with the mountain star, it is very auspicious for health and relationships, often referred to as "lucky for people."

Having significant backing is the key to fully realizing the chart's potential. Evidently, if you have a hill or mountain at the back of your house, this is extremely auspicious!

If not, you can create a "mountain" at the back with a very high, solid fence, dense landscaping, high ground, and so forth. If you have water at the back of the house, there could be serious illness in the house, especially for the woman/mother of the house. Also, you would have lost the opportunity to correctly extract the health- and people-luck available with this chart.

It is important that this home have a beautiful water feature such as a stream, Koi pond, waterfall, or fountain at the front of the property, place it as center of your garden as possible; however, do not directly align or block the front door.

If your home faces a natural lake, ocean, river, or pond and you have substantial support at the back, then this chart is fully activated. These essential exterior forms will bring incredible opportunities and luck to the occupants.

For those living in an apartment, high-rise building, townhome, condominium, or a rented space and who are not able to install a water feature outdoors, place one indoors in the recommended area. To activate the mountain in the recommended area, use a tall armoire, heavy bookcases, or stone statues; any of these items will sufficiently activate the energy.

These homes also may have a *Robbery Mountain Sha* formation if there is a jagged cliff, electrical tower, huge dead tree, lamppost, or a broken mountain in the Southeast; they indicate everyone in the household getting an unusual disease, injury by knives, and disasters.

Activating the Interior Environment

Master Bedroom + Family

There are two ways to activate great energy in the bedroom—location and direction; the direction of the bed will give you the most powerful results. Locate the master bedroom in the North, Northwest, West, or Northeast as these sectors have good mountain stars. ***Bed Directions:*** Place your headboard/bed to the North (1, 3, 4, or 9 Guas only), or to the Northwest direction (all Guas). These bed directions have a good mountain *and* facing star combination with excellent energy. Use the above directions when placing the bed for other family members; get their Life Guas in the Eight Mansions chart in chapter 4.

Home Office + Study

For the best energy, face North and Southeast (1, 3, 4, or 9 Guas only), or South, Northwest, and Southwest direction (all Guas). Choose one of these facing directions coupled with your +80 to enhance health, +70 for relationships, or +90 for wealth if possible. For example, if you are a 4 Gua, face South; this is your health direction and it has prosperous energy. If you are a 7 Gua, you could face Southwest, your +80 that also has wealth energy. For students, use the above directions to energize learning and success in exams.

Stoves and Toilets

The stove knobs, buttons, or controls should face to the North, South, Southwest, or Northwest. You will struggle with money, health, and relationships if there is a stove or toilet located in your +90, +80, or +70 sector of the house. Select a toilet located in one of your negative sectors of the house (-90, -80, -70, or -60). This house *cannot* have a kitchen or fireplace in the center of the home (2, 5 combination); it can bring serious health issues such as heart attacks and high blood pressure. This section applies to the head(s) of household or breadwinner.

Excellent Doors

Always use and activate good doors; the best ones for this chart are facing to the Southwest, North, South, Southeast, or Northwest. This applies to all exterior doors as well as an interior garage door used to enter the house. In modern homes, an interior garage door is often the main entry into the house, therefore it is extremely important. The front door (South) is the most excellent activating the most prosperous and benevolent energy.

PERIOD 8

Southwest 2 (217.6° to 232.5°)
Facing name: ***Kun***

Southwest 3 (232.6° to 247.5°)
Facing name: ***Shen*** and the ***Monkey***

Very Special Chart: ***Parent String***
(*Fu Mo San Poon Gua*)

N		NE		E
	7 1 4	5 8 2	9 3 6	
NW	3 6 9	2 5 8	1 4 7	SE
	4 7 1	8 2 5	6 9 3	
W		SW		S

Front

Figure 24: Southwest 2 & 3

Health Alerts of the Chart

This chart has one negative area to pay attention to regarding health; in certain years it becomes more dangerous. It is the ***Southwest*** (2 facing star), and it can bring real trouble in 2015, 2019, and 2022. No water (pools, fountains, etc.) or fire (stoves, fireplace/pits, or grills) should be placed in this area no matter the year—it will activate the negative energy.

Activating the External Environment

Need a Mountain in Front, Water at the Back

This property (Southwest 2 and 3) has a very special chart called a ***Parent String*** formation alleged to bring triple good luck to the occupants. Parent Strings are also noted for creating fast fortunes, wealth, powerful families, and turning bad deals into opportunities. These charts must be activated using a special technique; there must be a mountain in front and water at the back. The "mountain" can be higher ground, courtyard walls, landscape mounds, boulders (no sharp or jagged edges), or any combination (the mountain should be 3 feet or taller). Install a gorgeous water feature at the back of your house: a waterfall, large fountain, pond, or swimming pool. Keep it in the center of the garden.

For those living in an apartment, high-rise building, townhome, condominium, or a rented space and who are unable to install a water feature outdoors, place one indoors in the recommended area. To activate the mountain in the recommended area, use a tall armoire, heavy bookcases, or stone statues; any of these items will sufficiently activate the energy.

The ***Southwest 2*** homes have a possible *Eight Roads of Destruction* if a road/water comes from/exits certain areas of the South and West directions; they are noted for bringing disease, bankruptcy, and divorce. These homes also may have a *Robbery Mountain Sha* formation if there is a jagged cliff, electrical tower, huge dead tree, lamppost, or a broken mountain in the South; they indicate everyone in the household getting an unusual disease, injury by knives, and disasters.

The ***Southwest 3*** facing properties may have an *Eight Killing* formation if there is a mountain coming from the East, and will be worse in the years of the Pig, Rabbit, or Goat. These homes also may have a *Robbery Mountain Sha* formation if there is a jagged cliff, electrical tower, huge dead tree, lamppost, or a broken mountain in the Southwest.

Activating the Interior Environment

Master Bedroom + Family

There are two ways to activate great energy in the bedroom—location and direction; the direction of the bed will give you the most powerful results. Locate the master bedroom in the South, Southeast, Southwest, West, or East sectors of the house as these sectors have good mountain stars. ***Bed Directions:*** For ***Southwest 2*** homes, place your headboard/bed to the Northwest (2, 6, 7, or 8 Guas only and who are also lawyers or judges), or North, Southeast, or South (1, 3, 4, or 9 Guas only). Those in the West Life group (2, 6, 7, or 8) may also angle their bed to the Southeast between 142.6 and 157.5 degrees. For ***Southwest 3*** homes, place the headboard/bed to the Southeast or South (all Guas). These bed directions have a good mountain *and* facing star combination with excellent energy. Use the above directions when placing the bed for other family members; get their Life Gua in the Eight Mansions chart in chapter 4.

Home Office + Study

For the best energy in homes that face ***Southwest 2***, face your desk/body to the Northeast or Northwest (2, 6, 7, or 8 Guas only), or North, Southeast, or South (1, 3, 4, or 9 Guas only) directions. For homes that face ***Southwest 3***, face your desk/body to the Northeast, Northwest, Southeast, or South (all Guas), and North (1, 3, 4, or 9 Guas only) as these directions have good facing stars with wealth and harmonious energy.

Choose one of these facing directions coupled with your +80 to enhance health, +70 for relationships, or +90 for wealth if possible. For example, if you are a 3 Gua, face North: it's your +80 and has prosperous energy. For students, use the above directions to energize learning and success in exams.

Stoves and Toilets

The best directions for the stove knobs, buttons, or controls are Northeast, South, Southeast, or North. If there is a stove or toilet located in your +90, +80, or +70 sector of the house, health and money loss are at a high risk. Select a toilet located in one of your negative sectors of the house (-90, -80, -70, or -60). This house *cannot* have a kitchen or fireplace in the center of the home (2, 5 combination); it can bring serious health issues such as heart attacks and high blood pressure. This section applies to the head(s) of household or breadwinner.

Excellent Doors

Always use and activate good doors; the best ones for this chart are facing Northeast, Northwest, North, Southeast, and South. This applies to all exterior doors as well as an interior garage door used to enter the house. In modern homes, an interior garage door is often the main entry into the house; therefore, it is extremely important. The front door is a problem in this house; it has the "sickness" star. If this is your only door in and out, you will need to cure it with lots of metal next to or directly on the door. Brass, bronze, copper, pewter, and stainless steel are some high-vibrating metals to use, or you can hang large metal wind chimes. Keep in mind that these doors can never be fully cured, only weakened, as the movement/use of it will always keep it activated. Review the years it becomes really serious in the Health Alerts of the Chart section.

PERIOD 8

West 1 (247.6° to 262.5°)
Facing name: *Geng*

Chart: ***Double Stars Meet at Sitting***
(*Shuang Xing Dao Zuo*)

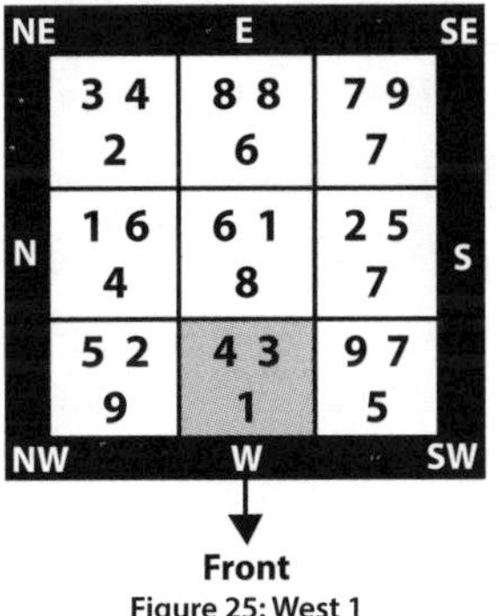

Figure 25: West 1

Health Alerts of the Chart

This chart has two negative areas to pay attention to regarding health; in certain years they become more dangerous. They are the ***South*** (2, 5) and the ***Northwest*** (5, 2). The South becomes more serious for illness in the years of 2017, 2020, and 2022. The Northwest can bring more sickness in the years of 2017, 2019, and 2023. No water (pools, fountains, etc.) or fire (stoves, fireplace/pits, or grills) should be placed in either area, no matter the year; it will activate the negative energy in these areas.

Activating the External Environment

Need a Mountain and Water at the Back

This property has the current prosperity and benevolent energy located at the back of the site known as ***Double Stars Meet at Sitting***. These properties produce well-educated, intelligent, polite, and charming people who can become very wealthy through good business management or involvement in politics. To activate this chart properly, you will need both water and a mountain at the back. The "mountain" could be a solid wall or fence comprised of stucco, brick, or stone; even smartly designed, tiered landscaping or a series of stacked terraces would work brilliantly. While designing this important feature, incorporate a large water feature proportionate to the size of your home and garden in the back.

If you live in an apartment, high-rise, townhome, condo, or a rented space and are not able to install an outdoor water feature, place one inside at the back of your space (East). Also, large heavy bookcases or armoires can represent your mountain; it should be place on the back wall as well.

The house does have a possible *Eight Roads of Destruction* formation if there is a road/driveway coming from and exiting Southwest; it is noted for bankruptcy, disease, or divorce. These homes also may have a *Robbery Mountain Sha* formation if there is a jagged cliff, electrical tower, huge dead tree, lamppost, or a broken mountain in the South; they indicate everyone in the household getting an unusual disease, injury by knives, and disasters.

Activating the Interior Environment

Master Bedroom + Family

There are two ways to activate great energy in the bedroom: location and direction. The direction of the bed will give you the most powerful results. Locate the master bedroom in the North, East, West, or Southwest as these sectors have good mountain stars. ***Bed Directions:*** Place your headboard/bed to the East (all Guas) or North (1, 3, 4, or 9 Guas only). These bed directions have a good mountain and facing star combination with excellent energy.

Take special caution regarding the South and Northwest; do not use if at all possible. If the master bedroom is already located there, make sure that the bed direction is not also South or Northwest. If so, reposition immediately; activating this direction indicates cancer, bankruptcy, leukemia, divorce, death, and all types of mishaps and disasters. Place high-quality metal in the room, such as wall art or statues made of bronze, brass, copper, pewter, or stainless steel. Additionally, use a soft neutral color palette such as whites, creams, taupes, and metal colors like silver and bronze. Do not use fire colors (reds, pinks, purple, or oranges) in the artwork, rugs, bedding, or wall color. These precautions will ensure that you are extracting the best energy possible and keep the 5 and 2 calm. Use the above directions when placing the bed for other family members; calculate their Life Gua in the Eight Mansions chart in chapter 4.

Home Office + Study

To enhance great energy, face your desk/body to the North or Southeast (1, 3, 4, or 9 Guas only), Northeast (2, 6, 7, and 8 Guas only), or East (all Guas). Choose one of these facing directions coupled with your +80 to enhance health, +70 for relationships, or +90 for wealth if possible. For example, if you are a 9 Gua, choose Southeast; it has wealth energy and it's your +80. If you are a 1 Gua, choose East—it has benevolent/wealth energy and is your health direction. For students, use the above directions to energize learning and success in exams.

Stoves and Toilets

The stove knobs, buttons, or controls can face East, Southeast, and Northeast. These directions have good facing stars. You will struggle with money, health, and relationships if there is a stove or toilet located in your +90, +80, or +70 sector of the house. Select a toilet located in one of your negative sectors of the house (-90, -80, -70, or -60). This section applies to the head(s) of household or breadwinner.

Excellent Doors

Always use and activate good doors; the best ones for this chart face North, Northeast, East, and Southeast. This applies to all exterior doors as well as an interior garage door used to enter the house. In modern homes, an interior garage door is often the main entry into the house; therefore, it is extremely important to include. In this chart, a South-facing door is the worst of the worst; avoid if at all possible. It has the evil 5 facing star and its energy can attract all types of disasters. If this is a well-used door or your only door in and out, you will need to cure it with lots of metal next to or directly on the door. Brass, bronze, copper, pewter, and stainless steel are some high-vibrating metals to use, or you can hang large metal wind chimes. Keep in mind that these doors can never be fully cured, only weakened, as the movement/use of it will always keep the energy activated. Review the years it becomes seriously dangerous in the Health Alerts of the Chart section.

PERIOD 8

West 2 (262.6° to 277.5°)
Facing name: *You* and the *Rooster*

West 3 (277.6° to 292.5°)
Facing name: *Xin*

Chart: ***Double Stars Meet at Facing*** (***Shuang Xing Dao Xiang***)

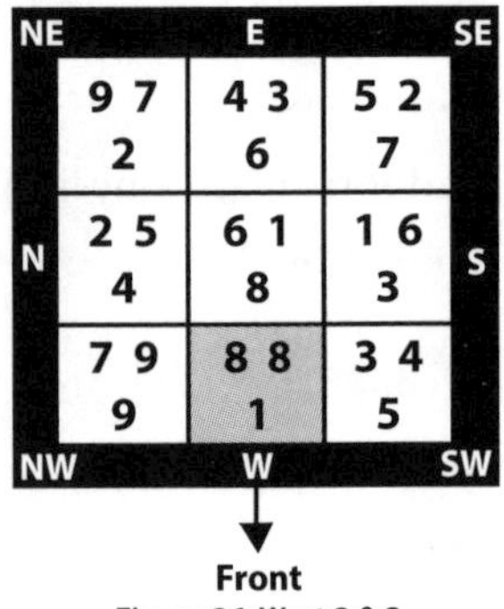

Figure 26: West 2 & 3

Health Alerts of the Chart

This chart has two negative areas to pay attention to regarding health; in certain years they become more dangerous. They are the ***North*** (2, 5) and the ***Southeast*** (5, 2); these sectors have very negative energy. The North becomes more serious for illness in the years of 2018, 2021, and 2023. The Southeast can bring more sickness in the years of 2015, 2017, and 2021. No water (pools, fountains, etc.), or fire (stoves, fireplace/pits, or grills) should be placed in either area no matter the year—doing so will activate the negative energy in these areas.

Activating the External Environment

Needs Mountain and Water in Front

This property is currently harnessing prosperity and the most benevolent energy (8s) in the front known as the ***Double Stars Meet at Facing.*** West-facing homes produce dynamic individuals who will be successful and able to accumulate great wealth rather quickly. It also supports powerful politicians, outstanding academic achievements, and super athletes. To fully capture this great energy, you will need to place a water feature and a mountain in the front garden. The "mountain" can be higher ground, courtyard walls, landscape mounds, boulders (no sharp or jagged edges), or any combination (the mountain should be 3 feet or taller). Install a beautiful water feature such as a fountain, stream, or koi pond in the front as well.

For those living in an apartment, high-rise building, townhome, condominium, or a rented space and who are unable to install a water feature outdoors, place one indoors in the recommended area. To activate the mountain in the recommended area, use a tall armoire, heavy bookcases, or stone statues; these will sufficiently activate the energy.

The ***West 2*** homes also have a possible *Eight Killing Forces* if there is mountain chi coming from the Southeast; it can hurt the body and cause things like blood-related accidents. These homes also may have a *Robbery Mountain Sha* formation if there is a jagged cliff, electrical tower, huge dead tree, lamppost, or a broken mountain in the south; they indicate everyone in the household getting an unusual disease, injury by knives, and disasters.

The *West 3* facing homes have a possible *Eight Roads of Destruction* formation if there is a road/driveway coming from and exiting Northwest; these indicate money loss. This direction also has a possible *Robbery Mountain Sha* in the Southwest.

Activating the Interior Environment

Master Bedroom + Family

There are two ways to health, harmony, and prosperity in the bedroom—location and direction; the *direction* of the bed will give you the most powerful results. Locate the master bedroom in the West (second floor), South, East, or the Northeast—these sectors have good mountain stars. ***Bed Directions:*** For homes that face ***West 2,*** place your headboard/bed to the West or Southwest (2, 6, 7, or 8 Guas only), or South (1, 3, 4, or 9 Guas only). For homes that face ***West 3*** place your headboard/bed to the South, Southwest, or West (all Guas). These bed directions have a good mountain and facing star combination with excellent energy.

Take special caution regarding the North and Southeast; do not use either if at all possible. If the master bedroom is already located there, make sure that the bed direction is not also North or Southeast. If so, reposition immediately; activating this direction indicates cancer, bankruptcy, leukemia, divorce, death, and all types of mishaps and disasters. Place high-quality metal in the room such as wall art or statues made of bronze, brass, copper, pewter, or stainless steel. Additionally, use a soft neutral color palette such as whites, creams, taupes, and metal colors like silver and bronze. Do not use fire colors (reds, pinks, purple, or oranges) in the artwork, rugs, bedding, or wall color. These precautions will ensure that you are extracting the best energy possible and keep the 5s and 2s calm. Use the above directions when placing the bed for other family members; get their Life Gua in the Eight Mansions chart in chapter 4.

Home Office + Study

For the best energy in ***West 2*** homes, face your desk/body West, Southwest, Northwest (2, 6, 7, or 8 Guas only), or South (1, 3, 4, or 9 Guas only) directions. For homes facing ***West 3***, place your desk/face to the South, Southwest, West, or Northwest (all Guas) as these directions have good facing stars with auspicious energy. Choose one of these facing directions coupled with your +80 to enhance health, +70 for relationships, or +90 for wealth if possible. For example, if you are a 6 Gua, face Southwest—this is your +70 and has romance, publishing, and writing energy. If you are an 8 Gua, choose West—this is your +90 and it has wealth energy. For students, use the above directions to support learning and success in exams, particularly the Southwest.

Stoves and Toilets

The best directions for the stove knobs, buttons, or controls are West, Southwest, or Northwest. You will struggle with money, health, and relationships if there is a stove or toilet located in your +90, +80, or +70 sector of the house. Select a toilet located in one of your negative sectors of the house (-90, -80, -70, or -60). This section applies to the head(s) of household or breadwinner.

Excellent Doors

Always use and activate good doors; the best ones for this chart are facing West, Southwest, Northwest, and South. This applies to all exterior doors as well as an interior garage door used to enter the house. In modern homes, an interior garage door is often the main entry into the house, making it extremely important. If one of these directions is also your +80, you will be very lucky with your health! A North-facing door, in this chart, is the worst of the worst; avoid if at all possible. It has the evil 5 facing star and its energy can attract all types of disasters. If this is your only door, in and out, you will need to cure it with lots of metal next to or directly on the door. Brass, bronze, copper, pewter, and stainless steel are some high-vibrating metals to use, or you can hang large metal wind chimes. However, these doors can never be fully cured, only weakened, as the movement/use of it will always keep it activated. Review the years it becomes particularly pernicious in the Health Alerts of the Chart section.

PERIOD 8

Northwest 1 (292.6° to 307.5°)
Facing name: ***Xu*** and the ***Dog***

Very Special Chart: ***Pearl String***
(*Lin Cu San Poon Gua*)

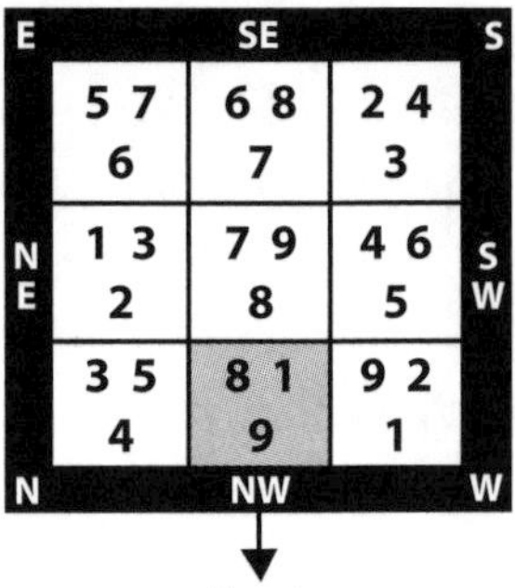

Figure 27: Northwest 1

Health Alerts of the Chart

This chart has two negative areas to pay attention to regarding health; in certain years they become more dangerous. They are the ***North*** (*5 facing star*) and the ***West*** (*2 facing star*). The North becomes more serious for illness in the years of 2018, 2021, and 2023. The West can bring more sickness in the years of 2015, 2018, and 2020. No water (pools, fountains, etc.) or fire (stoves, fireplace/pits, or grills) should be placed in either area no matter the year—doing so will activate the negative energy in these areas.

Activating the External Environment

Needs Mountain in Front and Water at Back

This property has the very desirable ***Pearl String*** formation, which is also referred to by some masters as the *Continuous Bead Formation.* This facing is famous for turning almost everything to an advantage, and it is especially true involving business. It's also said that when activated properly, this chart can bring the recipients triple good luck/opportunities. To fully capture the fabulous potential of this chart, you will need a mountain in front and water at the back. The "mountain" can be higher ground, courtyard walls, landscape mounds, boulders (no sharp or jagged edges), or any combination (the mountain should be 3 feet or taller). Keep these features as centered in the garden as possible, but do not block the front door. Place water at the back: install a pool, waterfall/pond, koi pond, lake, or spa.

If you're unable to activate this chart via the exterior, place water on the back wall using a wall fountain or large fish tank, then add two heavy objects (preferably stone, granite, or marble) on both sides of the front door, either interior or exterior.

These homes may have a *Robbery Mountain Sha* formation if there is a jagged cliff, electrical tower, huge dead tree, lamppost, or a broken mountain in the southwest; they indicate everyone in the household getting an unusual disease, injury by knives, and disasters.

Activating the Interior Environment

Master Bedroom + Family

There are two ways to activate great energy in the bedroom—location and direction; the direction of the bed will give you the most powerful results. Locate the master bedroom in the Southeast, West, Northeast, Southwest, or Northwest (second floor) as these rooms have good mountain stars. ***Bed Directions:*** Place your headboard/bed to the Northwest or Southwest (all Guas), or Southeast (1, 3, 4, or 9 Guas only). Use the above directions when placing the bed for other family members; get their Life Gua in the Eight Mansions chart in chapter 4.

Home Office + Study

Place your desk/face to the *Northwest, South,* and *Southwest* (all Guas), or *Southeast* (1, 3, 4, or 9 Guas only). These directions have great facing stars with benevolent energy. Choose one of these facing directions coupled with your +80 to enhance health, +70 for relationships, or +90 for wealth if possible. For students, use the above directions to energize learning and success in exams.

Stoves and Toilets

The best directions for the stove knobs, buttons, or controls are the Northwest, South, or Southeast. If there is a stove or toilet located in your +90, +80, or +70 sector of the house, health and money loss are at a high risk.

Select a toilet located in one of your negative sectors of the house (-90, -80, -70, or -60). This section applies to the head(s) of household or breadwinner.

Excellent Doors

Always use and activate good doors; the best ones for this chart are facing Northwest, South, Southwest, and Southeast.

This applies to all exterior doors as well as an interior garage door used to enter the house. In modern homes, an interior garage door is often the main entry into the house; therefore, it is extremely important.

If one of these directions is also your +80, you will be very lucky with your health. In this chart, a North-facing door is the worst of the worst; avoid if at all possible (5 facing star).

If this is a well-used door or your only door in and out, you will need to cure it with lots of metal next to or directly on the door. Brass, bronze, copper, pewter, and stainless steel are some high-vibrating metals to use, or you can hang large metal wind chimes.

Keep in mind that these doors can never be fully cured, only weakened, as the movement/use of it will always keep the negative energy activated. Review the years it becomes seriously dangerous in the Health Alerts of the Chart section.

PERIOD 8

Northwest 2 (307.6° to 322.5°)
Facing name: ***Chien***

Northwest 3 (322.6° to 337.5°)
Facing name: ***Hai*** and the ***Pig***

Special Chart: ***Prosperous Sitting*** and ***Facing*** (*Wang Shan Wang Shui*)

E		SE		S
	9 2 6	8 1 7	3 5 3	
NE	4 6 2	7 9 8	1 3 5	SW
	2 4 4	6 8 9	5 7 1	
N		NW		W

Front

Figure 28: Northwest 2 & 3

Health Alerts of the Chart

This chart has two negative areas to pay attention to regarding health; in certain years they become more dangerous. They are ***South*** (5 facing star) and ***East*** (2 facing star). The East becomes more serious for illness in the years of 2016, 2019, and 2023. The South can bring more sickness in the years of 2017, 2020, and 2022. No water (pools, fountains, etc.) or fire (stoves, fireplace/pits, or grills) should be placed in either area no matter the year—doing so will activate the negative energy in these areas.

Activating the External Environment

Needs Water in Front, Mountain in Back

This is a very auspicious chart known as ***Prosperous Sitting*** and ***Facing***; masters also affectionately called it "lucky for people, lucky for money." To fully extract the extraordinary potential of this chart, place a water feature in the front and make sure there is significant, solid backing emulating the energy of a mountain at the back. For example, it could be a tall, solid fence comprised of brick, wood, stucco, stone, or any combination thereof. Beautiful retaining walls or tiered landscaping would work perfectly as well. If there is a natural mountain, hill, or mound at the back of your site, you are very blessed.

In the event that you live in an apartment, high-rise, townhome, condo, or a rented space and who are unable to place an outdoor water feature, install one inside near the front door. Place tall heavy bookcases or an armoire on the back wall (Southeast). If you have a back patio, then place heavy stone, marble, or granite statues or planters there as your "mountain."

For homes that face *Northwest 2*, there is a possible *Eight Roads of Destruction* if you have a road coming from/exiting from either the West or North; they are infamous for bringing disharmony, bankruptcy, and divorce. These homes also may have a *Robbery Mountain Sha* formation if there is a jagged cliff, electrical tower, huge dead tree, lamppost, or a broken mountain in the North; they indicate everyone in the household getting an unusual disease, injury by knives, and disasters.

For the *Northwest 3* facing homes, you could have an *Eight Killing Forces* if mountain energy comes from the South. This formation will attract blood-related accidents and will worsen in the Horse, Tiger, and Dog years. These homes also may have a *Robbery Mountain Sha* formation if there is a jagged cliff, electrical tower, huge dead tree, lamppost, or a broken mountain in the West.

Activating the Interior Environment

Master Bedroom + Family

There are two ways to activate great energy in the bedroom—location and direction; the direction of the bed will give you the most powerful results. Locate the master bedroom in the East, Southeast, Southwest, Northeast, or Northwest (second floor) as these rooms all have good mountain stars. ***Bed Directions:*** For *Northwest 2* homes, place your headboard/bed to the Northwest and Northeast (2, 6, 7, or 8 Guas only), or Southeast (1, 3, 4, or 9 Guas only). For *Northwest 3* homes, place your headboard/bed to the Northwest, Southeast, or Northeast (all Guas). These bed directions have a good mountain and facing star combination with excellent energy. Use the above directions when placing the bed for other family members; get their Life Gua in the Eight Mansions chart in chapter 4.

Home Office + Study

For homes that face Northwest 2, place your desk/face Northwest and Northeast (2, 6, 7, or 8 Guas only), or Southeast and North (1, 3, 4, or 9 Guas only). For Northwest 3 homes, place your desk/face to the Northwest, Southeast, or Northeast (all Guas), or North (1, 3, 4, or 9 Guas only).

Choose one of these facing directions coupled with your +80 to enhance health, +70 for relationships, or +90 for wealth if possible. For example if you are a 3 Gua, face North—it is your health direction. It connotes a public persona, romance, and being blessed by the Heavenly Doctor and unexpected wealth from the heavens (Tien Yi). For students, use the above directions to energize learning and success in exams.

Stoves and Toilets

The best directions for stove knobs, buttons, or controls are Northwest, North, or Southeast as these are good facing stars. You will struggle with money, health, and relationships if there is a stove or toilet located in your +90, +80, or +70 sector of the house. Choose a toilet in your negative sectors of the house (-90, -80, -70, or -60). This section applies to the head(s) of household or breadwinner.

Excellent Doors

Always use and activate good doors; the best ones for this chart are facing Northwest, Northeast, Southeast, and North. This applies to all exterior doors as well as an interior garage door used to enter the house. In modern homes, an interior garage door is often the main entry into the house, making it extremely important. If one of these directions is also your +80, you will be very lucky with your health.

PERIOD 8

North 1 (337.6° to 352.5°)
Facing name: ***Ren***

Chart: ***Double Stars Meet at the Facing*** (*Shuang Xing Dao Xiang*)

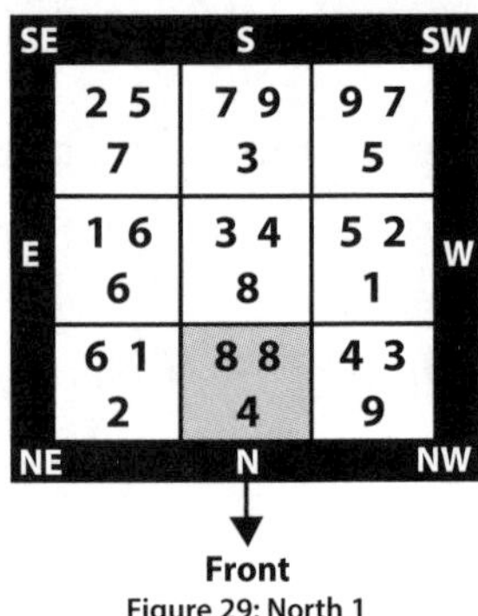

Figure 29: North 1

Health Alerts of the Chart

This chart has two negative areas to pay attention to regarding health; in certain years they become more dangerous. They are the ***Southeast*** (2, 5) and the ***West*** (5, 2). The Southeast becomes more serious for illness in the years of 2015, 2017, and 2021. The West can bring more sickness in the years of 2015, 2018, and 2020. No water (pools, fountains, etc.) or fire (stoves, fireplace/pits, or grills) should be placed in either area no matter the year—doing so will activate the negative energy in these areas.

Activating the External Environment

Needs Water and Mountain in Front

This property has the two 8 stars in the front known as ***Double Stars Meet at the Facing.*** The North-facing properties indicate success, charismatic people, and wealth-luck. In order for this chart to support health and money, it's very important to install a water feature and a "mountain" in the front garden. You can fulfill the criteria for both if you install a tall, heavy concrete or marble fountain near (but not blocking) the front door. If you wish to construct two separate features, another way to activate the "mountain" is with higher ground, courtyard walls, landscape mounds, boulders (no sharp or jagged edges), or any combination (the mountain should be 3 feet or taller). The water feature may be a stream, koi pond, waterfall (flowing towards the house, not away from it), or fountain.

If you are unable to place these features exterior to your site, install a water fountain near the front door inside. Place two heavy statues or stone planters on either side of the front door (inside or out). North is one of the best facings for all those in the East Life group (1, 3, 4, or 9 Guas), and you will benefit greatly by living in one.

There is a possible *Eight Roads of Destruction* with this facing if there is a road coming from/exiting the Northwest direction; they are famous for bringing money loss and disasters. These homes also may have a *Robbery Mountain Sha* formation if there is a jagged cliff, electrical tower, huge dead tree, lamppost, or a broken mountain in the West; they indicate everyone in the household getting an unusual disease, injury by knives, and disasters.

Activating the Interior Environment

Master Bedroom + Family

There are two ways to activate great energy in the bedroom—location and direction; the direction of the bed will give you the most powerful results. Locate the master bedroom in the East, Southwest, North (second floor), or Northeast sectors of the house as they are good mountain stars. ***Bed Directions:*** Place your headboard/bed to the North (1, 3, 4, or 9 Guas only), East (all Guas), or Northeast (2, 6, 7, or 8 Guas only). These bed directions have a good mountain and facing star combination with excellent energy.

Take special care regarding the West and Southeast—do not use either if at all possible. If the master bedroom is already located there, make sure that the bed direction is not also West or Southeast. If so, reposition immediately; activating this direction indicates cancer, bankruptcy, leukemia, divorce, death, and all types of mishaps and disasters. Place high-quality metal in the room such as wall art or statues made of bronze, brass, copper, pewter, or stainless steel. Additionally, use a soft neutral color palette such as whites, creams, taupes, and metal colors like silver and bronze. Do not use fire colors (reds, pinks, purple, or oranges) in the artwork, rugs, bedding, or wall color. These precautions will ensure that you are extracting the best energy possible and keep the 5 and 2 calm. Use the above directions when placing the bed for other family members; get their Life Gua in the Eight Mansions chart in chapter 4.

Home Office + Study

Place your desk/face to the North (1, 3, 4, or 9 Guas only), East (all Guas), Northeast (2, 6, 7, or 8 Guas only), or South (all Guas). Choose one of these facing directions coupled with your +80 to enhance health, +70 for relationships, or +90 for wealth if possible. For example, if you are a 6 Gua, face Northeast—it has romance and wealth energy, and is also your Tien Yi (the Heavenly Doctor offers you protection and unexpected wealth from the heavens). For students, use the above directions to energize learning and success in exams.

Stoves and Toilets

The best directions for the stove knobs, buttons, or controls are North, Northeast, and South; they have good facing stars. You will struggle with money, health, and relationships if there is a stove or toilet located in your +90, +80, or +70 sector of the house. Select a toilet located in one of your negative sectors of the house (-90, -80, -70, or -60). This section applies to the head(s) of household or breadwinner.

Excellent Doors

Always use and activate good doors; the best ones for this chart are facing to the North, East, Northeast, and South. This applies to all exterior doors as well as an interior garage door used to enter the house. In modern homes, an interior garage door is often the main entry into the house and is therefore extremely important. Two doors will be a problem at this property—a Southeast (5 facing star) and West (2 facing star) door. If either of these are well-used or your only door in and out, you will need to cure it with lots of metal next to or directly on the door. Brass, bronze, copper, pewter, and stainless steel are some high-vibrating metals to use, as are large metal wind chimes. Keep in mind that these doors can never be fully cured, only weakened, as the movement/use of it will always keep the negative energy activated. Review the years it becomes particularly pernicious in the Health Alerts of the Chart section.

PERIOD 8

North 2 (352.6° to 7.5°)
Facing name: *Tzi* and the *Rat*

North 3 (7.6° to 22.5)
Facing name: *Kwei*

Chart: ***Double Stars Meet at Sitting***
(*Shuang Xing Dao Zuo*)

SE	S	SW
4 3 7	8 8 3	6 1 5
E: 5 2 6	3 4 8	1 6 1 :W
9 7 2	7 9 4	2 5 9
NE	N	NW

Front

Figure 30: North 2 & 3

Health Alerts of the Chart

This chart has two negative areas to pay attention to regarding health; in certain years they become more dangerous. They are the *Northwest* (2,5) and the *East* (5,2). The Northwest becomes more serious for illness in the years of 2017, 2019, and 2023. The East can bring more sickness in the years of 2016, 2020, and 2023. No water (pools, fountains, etc.) or fire (stoves, fireplace/pits, or grills) should be placed in either area no matter the year; doing so will activate the negative energy in these areas.

Activating the External Environment

Needs Mountain and Water at the Back

This chart has the two 8s at the back known as ***Double Stars Meet at Sitting***; two important features are needed to completely realize the powerful, positive energy of this chart—a mountain and water. Install a pool with a rock waterfall, and both elements will be fully represented at the rear of the site. Make sure the house has substantial backing with high ground, terraced landscaping against a solid fence/wall. Keep the water as center as possible. If there is a natural hill or mountain already at the back, this is extremely auspicious.

If you are unable to activate this chart on the exterior level, then install a water fountain near the back door. Place two stone planters or statues outside if you have a balcony or patio. If not, place them near the back door inside your living space. The North-facing charts can bring the occupants success in business and business relationships that will take them all over the world.

The *North 2* properties may have a *Robbery Mountain Sha* formation if there a jagged cliff, electrical tower, huge dead tree, lamppost, or a broken mountain in the West; they indicate everyone in the household getting an unusual disease, injury by knives, and disasters.

For homes that face *North 3*, there is a possible *Eight Roads of Destruction* if you have a road/driveway coming from and exiting the Northeast direction and they are notorious for bringing extramarital/scandalous affairs, bankruptcy, and divorce. These homes also may have a *Robbery Mountain Sha* formation if there is a jagged cliff, electrical tower, huge dead tree, lamppost, or a broken mountain in the Northeast.

Activating the Interior Environment

Master Bedroom + Family

There are two ways to activate great energy in the bedroom—location and direction; the direction of the bed will give you the most powerful results. Locate the master bedroom in the South, Southwest, Southeast, West, or Northeast as all of these areas have good mountain stars. ***Bed Directions:*** For homes that face *North 2*, place your headboard/bed to the South (1, 3, 4, or 9 Guas only), Southwest, or West (2, 6, 7, or 8 Guas only). If the home faces to *North 3*, place your headboard/bed to the South, West, or Southwest (all Guas). These bed directions have a good mountain and facing star combination with excellent energy.

Take care regarding the Northwest and East—do not use either if at all possible. If the master bedroom is already located there, make sure that the bed direction is not also Northwest or East. If so, reposition immediately; activating this direction indicates cancer, bankruptcy, leukemia, divorce, death, and all types of mishaps and disasters. Place high-quality metal in the room such as wall art or statues made of bronze, brass, copper, pewter, or stainless steel. Additionally, use a soft neutral color palette such as whites, creams, taupes, and metal colors like silver and bronze. Do not use fire colors (reds, pinks, purple, or oranges) in the artwork, rugs, bedding, or wall color. These precautions will ensure that you are extracting the best energy possible and keep the 5 and 2 calm. Use the above directions when placing the bed for other family members; get their Life Gua in the Eight Mansions chart in chapter 4.

Home Office + Study

For *North 2* facing properties, place your desk/face to the South, Southeast, or North (1, 3, 4, or 9 Guas only), Southwest or West (2, 6, 7, or 8 Guas only). If the home faces to *North 3*, place your desk/face to the South, West, or Southwest (all Guas), and North (1, 3, 4, or 9 Guas only). Choose one of these facing directions coupled with your +80 to enhance health, +70 for relationships, or +90 for wealth if possible. For example, face South if you are a 4 Gua: it has wealth energy and it's your +80. It is an arrangement that indicates recognition at work or a promotion and good health. For students, use the above directions to energize learning and success in exams.

Stoves and Toilets

The best directions for the stove knobs, buttons, or controls are the South, North, or Southwest. You will struggle with money, health, and relationships if there is a stove or toilet located in your +90, +80, or +70 sector of the house. Select a toilet located in one of your negative sectors of the house (-90, -80, -70, or -60). This section applies to the head(s) of household or breadwinner.

Excellent Doors

Always use and activate good doors; the best ones for this chart are facing to the South, North, Southwest, and West. This applies to all exterior doors as well as an interior garage door used to enter the house. In modern homes, an interior garage door is often the main entry into the house, making it extremely important. If one of these directions is also your +80, you will be very lucky with your health. A Northwest-facing door is the worst of the worst in this chart; avoid if at all possible. It has the evil 5 facing star, and its energy attracts all types of disasters. If this is your only door in and out, you will need to cure it with lots of metal next to or directly on the door. Brass, bronze, copper, pewter, and stainless steel are some high-vibrating metals you can use, as well as large metal wind chimes. Keep in mind these doors can never be fully cured, only weakened, as the movement/use of it will always keep the negative energy activated. Review the years it becomes magnified in the Health Alerts of the Chart section.

PERIOD 8

Northeast 1 (22.6° to 37.5°)

Facing name: ***Chou*** and the ***Ox***

Very Special Chart: ***Combination of Ten*** (*He Shih Chu*) and ***Prosperous Sitting and Facing*** (*Wang Shan Wang Shui*)

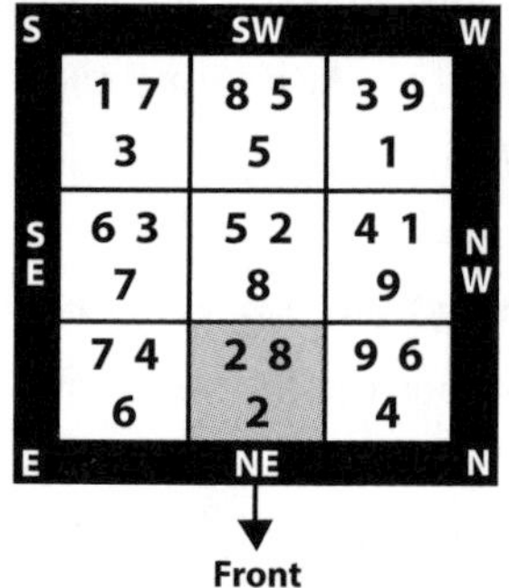

Figure 31: Northeast 1

Health Alerts of the Chart

This chart has one negative area to pay attention regarding health; in certain years it becomes more dangerous. It is the ***Southwest*** (5 facing star) and is more serious for illness in the years of 2015, 2019, and 2022. No water (pools, fountains, etc.) or fire (stoves, fireplace/pits, or grills) should be placed in this area no matter the year—it will activate the negative energy there.

Activating the External Environment

Needs Water in Front, Mountain at Back

This is one of the most auspicious charts of Period 8 boasting two very special aspects; it's a ***Combination of Ten*** and ***Prosperous Sitting and Facing.*** This chart can bring great prosperity and nobility to the occupants; it's very lucky for both people and money. To fully activate the enormous promise of this chart, you will need substantial backing such as a solid fence comprised of stucco, brick, rock, or wood, or any combination of these elements. Installing tiered or terraced garden beds in front of the solid fence will magnify the effect. Place a beautiful water feature such as a stream, koi pond, water fountain, or waterfall in the front. (It should flow toward the home.)

For those living in an apartment, high-rise building, townhome, condominium, or a rented space and who are unable to install a water feature outdoors, place one indoors in the recommended area. To activate the mountain in the recommended area, use a tall armoire, heavy bookcases, or stone statues; these will sufficiently activate the energy.

These sites may also have a *Robbery Mountain Sha* formation if there is a jagged cliff, electrical tower, huge dead tree, lamppost, or a broken mountain in the North; they indicate everyone in the household getting an unusual disease, injury by knives, and disasters.

Activating the Interior Environment

Master Bedroom + Family

There are two ways to activate great energy in the bedroom—location and direction; the direction of the bed will give you the most powerful results. Locate the master bedroom in the South, Southwest, North, or Southeast as these areas all have good mountain stars. ***Bed Directions:*** Place your headboard/bed to the Northwest (all Guas) or North (1, 3, 4, or 9 Guas only). These bed directions have a good mountain and facing star combination with excellent energy. Use the above directions when placing the bed for other family members; get their Life Gua in the Eight Mansions chart in chapter 4.

Home Office + Study

While sitting at your desk, face to the Northeast (2, 6, 7, or 8 Guas only), Northwest, East, and West (all Guas), or North (1, 3, 4, or 9 Guas only) directions. Choose one of these facing directions coupled with your +80 to enhance health, +70 for relationships, or +90 for wealth if possible. For example, face the Northwest if you are an 8 Gua; it has strong money/scholarly energy and is your Tien Yi (Heavenly Doctor) direction, also indicating unexpected wealth "from the heavens." For students, use the above directions to energize learning and success in exams.

Stoves and Toilets

The stove knobs, buttons, or controls should face Northeast, East, Northwest, or West. If there is a stove or toilet located in your +90, +80, or +70 sector of the house, health and money loss are at a high risk. Select a toilet located in one of your negative sectors of the house (-90, -80, -70, or -60). This section applies to the head(s) of household or breadwinner. This house *cannot* have a kitchen or fireplace in the center of the home (5, 2 combination); it can bring serious health issues such as heart attacks and high blood pressure.

Excellent Doors

Always use and activate good doors; the best ones for this chart are facing to the Northeast, Northwest, West, North, and East. This applies to all exterior doors as well as an interior garage door used to enter the house. In modern homes, an interior garage door is often the main entry into the house, making it extremely important. If one of these directions is also your +80, you will be very lucky with your health. In this chart, a Southwest-facing door (the back door of these properties) is the worst of the worst; avoid if at all possible. It has the evil 5-facing star and is very strong in the Southwest. If this is your only door in and out, you will need to cure it with lots of metal next to or directly on the door. Brass, bronze, copper, pewter, and stainless steel are some high-vibrating metals to use, or you can hang large metal wind chimes. Keep in mind that these doors can never be fully cured, only weakened, as the movement/use of it will always keep the negative energy activated. Review the years it becomes particularly pernicious in the Health Alerts of the Chart section.

PERIOD 8

Northeast 2 (37.6° to 52.5°)
Facing name: *Gen*

Northeast 3 (52.6° to 67.5°)
Facing name: *Yin* and the *Tiger*

Very Special Chart: *Parent String*
(Fu Mu San Poon Gua)

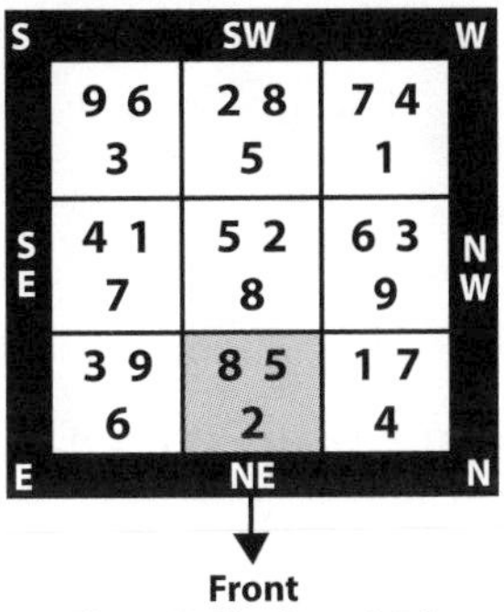

S	SW	W
9 6 3	2 8 5	7 4 1
4 1 7	5 2 8	6 3 9
3 9 6	8 5 2	1 7 4
E	NE	N

(Left side: SE; right side: NW)

Front

Figure 32: Northeast 2 & 3

Health Alerts of the Chart

This chart has one negative area to pay attention to regarding health; in certain years it becomes more dangerous. It is the *Northeast* (5 facing star) and it is more serious for illness in the years of 2016, 2019, and 2021. No water (pools, fountains, etc.) or fire (stoves, fireplace/pits, or grills) should be placed in this area no matter the year—it will activate the negative energy in these areas.

Activating the External Environment

Need Mountain in Front, Water at the Back

This property boasts one of the very special charts known as a *Parent String*. Properties that face the Northeast can produce open-minded and kindhearted people, intelligent children, and the householders can amass fortunes. However, these special charts must be energized in a specific way: a mountain in the front and water at the back. The "mountain" can be higher ground, courtyard walls, landscape mounds, boulders (no sharp or jagged edges), or any combination (the mountain should be 3 feet or taller). Keep the mountain as centered in the garden as possible without blocking the front door. Install a beautiful water feature such as a pool, waterfall, koi pond, or small lake in the center of the back garden.

For those living in an apartment, high-rise building, townhome, condominium, or a rented space and who are unable to install a water feature outdoors, place one indoors in the recommended area. To activate the mountain in the recommended area, use a tall armoire, heavy bookcases, or stone statues; these will sufficiently activate the energy.

For homes facing *Northeast 2* there is a possible *Eight Roads of Destruction* if you have a road/driveway coming from and exiting the North and East. This formation can harm health, devastate people's lives, and kill wealth and harmony. These properties may also have a *Robbery Mountain Sha* formation if there is a jagged cliff, electrical tower, huge dead tree, lamppost, or a broken mountain in the East; they indicate everyone in the household getting an unusual disease, injury by knives, and disasters.

For *Northeast 3* facing properties, there is a possible *Eight Killing Forces* if there is a mountain in front of the property on the left-hand side (Northeast); this formation will attract blood-related accidents and disasters of all types. There is also a possible *Robbery Mountain Sha* formation if there is a jagged cliff, electrical tower, huge dead tree, lamppost, or a broken mountain in the North.

Activating the Interior Environment

Master Bedroom + Family

There are two ways to activate great energy in the bedroom—location and direction. The direction of the bed will give you the most powerful results. Locate the master bedroom in the South, North, Northwest, or Northeast (second floor) as these areas have good mountain stars. ***Bed Directions:*** For homes that face *Northeast 2*, place your headboard/bed to the Southeast or South (1, 3, 4, or 9 Guas only); those who are part of the West Life Group (2, 6, 7, or 8 Guas only) can use the Southeast between 142 and 157 degrees and the South between 187 and 202 degrees. For homes that face ***Northeast 3***, place your headboard to the Southeast or South directions (all Guas). These bed directions have a good mountain and facing star combination with excellent energy. Use the above directions when placing the bed for other family members; get their Life Gua in the Eight Mansions chart in chapter 4.

Home Office + Study

For ***Northeast 2*** homes, place your desk/face to the Southwest or West (2, 6, 7, or 8 Guas only), Southeast, South, or East (1, 3, 4, or 9 Guas only) as these directions have good facing stars with romance, health, or prosperity energy. For ***Northeast 3*** homes, place your desk/face Southwest, West, Southeast, South, or East—these directions support all Guas.

Choose one of these facing directions coupled with your +80 to enhance health, +70 for relationships, or +90 for wealth if possible. For example, face the Southwest if you are a 7 Gua; it has prosperity energy and is your personal health direction; Tien Yi (the Heavenly Doctor) will protect you. For students, use the above directions to energize learning and success in exams.

Stoves and Toilets

The best directions for the stove knobs, buttons, or controls are Southeast, Southwest, West, or East. You will struggle with money, health, and relationships if there is a stove or toilet located in your +90, +80, or +70 sector of the house. Select a toilet located in one of your negative sectors of the house (-90, -80, -70, or -60). This section applies to the head(s) of household or breadwinner. This house *cannot* have a kitchen or fireplace in the center of the home (5, 2 combination); it can bring serious health issues such as heart attacks and high blood pressure.

Excellent Doors

Always use and activate good doors; the best ones for this chart are facing West, Southwest, Southeast, South, and East. This applies to all exterior doors as well as an interior garage door used to enter the house. In modern homes, an interior garage door is often the main entry into the house and is therefore extremely important. If one of these directions is also your +80, you will be very lucky with your health. Unfortunately, a Northeast-facing front door is the worst of the worst in this chart; avoid if at all possible. It has the evil 5 facing star and is really strong in the Northeast. If this is a well-used door or your only door in and out, you will need to cure it with lots of metal next to or directly on the door. Brass, bronze, copper, pewter, and stainless steel are some high-vibrating metals to use, or you can hang large metal wind chimes. These doors can never be fully cured, only *weakened*, as the movement/use of it will always keep the negative energy activated. Review the years it becomes seriously dangerous in the Health Alerts of the Chart section.

PERIOD 8

East 1 (*67.6° to 82.5°*)
Facing name: *Jia*

Chart: *Double Stars Meet at Facing (Shuang Xing Dao Xiang)*

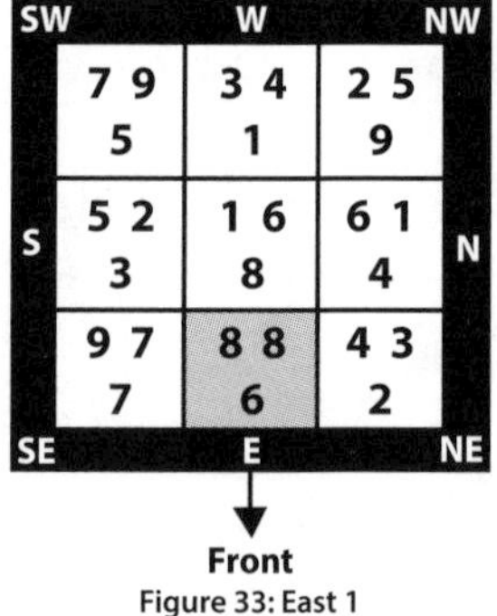

Figure 33: East 1

Health Alerts of the Chart

This chart has two negative areas to pay attention to regarding health; in certain years they become more dangerous. They are the ***Northwest*** (2, 5) and the ***South*** (5, 2). The Northwest becomes more serious for illness in the years of 2017, 2019, and 2023. The South can bring more sickness in the years of 2017, 2020, and 2022. No water (pools, fountains, etc.) or fire (stoves, fireplace/pits, or grills) should be placed in either area no matter the year—it will activate the negative energy in these areas.

Activating the External Environment

Need Water and Mountain in Front

These properties are referred to as the ***Double Stars Meet at Facing***, and they have the two 8s in the front. When this chart is fully energized, it can produce residents with high academic achievements or great successes in the educational field.

To capture this great energy, you will need both a mountain and beautiful water feature in the front garden area. The "mountain" can be higher ground, courtyard walls, landscape mounds, boulders (no sharp or jagged edges), or any combination (the mountain should be 3 feet or taller).

Install a water feature such as a koi pond, waterfall, or stream in the front garden. You could place a large, tall, stone or marble fountain in the front yard; this would fulfill the criteria of both mountain and water.

For those living in an apartment, high-rise building, townhome, condominium, or a rented space and who are unable to install a water feature outdoors, place one indoors in the recommended area. To activate the mountain in the recommended area, use a tall armoire, heavy bookcases, or stone statues; these will sufficiently activate the energy.

There is a possible *Eight Roads of Destruction* formation if you have a road/driveway coming from and exiting Northeast; they are notorious for bringing illness, bankruptcy, and divorce. There is also a possible *Robbery Mountain Sha* formation if there is a jagged cliff, electrical tower, huge dead tree, lamppost, or a broken mountain in the South; they indicate everyone in the household getting an unusual disease, injury by knives, and disasters.

Activating the Interior Environment

Master Bedroom + Family

There are two ways to activate great energy in the bedroom—location and direction. The direction of the bed will give you the most powerful results. Locate the master bedroom in the North, East, or Southeast as these areas have good mountain stars with great energy. ***Bed Directions:*** Place your headboard/bed to the North (1, 3, 4, or 9 Guas only) or East (all Guas). These bed directions have a good mountain and facing star combination with superior energy.

Take special caution regarding the Northwest and South; do not use either if at all possible. If the master bedroom is already located there, make sure that the bed direction is not also Northwest or South. If so, reposition immediately; activating this direction indicates cancer, bankruptcy, leukemia, divorce, death, and all types of mishaps and disasters. Place high-quality metal in the room such as wall art or statues made of bronze, brass, copper, pewter, or stainless steel. Additionally, use a soft neutral color palette such as whites, creams, taupes, and metal colors like silver and bronze. Do not use fire colors (reds, pinks, purple, or oranges) in the artwork, rugs, bedding, or wall color. These precautions will ensure you extract the best energy possible and keep the 5 and 2 calm. Use the above directions when placing the bed for other family members; get their Life Gua in the Eight Mansions chart in chapter 4.

Home Office + Study

While sitting at your desk, face to the North (1, 3, 4, or 9 Guas only), East, West, or Southwest (all Guas)—these are all good facing stars that will support many opportunities. Choose one of these facing directions coupled with your +80 to enhance health, +70 for relationships, or +90 for wealth if possible. For example, choose East if you are a 1 Gua; it has wealth energy and indicates recognition at work or a promotion in the workplace. For students, use the above directions to energize learning and success in exams.

Stoves and Toilets

The best directions for the stove knobs, buttons, or controls to face are North, West, Southwest, or East. You will struggle with money, health, and relationships if there is a stove or toilet located in your +90, +80, or +70 sector of the house. Select a toilet located in one of your negative sectors of the house (-90, -80, -70, or -60). This section applies to the head(s) of household or breadwinner.

Excellent Doors

Always use and activate good doors; the best ones for this chart face the North, East, West, and Southwest. This applies to all exterior doors as well as an interior garage door used to enter the house.

In modern homes, an interior garage door is often the main entry into the house; therefore, it is extremely important. If one of these directions is also your +80, you will be very lucky with your health.

The worst of the worst in this chart is a Northwest-facing door; avoid if at all possible. It has the evil 5 facing star and its energy attracts all types of disasters.

If this is a well-used door or your only door in and out, you will need to cure it with lots of metal next to or directly on the door. Brass, bronze, copper, pewter, and stainless steel are some high-vibrating metals, or you can hang large metal wind chimes.

Keep in mind that these doors can never be fully cured, only weakened, as the movement/use of it will always keep the negative energy activated. Review the years it becomes really serious in the Health Alerts of the Chart section.

PERIOD 8

East 2 (82.6° to 97.5°)

Facing name: *Mao* and the *Rabbit*

East 3 (97.6° to 112.5°)

Facing name: *Yi*

Chart: *Double Stars Meet at the Sitting* (*Shuang Xing Dao Zuo*)

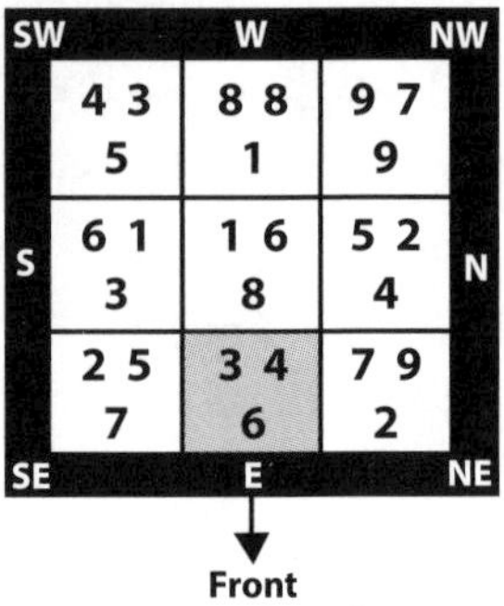

SW	W	NW
4 3 5	8 8 1	9 7 9
6 1 3	1 6 8	5 2 4
2 5 7	3 4 6	7 9 2
SE	E	NE

S (left) · N (right)

Front

Figure 34: East 2 & 3

Health Alerts of the Chart

This chart has two negative areas to pay attention to regarding health; in certain years they become more dangerous. They are the ***Southeast*** (2, 5) and the ***North*** (5, 2). The Southeast becomes more serious for illness in 2015, 2017, and 2021. The North can bring more sickness in 2018, 2021, and 2023. No water (pools, fountains, etc.) or fire (stoves, fireplace/pits, or grills) should be placed in either area no matter the year—doing so will activate the negative energy.

Activating the External Environment

Needs Mountain and Water at Back

This property is known as ***Double Stars Meet at Sitting*** and has the two 8s located at the back of the structure. The East-facing charts can produce righteous, charismatic, loyal, faithful professionals such as doctors, lawyers, and philosophers who are both wealthy and noble. In order to fully energize this chart, you will need a mountain and water in the West (backyard), and yes, installing both features is important. Be diligent in creating substantial backing such as a solid fence made of brick, stucco, wood, or any combination thereof. You could create tiered or terraced garden beds in front of the solid fencing to increase the effect. If you have a natural mountain, hill, or mound located at the back, you are blessed indeed! Install a beautiful water feature such as a pool, fountain, koi pond, or stream. If you have a pool with a large rock waterfall, the criteria for activating this chart are met if they are located in the center back.

For those living in an apartment, high-rise building, townhome, condominium, or a rented space and who are unable to install a water feature outdoors, place one indoors in the recommended area. To activate the mountain in the recommended area, use a tall armoire, heavy bookcases, or stone statues; these will sufficiently activate the energy.

For homes facing ***East 2*** there is a possible *Eight Killings* formation if there is a mountain from the Southwest, a direction noted for activating blood-related accidents. For homes that face ***East 3***, there is a possible *Eight Roads of Destruction* if there is a road/driveway coming from and exiting from the Southeast direction; they are notorious for illness, bankruptcy, and divorce. There is also a possible *Robbery Mountain Sha* formation if there is a jagged cliff, electrical tower, huge dead tree, lamppost, or a broken mountain in the Northeast for *both* East 2 and East 3 homes; they indicate everyone in the household getting an unusual disease, injury by knives, and disasters.

Activating the Interior Environment

Master Bedroom + Family

There are two ways to activate great energy in the bedroom—location and direction; the direction of the bed will give you the most powerful results. Locate the master bedroom in the South, Northwest, or West as these areas have good mountain stars. ***Bed Directions:*** For homes that face ***East 2***, place your headboard/bed to the West (2, 6, 7, or 8 Guas only) or South (1, 3, 4, or 9 Guas only). For homes that face ***East 3***, place your headboard/bed to the West or South (all Guas); these directions have a good facing and mountain star combination that will enhance health, prosperity, and harmony in the house.

Take special caution regarding the North and Southeast; do not use either if at all possible. If the master bedroom is already located there, make sure that the bed direction is not also North or Southeast. If so, reposition immediately; activating this direction indicates cancer, bankruptcy, leukemia, divorce, death, and all types of mishaps and disasters. Place high-quality metal in the room such as wall art or statues made of bronze, brass, copper, pewter, or stainless steel. Additionally, use a soft neutral color palette such as whites, creams, taupes, and metal colors like silver and bronze.

Do not use fire colors (reds, pinks, purple, or oranges) in the artwork, rugs, bedding, or wall color. These precautions will ensure that you are extracting the best energy possible and keep the 5 and 2 calm. Use the above directions when placing the bed for other family members; get their Life Gua in the Eight Mansions chart in chapter 4.

Home Office + Study

For *East 2* homes, place your desk/face to the West or Northeast (2, 6, 7, or 8 Guas only), or to the East or South (1, 3, 4, or 9 Guas only). For *East 3* homes, place your desk/face East, West, Northeast, or South; these directions support all Guas.

Choose one of these facing directions coupled with your +80 to enhance health, +70 for relationships, or +90 for wealth if possible. For example, if you are a 4 Gua, South is your +80, and it has wonderful wealth energy. For students, use the above directions to energize learning and success in exams.

Stoves and Toilets

The best directions for the stove knobs, buttons, or controls are East, West, South, or Northeast; these directions activate household-harmony, prosperity, and health. You will struggle with money, health, and relationships if there is a stove or toilet located in your +90, +80, or +70 sector. Select a toilet located in one of your negative sectors of the house (-90, -80, -70, or -60). This section applies to the head(s) of household or breadwinner.

Excellent Doors

Always use and activate good doors; the best ones for this chart face West, Northeast, East, and South. This applies to all exterior doors as well as an interior garage door used to enter the house. In modern homes, the interior garage door is often the main entry into the house; therefore, it is extremely important. If one of these directions is also your +80, you will be very lucky with health. In this chart, a Southeast-facing door is the worst of the worst—it has the evil 5 facing star, and its energy attracts all types of disasters. If this is a well-used door or your only door in and out, you will need to cure it with lots of metal next to or directly on the door. Brass, bronze, copper, pewter, and stainless steel are some high-vibrating metals to use, or you can hang large metal wind chimes. Keep in mind that these doors can never be fully cured, only weakened, as the movement/use will always keep the negative energy activated. Review the years it becomes seriously dangerous in the Health Alerts of the Chart section.

PERIOD 8

Southeast 1 (112.6° to 127.5°)
Facing name: *Chen* and the *Dragon*

Very Special Chart: *Pearl String* (*Lin Cu San Poon Gua*)

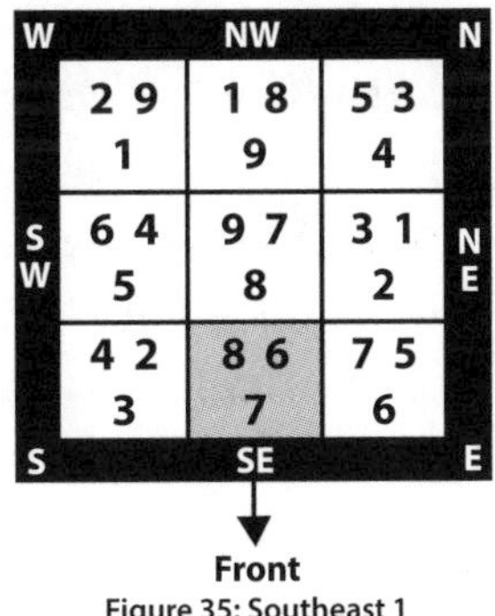

Figure 35: Southeast 1

Health Alerts of the Chart

This chart has two negative areas to pay attention to regarding health; in certain years they become more dangerous. They are the *East* (5 facing star) and the *South* (2 facing star). The East becomes more serious for illness in the years of 2016, 2019, and 2023. The South can bring more sickness in the years of 2017, 2020, and

2022. No water (pools, fountains, etc.) or fire (stoves, fireplace/pits, or grills) should be placed in either area no matter the year—doing so will activate the negative energy in these areas.

Activating the External Environment

Needs Mountain in Front, Water at the Back

The *Pearl String* charts are very special and must be energized with a mountain in front and water at the back to fully realize its potential to bring triple good luck. These Southeast-facing properties can produce great talent in all sports, including martial arts. The children of this house may also excel in sciences, especially those requiring technical expertise. To create the "mountain" in front, you may use high ground, landscape mounds (like those on golf courses), massive boulders (no jagged or pointed edges), or courtyard walls. Keep the mountain as centered as possible in the front yard without blocking the front door. At the back, install a koi pond, swimming pool, waterfall, or large fountain.

If you are unable to activate the exterior of your site, install a fountain near the back door, inside or outside on the balcony or patio, if you have one. Place two stone statues or planters on either side of the front door; tall bookcases, or armoire also work well as an interior "mountain."

An *Eight Killings* formation is possible if there is a mountain bringing energy to the house from the North direction. There is also a possible *Robbery Mountain Sha* formation if there is a jagged cliff, electrical tower, huge dead tree, lamppost, or a broken mountain in the Northeast; they indicate everyone in the household getting an unusual disease, injury by knives, and disasters.

Activating the Interior Environment

Master Bedroom + Family

There are two ways to activate great energy in the bedroom—location and direction; the direction of the bed will give you the most powerful results. Locate the master bedroom in the Southwest, Northwest, or

Southeast (second floor), as these areas have good mountain stars. ***Bed Directions:*** Place your headboard/bed to the Northwest, Southwest (all Guas), or Southeast (1, 3, 4, or 9 Guas only). These bed directions have a good mountain and facing star combination with excellent energy. Use the above directions when placing the bed for other family members; get their Life Gua in the Eight Mansions chart in chapter 4.

Home Office + Study

While sitting at your desk, face to the Northwest, Southwest, or West (all Guas), Northeast (2, 6, 7, or 8 Guas only), or Southeast (1, 3, 4, or 9 Guas only). Choose one of these facing directions coupled with your +80 to enhance health, +70 for relationships, or +90 for wealth if possible. For example if you are a 7 Gua face the Southwest—it has good romance/writing energy and it's your +80. Tien Yi (the Heavenly Doctor) will watch over you, and you will also be granted unexpected wealth from the heavens with this arrangement. For students, use the above directions to energize learning and success in exams.

Stoves and Toilets

The best directions for the stove knobs, buttons, or controls are Northwest, Northeast, or West; these directions support harmony, prosperity, and romance. If there is a stove or toilet located in your +90, +80, or +70 sector of the house, you are at a high risk for health and money loss. Select a toilet located in one of your negative sectors of the house (-90, -80, -70, or -60). This section applies to the head(s) of household or breadwinner.

Excellent Doors

Always use and activate great doors; for this chart they are facing Northwest, West, Northeast, Southeast, and Southwest. This applies to all exterior doors as well as an interior garage door used to enter the house. In modern homes, an interior garage door is often the main entry into the house, making it extremely important. If one of these directions is also your +80, you will have great health-luck.

PERIOD 8

Southeast 2 (127.6° to 142.5°)
Facing name: *Xun*

Southeast 3 (142.6° to 157.5°)
Facing name: *Su* and the *Snake*

Chart: *Prosperous Sitting, Prosperous Facing* (*Wang Shan Wang Shui*)

W	NW	N
7 5 1	8 6 9	4 2 4
SW: 3 1 5	9 7 8	NE: 6 4 2
5 3 3	1 8 7	2 9 6
S	SE	E

Front

Figure 36: Southeast 2 & 3

Health Alerts of the Chart

This chart has two negative areas to pay attention to regarding health; in certain years they become more dangerous. They are the *West* (5 facing star) and the *North* (2 facing star). The West becomes more serious for illness in the years of 2018 and 2020. The North can bring more sickness in the years of 2018, 2021, and 2023. No water (pools, fountains, etc.) or fire (stoves, fire place/pits, or grills) should be placed in either area no matter the year—doing so will activate the negative energy in these areas.

Activating the External Environment

Needs Water in Front, Mountain in Back

Feng Shui masters refer to these properties as "lucky for people, lucky for money" and they are formally called *Prosperous Sitting, Prosperous Facing* (*Wang Shan, Wang Shui*). This chart can produce those who have high morals, nobility, trustworthiness; the Southeast-facing is suited for philosophers, performers, singers, and artists. In order to fully energize the potential, you will need significant backing with a solid fence made of stone, stucco, bricks, wood, or any combination thereof. If there is a natural mountain, hill, or mound behind the property, this is very auspicious. Place a beautiful water feature in the front such as a fountain, stream, koi pond, or waterfall.

If you are unable to activate the exterior of your site, install a fountain near the front door (inside or out). Place two stone planters or statues near the back door (inside or out). You may also use a tall armoire or bookcases near the back door; they work very well as an internal mountain. There is a possible *Eight Roads of Destruction* if the house faces ***Southeast 2*** and a road/driveway comes from/exits the South or East; they indicate sickness, bankruptcy, and divorce.

An *Eight Killings* formation is possible for homes facing ***Southeast 3*** if there is a mountain bringing energy to the house from the West direction; this formation will cause blood-related accidents. There is also a possible *Robbery Mountain Sha* formation if there is a jagged cliff, electrical tower, huge dead tree, lamppost, or a broken mountain in the East for both facings; they indicate everyone in the household getting an unusual disease, injury by knives, and disasters.

Activating the Interior Environment

Master Bedroom + Family

There are two ways to activate great energy in the bedroom—location and direction; the direction of the bed will give you the most powerful results. Locate the master bedroom in the Northwest, Northeast, or the Southeast (second floor) as these have good mountain stars. ***Bed Directions:*** For homes that face ***Southeast 2,*** place your headboard/bed to the Northwest or Northeast (2, 6, 7, or 8 Guas only) or Southeast (1, 3, 4 or 9 Guas only). For homes facing ***Southeast 3,*** place your headboard/bed to the Southeast, Northwest, or Northeast direction (all Guas). These bed directions have a good mountain and facing star combination with excellent energy. Use the above directions when placing the bed for other family members; get their Life Gua in chapter 4.

Home Office + Study

For ***Southeast 2*** homes, place your desk/face to the Southeast or East (1, 3, 4, or 9 Guas only), Northwest, Southwest, or Northeast (2, 6, 7, or 8 Guas only) directions. For ***Southeast 3*** homes, place your desk/face to the Southeast, Northwest, Northeast, Southwest, or East direction (all Guas). Choose one of these facing directions coupled with your +80 to enhance health, +70 for relationships, or +90 for wealth if possible. For example, if you are a 9 Gua, face to the Southeast—this arrangement indicates that the Heavenly Doctor (Tien Yi) protects you and brings you unexpected wealth "from the heavens."

Stoves and Toilets

The best directions for the stove knobs, buttons, or controls are Southeast, East, Northeast, or Southwest; these directions support harmony, prosperity, and health. You will struggle with money, health, and relationships if there is a stove or toilet located in your +90, +80, or +70 sector. Select a toilet located in one of your negative sectors of the house (-90, -80, -70, or -60). This section applies to the head(s) of household or breadwinner.

Excellent Doors

Always use and activate good doors; the best ones for this chart are facing to the Southeast, Northeast, East, or Southwest directions. This applies to all exterior doors as well as an interior garage door used to enter the house. In modern homes, an interior garage door is often the main entry into the house, making it extremely important. If one of these directions is also your +80, you will be very lucky with health.

Seven

Period 7 Charts: How to Extract Health, Wealth & Longevity

Physical fitness is not only one of the most important keys to a healthy body, it is the basis of dynamic and creative intellectual activity.

John F. Kennedy

The Period 7 homes have lost much of their vitality as of February 4, 2004, and they will need to be reenergized in very precise and particular ways. The following information will guide you to do just that! Prepare before proceeding, review the introduction in chapter 6. If you moved in between February 4, 1984, and February 3, 2004, and have done no renovations or remodeling, the following Period 7 Natal Star charts apply.

PERIOD 7

South 1 (157.6° to 172.5°)

Facing Name: ***Bing***

Chart: ***Double Stars Meet at Facing***

(*Shuang Xing Dao Xiang*)

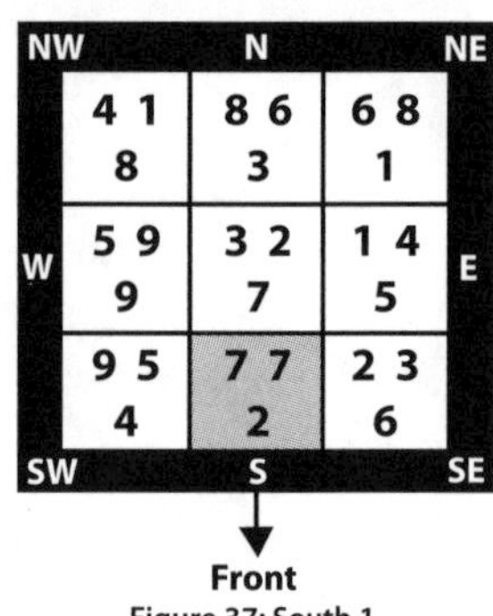

Figure 37: South 1

Health Alerts of the Chart

This chart has two negative areas to pay attention to regarding health; in certain years it becomes more dangerous. It is the ***Southwest*** (5 facing star), and it becomes more serious for illness in the years of 2015, 2019, and 2022. Also, sleeping to the ***West*** is unsafe for health (5, 9). No water (pools, fountains, etc.) or fire (stoves, fireplace/pits, or grills) should be placed in the Southwest area no matter the year—it will activate the negative energy.

Activating the External Environment

Enhancements: *Needs Water in the Northeast, Mountain in North*
Cures: *Paint front door red and place small still water near it*

This chart has the two 7s in the front of the property known as ***Double Stars Meet at Facing***. It was quite prestigious until February 4, 2004. In general, South-facing structures support people of authority, charismatic people, and a family that can accumulate lots of property. It can also bring descendants who will achieve high-ranking positions in politics if activated accordingly.

To reenergize this chart now that we are in Period 8, make sure you have substantial backing with a solid fence composed of stucco, brick, wood, or any combination thereof. You could also make clever use of tiered or terraced garden beds in front of the fence to increase the effect. Water located in the Northeast ushers in the most benevolent and prosperous energy; place it there. Although the South reduces the negative 7 stars, place a small water feature or birdbath near the front door. Also, paint the door red; these cures will further exhaust the negative energy. If you are unable to activate this chart exterior to your site, place two stone statues or planters inside near the back door and a tall floor fountain in the Northeast corner. If you are not allowed to paint the front door red on the exterior, paint the interior side red.

This house also has a potential *Eight Roads of Destruction* if there is a road/driveway coming from and exiting the Southeast. It activates disease, bankruptcy, and divorce. There is also a possible *Robbery Mountain Sha* formation if there is a jagged cliff, electrical tower, huge dead tree, lamppost, or a broken mountain in the Southwest; they indicate everyone in the household getting an unusual disease, injury by knives, and disasters.

Activating the Interior Environment

Master Bedroom + Family

There are two ways to activate great energy in the bedroom—location and direction; the direction of the bed will give you the most powerful results. Locate the master bedroom in the North, Northeast, East, or Northwest as these areas have good mountain stars. ***Bed Directions:*** Place your headboard/bed to the North (1, 3, 4, or 9 Guas only), Northeast (2, 6, 7, or 8 Guas only), or East and Northwest directions (all Guas). These bed directions have a good mountain and facing star combination with excellent energy.

Take special caution regarding the West and Southwest; do not use either if at all possible. If the master bedroom is already located there, make sure that the bed direction is not also West and Southwest. If so, reposition immediately; activating this direction indicates cancer, bankruptcy, leukemia, divorce, death, and all types of mishaps and disasters. Place high-quality metal in the room such as wall art or statues made of bronze, brass, copper, pewter, or stainless steel. Also make sure to use a soft neutral color palette such as whites, creams, taupes, and metal colors like silver and bronze. Do not use fire colors (reds, pinks, purple, or oranges) in the artwork, rugs, bedding, or wall color. These precautions will ensure that you are extracting the best energy possible and keep the aggressive 5 star calm. Use the above directions when placing the bed for other family members; get their Life Gua in the Eight Mansions chart in chapter 4.

Home Office + Study

Place your desk/face North (1, 3, 4, or 9 Guas only), Northeast (2, 6, 7, or 8 Guas only), or West, East, and Northwest (all Guas). Choose one of these facing directions coupled with your +80 to enhance health, +70 for relationships, or +90 for wealth if possible. For example if you are an 8 Gua, face Northwest. This is your Tien Yi (Heavenly Doctor) or health direction, and it will protect you and bring unexpected wealth "from the heavens." The stars in this direction also have energy that supports romance and writing. For students, use the above directions to energize learning and success in exams.

Stoves and Toilets

The stove knobs, buttons, or controls should face Northeast, Northwest, or West. This house *cannot* have fire (kitchen, stove, or fireplace) in the center (3, 2) of the house; it can cause serious illness, especially the liver or stomach. You will struggle with money, health, and relationships if there is a stove or toilet located in your +90, +80, or +70 sector of the house. Select a toilet located in one of your negative sectors of the house (-90, -80, -70, or -60). This section applies to the head(s) of household or breadwinner.

Excellent Doors

Always use and activate good doors; the best ones for this chart are facing to the North, Northeast, West, and Northwest. This applies to all exterior doors as well as an interior garage door used to enter the house. In modern homes, an interior garage door is often the main entry into the house, making it extremely important. If one of these directions is also your +80, you will be very lucky with your health.

PERIOD 7

South 2 (172.6° to 187.5°)

Facing Name: *Wu* and the *Horse*

South 3 (187.6° to 202.5°)

Facing Name: *Ting*

Chart: *Combination of Ten* (*He Shih Chu*) and *Double Stars Meet at Back* (*Shuang Xing Dao Zuo*)

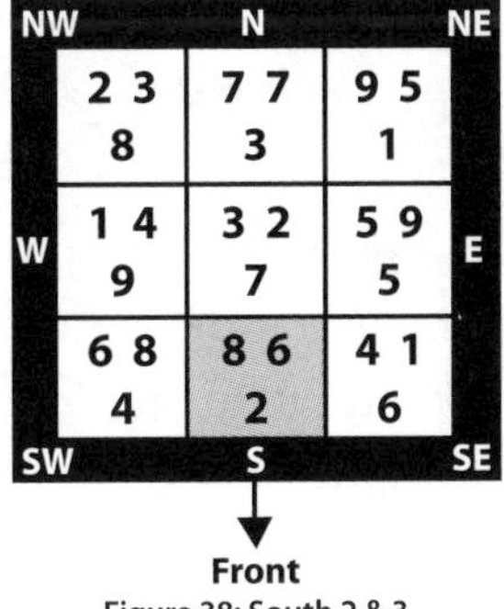

Figure 38: South 2 & 3

Health Alerts of the Chart

This chart has one negative area to pay attention to regarding health; in certain years it becomes more dangerous. It is the *Northeast* (5 facing star) and it becomes more serious for illness in the years of 2016, 2019, and 2021. No water (pools, fountains, etc.) or fire (stoves, fireplace/pits, or grills) should be placed in this area no matter the year—it will be activated.

Activating the External Environment

Enhancement: Place Water in Southwest, Mountain in South

Cures: Paint the back door red, and place small, still water near it

This chart has the two 7s at the back of the property known as ***Double Stars Meet at Sitting*** and a ***Combination of Ten***; it was extremely auspicious until February 4, 2004, when much of its vitality was lost. However, the South-facing homes support entrepreneurs and success in scholarly pursuits if activated accordingly. To reenergize this chart now that we are in Period 8, you will need to install a water feature in the front and simulate a mountain near the front door without blocking it. Water located in the Southwest ushers in the most benevolent and prosperous energy and should be placed there. The mountain can be courtyard walls, boulders (no sharp jagged edges), or landscaping mounds like on golf courses. Paint the back door red, and place a small water feature such as a birdbath to weaken the negative energy there. If you are unable to activate the chart exterior to your site, place a water fountain in the Southwest corner inside. Install two stone statues or planters on either side of the front door (inside or out).

For homes that face ***South 2***, there is a possible *Eight Killing Forces* formation if there is a mountain coming from the Northwest direction; this formation will invite blood-related accidents. For homes that face to ***South 3***, there is a possible *Eight Roads of Destruction* if there is a road/driveway coming from and exiting the Southwest direction; this formation will activate illness, bankruptcy, and divorce. South 2 and 3 may have a possible *Robbery Mountain Sha* formation if there is a jagged cliff, electrical tower, huge dead tree, lamppost, or a broken mountain in the Southeast; they indicate everyone in the household getting an unusual disease, injury by knives, and disasters.

Activating the Interior Environment

Master Bedroom + Family

There are two ways to activate great energy in the bedroom: location and direction. The direction of the bed will give you the most powerful results. Locate the master bedroom in the West, South, Southeast, or Southwest as these areas have good mountain stars. ***Bed Directions:*** For homes that face ***South 2***, place your headboard/bed to the South or Southeast (1, 3, 4, or 9 Guas only), and West or Southwest (2, 6, 7, or 8 Guas only). For homes that face ***South 3***, place your headboard/bed to the South, Southeast, West, or Southwest (all Guas). These bed directions have a good mountain and facing star combination with excellent energy.

Take special caution regarding the East and Northeast; do not use if at all possible. If the master bedroom is already located there, make sure that the bed direction is not also East or Northeast. If so, reposition immediately; activating this direction indicates cancer, bankruptcy, leukemia, divorce, death, and all types of mishaps and disasters. Place high-quality metal in the room such as wall art or statues made of bronze, brass, copper, pewter, or stainless steel. Also, make sure to use a soft neutral color palette such as whites, creams, taupes, and metal colors like silver and bronze. Do not use fire colors (reds, pinks, purple, or oranges) in the artwork, rugs, bedding, or wall color. These precautions will ensure that you are extracting the best energy possible and keep the aggressive 5 star calm. Use the above directions when placing the bed for other family members; get their Life Gua in the Eight Mansions chart in chapter 4.

Home Office + Study

For the ***South 2*** homes, place your desk/face to the South, East or Southeast (1, 3, 4, or 9 Guas only), West, or Southwest (2, 6, 7, or 8 Guas only). For ***South 3*** homes, place your desk/face the South, Southwest, West, East, or Southeast (all Guas). Choose one of these facing directions coupled with your +80 to enhance health, +70 for relationships, or +90 for wealth if possible.

For example if you are a 9 Gua, face the Southeast. This direction has great romance and wealth energy *plus* it's your personal Tien Yi (Heavenly Doctor) direction that secures health. For students, use the above directions to energize learning and success in exams; in this chart the West and Southeast have the strongest scholarly chi.

Stoves and Toilets

The best directions for stove knobs, buttons, or controls are Southwest, Southeast, West, or East. If there is a stove or toilet located in your +90, +80, or +70 sector of the house, health and money loss are at a high risk. Select a toilet located in one of your negative sectors of the house (-90,

-80, -70, or -60). This house *cannot* have a kitchen or fireplace in the center of the home (3, 2 combination); it can bring serious health issues such as heart attacks and high blood pressure. This section applies to the head(s) of household or breadwinner.

Excellent Doors

Always use and activate good doors; the best ones for this chart are facing to the South, East, Southeast, West, and Southwest. This applies to all exterior doors as well as an interior garage door used to enter the house. In modern homes, an interior garage door is often the main entry into the house, making it extremely important. If one of these directions is also your +80, you will be very lucky with your health.

PERIOD 7

Southwest 1 (202.6° to 217.5°)

Facing Name: ***Wei*** and the ***Goat***

Chart: ***Double Stars Meet at Facing (Shuang Xing Dao Xiang)***

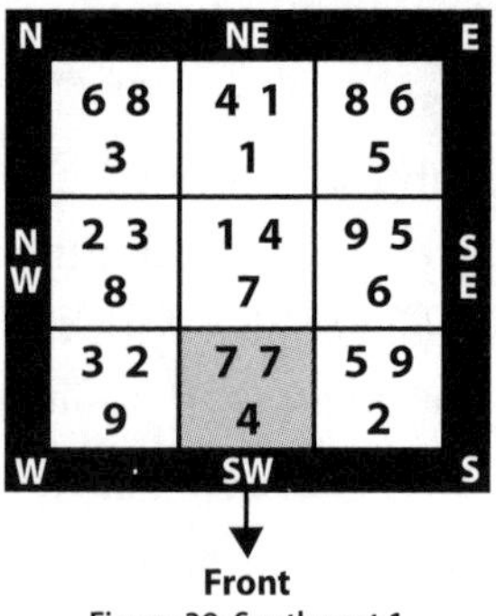

Figure 39: Southwest 1

Health Alerts of the Chart

This chart has two negative areas to pay attention to regarding health; in certain years they become more dangerous. They are the ***Southeast*** (9, 5) and the ***West*** (2 facing star). The Southeast becomes more serious for illness in the years of 2015, 2017, and 2021. The West can bring more sickness in the years of 2015, 2018, and 2020. No water (pools, fountains, etc.) or fire (stoves, fireplace/pits, or grills) should be placed in either area no matter the year—it will activate the negative energy in these areas.

Activating the External Environment

Enhancements: *Needs Water in North or Northeast, Mountain in East*
Cures: *Paint front door red and place small still water near door*

This property is known as ***Double Stars Meet at Facing*** and it has two 7s at the front of the site; this was very auspicious until February 4, 2004, when much of its vitality was lost. However, Southwest-facing properties are also known for turning bad fortunes into lucrative opportunities and may also denote the birth of an intelligent, wealthy, and prosperous person *if* activated properly. To reenergize this chart now that we are in Period 8, you will need to create a mountain in the East corner of your back garden. The "mountain" could be boulders (no sharp or jagged edges), basalt pillars, or landscape mounds like those in golf courses. Install a water feature in the North corner of your backyard; but take care that it is not located between 352° to 7° degrees; this will create a *Peach Blossom Sha* that could stir up illicit affairs.[37] Water is better placed in the center of the back garden, the Northeast. This can be a waterfall, koi pond, swimming pool, or fountain. If you're unable to energize the exterior of the property, place a water fountain on the Northeast wall inside your home. Place a tall, heavy armoire or bookcases angled in the East corner to represent your "mountain."

There is a possible *Robbery Mountain Sha* formation if there is a jagged cliff, electrical tower, huge dead tree, lamppost, or a broken mountain in the Southeast; they indicate everyone in the household getting an unusual disease, injury by knives, and disasters.

Activating the Interior Environment

Master Bedroom + Family

There are two ways to activate great energy in the bedroom—location and direction; the direction of the bed will give you the most powerful

---

37. To learn more about good and bad Peach Blossoms aka flowers of romance, refer to the author's book *Classical Feng Shui for Romance, Sex & Relationships* (2015, Llewellyn).

results. Locate your master bedroom in the North, East, or Southeast as these areas have good mountain stars with great energy. ***Bed Directions:*** Place your headboard/bed to the North (1, 3, 4, or 9 Guas only), Northeast (2, 6, 7, or 8 Guas only), or East (all Guas). These bed directions have a good mountain and facing star combination with excellent energy.

Take special caution regarding the Southeast and South; do not use either if at all possible. If the master bedroom is already located there, make sure that the bed direction is not also Southeast or South. If so, reposition immediately; activating this direction indicates cancer, bankruptcy, leukemia, divorce, death, and all types of disasters. Place high-quality metal in the room such as wall art or statues made of bronze, brass, copper, pewter, or stainless steel. Also, make sure to use a soft neutral color palette such as whites, creams, taupes, and metal colors like silver and bronze. Do not use fire colors (reds, pinks, purple, or oranges) in the artwork, rugs, bedding, or wall color. These precautions will ensure that you are extracting the best energy possible and keep the aggressive 5 star calm. Use the above directions when placing the bed for other family members; get their Life Gua in the Eight Mansions chart in chapter 4.

Home Office + Study

Place your desk/face to the North (1, 3, 4, or 9 Guas only), Northeast (2, 6, 7, or 8 Guas only), East, or South (all Guas). Choose one of these facing directions coupled with your +80 to enhance health, +70 for relationships, or +90 for wealth if possible. For example, if you are a 3 Gua, face North as this is your +90 (wealth); this arrangement indicates recognition at work and a promotion. If you're a 6 Gua, face Northeast. This direction has romance, money, and writing energy *and* the protection of Tien Yi, the Heavenly Doctor.

Stoves and Toilets

The best directions for the stove knobs, buttons, or controls are North, Northeast, or South. You will struggle with money, health, and relationships if there is a stove or toilet located in your +90, +80, or +70 sector of the house.

Select a toilet located in one of your negative sectors of the house (-90, -80, -70, or -60). This section applies to the head(s) of household or breadwinner.

Excellent Doors

Always use and activate good doors; the best ones for this chart are facing North, Northeast, East, and South; this applies to all exterior doors as well as an interior garage door used to enter the house.

In modern homes, an interior garage door is often the main entry into the house; therefore, it is extremely important.

If one of these directions is also your +80, you will be very lucky with your health. In this chart, a Southeast-facing door is the worst of the worst; avoid if at all possible. It has the evil 5 facing star, and its energy attracts all types of disasters.

If this is a well-used door or your only door in and out, you will need to cure it with lots of metal next to or directly on the door.

Brass, bronze, copper, pewter, and stainless steel are some high-vibrating metals to use, or you can hang large metal wind chimes. These doors can never be fully cured, only weakened, as the movement/use will always keep the energy activated.

Review the years it becomes particularly pernicious in the Health Alerts of the Chart section.

PERIOD 7

Southwest 2 (217.6° to 232.5°)
Facing Name: *Kun*

Southwest 3 (232.6° to 247.5°)
Facing name: *Shen* and the *Monkey*

Chart: *Double Stars Meet at Sitting* (*Shuang Xing Dao Zuo*)

N	NE	E
5 9 3	7 7 1	3 2 5
9 5 8	1 4 7	2 3 6
8 6 9	4 1 4	6 8 2
W	SW	S

(NW on the left side, SE on the right side)

Front

Figure 40: Southwest 2 & 3

Health Alerts of the Chart!

This chart has two negative areas to pay attention to regarding health; in certain years they become more dangerous. They are the *Northwest* (9, 5 facing star) and the *East* (2 facing star). The Northwest is more serious for illness in the years of 2017, 2019, and 2023. The East can bring more sickness in the years of 2016, 2020, and 2023. No water (pools, fountains, etc.) or fire (stoves, fireplace/pits, or grills) should be placed in either area no matter the year—doing so will activate the negative energy in these areas.

Activating the External Environment

Enhancements: Place Water in South, Mountain in West
Cures: Place a birdbath near the back door and paint it red

This property has the two 7s at the back of the property called ***Double Stars Meet at the Sitting***; this was very lucky for health and money until February 4, 2004, when much of its vitality was lost. However, the Southwest-facing properties are known for turning bad fortunes into lucrative opportunities and may also denote in the birth of an intelligent, wealthy and prosperous person *if* activated properly. In order to reenergize the chart now that we are in Period 8, you will need to place a water feature such as a fountain in the South of your front garden. Water located in the South ushers in the most benevolent and prosperous energy and should be placed there. Simulate a mountain in the West of your front yard by installing a landscape mound (like those in golf courses), boulders, basalt pillars, or courtyard walls activate this energy. Southwest, near the front door, is an alternate placement for a water feature. Place a small water feature such as a birdbath near the back door and paint it red; the color will exhaust the negative energy there.

If you are unable to activate the exterior of your site, place a water fountain angled in the South corner inside your home. Place a tall, heavy armoire, or bookcases angled in the West corner of your interior space.

Homes facing to ***Southwest 2*** could have an *Eight Roads of Destruction* formation if a road/driveway comes from or exits the South or West directions; they are notorious for bringing ill health, bankruptcy, kill good business deals/relationships, and divorce. There is a possible *Robbery Mountain Sha* formation if there is a jagged cliff, electrical tower, huge dead tree, lamppost, or a broken mountain in the South; they indicate everyone in the household getting an unusual disease, injury by knives, and disasters.

The ***Southwest 3*** facing homes may have an *Eight Killings* formation if there is a mountain coming from the East direction; this formation will unsettle relationships in the house. There is a possible *Robbery Mountain Sha* formation if there is a jagged cliff, electrical tower, huge dead tree, lamppost, or a broken mountain in the Southwest.

Activating the Interior Environment

Master Bedroom + Family

There are two ways to activate great energy in the bedroom—location and direction. The direction of the bed will give you the most powerful results. Locate your master bedroom in the Southwest, South, or West; these sectors of the house have good mountain stars. ***Bed Directions:*** For homes that face ***Southwest 2***, place your headboard/bed to the place your headboard/bed to the South (1, 3, 4, or 9 Guas only), Southwest, or West (2, 6, 7, or 8 Guas only). For homes that face ***Southwest 3***, place your headboard/bed to the South, Southwest, or West (all Guas). These bed directions have a good mountain and facing star combination with excellent energy.

Take special caution regarding the North and Northwest; do not use either if at all possible. If the master bedroom is already located there, make sure that the bed direction is not also North and Northwest. If so, reposition immediately; activating this direction indicates cancer, bankruptcy, leukemia, divorce, death, and all types of disasters. Place high-quality metal in the room such as wall art or statues made of bronze, brass, copper, pewter, or stainless steel. Additionally, use a soft neutral color palette such as whites, creams, taupes, and metal colors like silver and bronze. Do not use fire colors (reds, pinks, purple, or oranges) in the artwork, rugs, bedding, or wall color. These precautions will ensure that you are extracting the best energy possible and keep the aggressive 5 star calm. Use the above directions when placing the bed for other family members; get their Life Gua in the Eight Mansions chart in chapter 4.

Home Office + Study

For the ***Southwest 2*** homes, place your desk/face to the North or South (1, 3, 4, or 9 Guas only), Southwest, or West (2, 6, 7, or 8 Guas only). For the ***Southwest 3*** homes, place your desk/face to the North (1, 3, 4, or 9 Guas only), South, Southwest, or West (all Guas). Choose one of these facing directions coupled with your +80 to enhance health, +70 for relationships, or +90 for wealth if possible. For example if you are a 3 Gua, face South as it is your +90 (wealth) direction. If you are a 7 Gua, face the Southwest, your +80 that also has good romance, writing, and wealth energy. Since it is also your unique health direction, the Heavenly Doctor (Tien Yi) will protect you and bring you unexpected wealth "from the heavens." For students, use the above directions to energize learning and success in exams.

Stoves and Toilets

The best directions for the stove knobs, buttons, or controls are to the South, Southwest, or North. You will struggle with money, health, and relationships if there is a stove or toilet located in your +90, +80, or +70 sector of the house. Select a toilet located in one of your negative sectors of the house (-90, -80, -70, or -60). This section applies to the head(s) of household or breadwinner.

Excellent Doors

Always use and activate good doors; the best ones for this chart are facing North, South, Southwest and West. This applies to all exterior doors as well as an interior garage door used to enter the house. In modern homes, an interior garage door is often the main entry into the house, making it extremely important. In this chart, a Northwest-facing door is the worst of the worst; avoid if at all possible. It has the evil 5 facing star and its energy attracts all types of disasters. If this is a well-used door, you will need to cure it with lots of metal next to or directly on the door. Brass, bronze, copper, pewter, and stainless steel are some high-vibrating metals to use, or you can hang large metal wind chimes. These doors can never be fully cured, only weakened, as the movement/use will always keep the energy activated. Review the years it becomes seriously dangerous in the Health Alerts of the Chart section.

PERIOD 7

West 1 (247.6° to 262.5°)

Facing Name: *Geng*

Chart: *Reverse Formation*

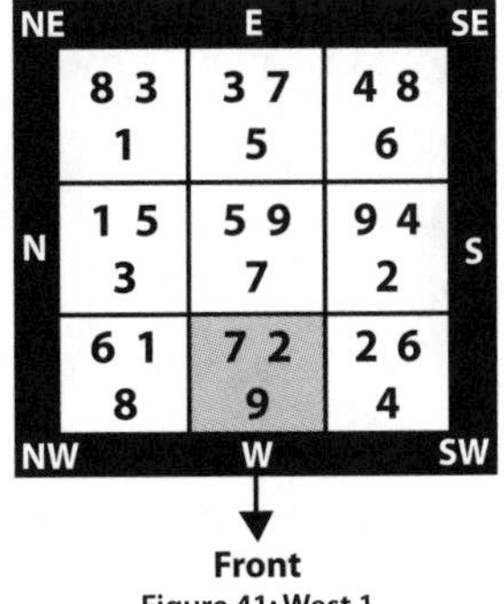

Figure 41: West 1

Health Alerts of the Chart

This chart has two negative areas to pay attention to regarding health; in certain years they become more dangerous. They are the *North* (5 facing star) and the *West* (2 facing star). The

North becomes more serious for illness in the years of 2018, 2021, and 2023. The West can bring more sickness in the years of 2015, 2018, and 2020. No water (pools, fountains, etc.) or fire (stoves, fireplace/pits, or grills) should be placed in either area no matter the year—doing so will activate the negative energy in these areas.

Activating the External Environment

Enhancements: *Needs Water in Southeast, Mountain in Northeast*
Cures: *Place small water and paint back door red; place metal on/near the front door*

This chart is known as a ***Reverse Formation.*** It was not particularly auspicious even in Period 7; it has worsened in Period 8. However, the West-facing properties produce well-educated, intelligent, polite, and charming people who can become very wealthy through good business management, or getting involved in politics *if* activated accordingly. In order to re-energize this property you will need to create a mountain in the Northeast of your back garden; this can be accomplished by using boulders (no sharp or jagged edges), landscape mounds, tiered or terraced garden beds, basalt pillars, or high ground/ mounds like those at golf courses. Install a large water feature in the Southeast corner of your back yard. This can be a waterfall, koi pond, swimming pool, or large fountain. Water located in the Southeast ushers in the most benevolent and prosperous energy and should be placed there. If you are unable to activate this chart exterior to your site, install a water fountain indoors in the Southeast corner. Place a tall armoire or bookcases in the Northeast corner at the back of your space.

Unfortunately, the front door (West-facing) and back door (East-facing) ***must*** be cured or you may be plagued with sickness and robberies. The front door will need lots of metal such as brass, copper, bronze, pewter, stainless steel, or large metal wind chimes; remove any water feature placed here. Place small water such as a birdbath near the back door and paint it red.

The house does have a possible *Eight Roads of Destruction* formation if there is a road/driveway coming from and exiting the Southwest direction; they are notorious for bringing ill health, bankruptcy, and divorce. There is a possible *Robbery Mountain Sha* formation if there is a jagged cliff, electrical tower, huge dead tree, lamppost, or a broken mountain in the South; they indicate everyone in the household getting an unusual disease, injury by knives, and disasters.

Activating the Interior Environment

Master Bedroom + Family

There are two ways to activate great energy in the bedroom—location and direction; the direction of the bed will give you the most powerful results. Locate your master bedroom in the Northeast, South, or Northwest as these sectors have good mountain stars. ***Bed Directions:*** Place your headboard/bed to the Northwest and South (all Guas), and Southeast (1, 3, 4, or 9 Guas only) directions. These bed directions have a good mountain and facing star combination with excellent energy. Use the above directions when placing the bed for other family members; get their Life Gua in the Eight Mansions chart in chapter 4.

Home Office + Study

For the best health, business opportunities, and romance-luck, face your desk/body Northwest, South, or Southwest (all Guas), and Southeast (1, 3, 4, or 9 Guas only). Choose one of these facing directions coupled with your +80 to enhance health, +70 for relationships, or +90 for wealth if possible. For example, if you are a 1 Gua, face Southeast, your +90 (wealth) direction. This arrangement indicates recognition and a promotion in the workplace. If you are an 8 Gua, face the Northwest as this is your +80 (health) and the Heavenly Doctor (Tien Yi) will protect your health. The stars in the Northwest also indicate good romance and writing energy.

For students, use the above directions to energize learning and success in exams.

Stoves and Toilets

The best directions for the stove knobs, buttons or controls are Southeast, South, and Northwest.

If there is a stove or toilet located in your +90, +80, or +70 sector of the house, health and money loss are at high risk. Select a toilet located in one of your negative sectors of the house (-90, -80, -70, or -60).

This section applies to the head(s) of household or breadwinner. This house *cannot* have a kitchen or fireplace in the center of the home (5, 9 combination); it can bring serious health issues such as heart attacks and high blood pressure.

Excellent Doors

Always use and activate good doors; the best ones for this chart are facing Northwest, South, Southwest, and Southeast; this applies to all exterior doors as well as any interior garage doors used to enter the house.

In modern homes, an interior garage door is often the main entry into the house, making it extremely important.

In this chart, a North-facing door is the worst of the worst and will need to be cured with lots of metal next to or directly on the door.

Brass, bronze, copper, pewter, and stainless steel are some high-vibrating metals you can use, or you can hang large metal wind chimes.

These doors can never be fully cured, only weakened, as movement/use will always keep the energy activated. Review the years it becomes aggressive in the Health Alerts of the Chart section.

PERIOD 7

West 2 (262.6° to 277.5°)
Facing Name: *You* and the ***Rooster***

West 3 (277.6° to 292.5°)
Facing Name: *Xin*

Chart: ***Prosperous Sitting and Facing***
(*Wang Shan Wang Shui*)

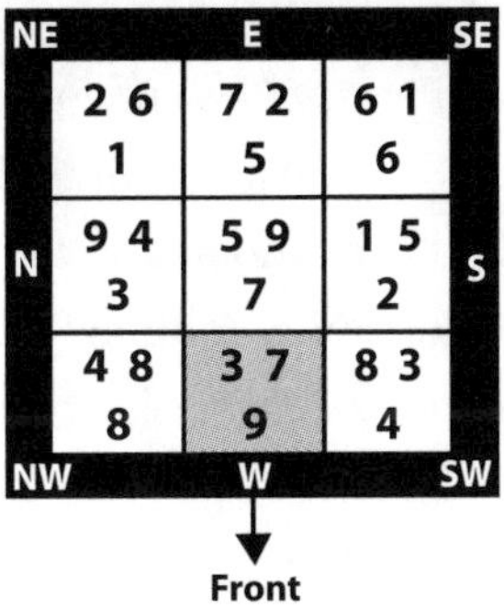

NE	E	SE
2 6 1	7 2 5	6 1 6
9 4 3	5 9 7	1 5 2
4 8 8	3 7 9	8 3 4
NW	W	SW

N (left side) · S (right side)

Front

Figure 42: West 2 & 3

Health Alerts of the Chart!

This chart has two negative areas to pay attention to regarding health; in certain years they become more dangerous. They are the ***South*** (5 facing star) and the ***East*** (2 facing star). The South becomes more serious for illness in the years of 2017, 2019, and 2022. The East can bring more sickness in the years of 2016, 2020, and 2023. No water (pools, fountains, etc.) or fire (stoves, fireplace/pits, or grills) should be placed in either area no matter the year—doing so will activate the negative energy in these areas.

Activating the External Environment

Enhancements: *Needs Water in Northwest, Mountain in Southwest; Alternate water in Southeast*
Cures: *Place small water and paint the front door red; place wind chimes near the back door*

This chart had the two 7s perfectly placed in Period 7 known as ***Prosperous Sitting and Facing***; it was very prestigious until February 4, 2004, when it turned harmful. However, West-facing properties produce people who can be powerful in the politics, super athletes, and those very accomplished in academia *if* activated accordingly. In order to reenergize this property, you will need to install a large water feature in your front garden in the Northwest. This can be a fountain, koi pond, or waterfall, and it must flow towards the house. Water located in the Northwest ushers in the most benevolent and prosperous energy and should be placed there.

Create a mountain in the Southwest area of your front garden using boulders (no sharp or jagged edges), basalt pillars, courtyard walls, or landscaping mounds like those you see on golf courses. If you are unable to activate this chart exterior to your site, place a water fountain in the Northwest corner indoors. Place a heavy armoire or tall bookcases in the Southwest corner inside.

Unfortunately, the front door (West-facing) and back door (East-facing) ***must*** be cured or you may be plagued with sickness and robberies. The front door will need to be painted red, as well as small water such as a birdbath. The back door will need lots of metal such as brass, copper, bronze, pewter, stainless steel, or large metal wind chimes; remove any water feature placed here.

The *West 2* homes also have a possible *Eight Killing Forces* if there is mountain chi coming from the Southeast direction and invites blood-related accidents. The *West 3* facing homes have a possible *Eight Roads of Destruction* formation if there is a road/driveway coming from and exiting the Northwest direction; they are notorious for bringing ill health, bankruptcy, and divorce. There is a possible *Robbery Mountain Sha* formation for both facings if there is a jagged cliff, electrical tower, huge dead tree, lamppost, or a broken mountain in the South or Southwest; they indicate everyone in the household getting an unusual disease, injury by knives, and disasters.

Activating the Interior Environment

Master Bedroom + Family

There are two ways to activate great energy in the bedroom—location and direction. The direction of the bed will give you the most powerful results. Locate your master bedroom in the North, Southwest, Northwest, or

Southeast as these sectors have good mountain stars. ***Bed Directions:*** For homes that face ***West 2***, place your headboard/bed to the Northwest (2, 6, 7, or 8 Guas only), North, or Southeast (1, 3, 4, or 9 Guas only). For homes that face to ***West 3***, place your headboard/bed to the Northwest, Southeast (all Guas), or North (1, 3, 4, or 9 Guas. These bed directions have a good mountain and facing star combination with excellent energy. Use the above directions when placing the bed for other family members; get their Life Gua in the Eight Mansions chart in chapter 4.

Home Office + Study

For the ***West 2*** homes, place your desk/face to the Northwest or Northeast (2, 6, 7, or 8 Guas only), North or Southeast (1, 3, 4, or 9 Guas only). For the ***West 3*** homes, place your desk/face to the Northwest, Northeast, or Southeast (all Guas) or North (1, 3, 4, or 9 Guas only). Choose one of these facing directions coupled with your +70 for relationships, +80 to enhance health, or +90 for wealth if possible. For example, if you're a 9 Gua face Southeast, your unique health direction (+80). The stars in this location indicate wealth, romance, and writing energy. If you are a 2 Life Gua, Northwest is your +70 (relationships), and it has extremely prosperous energy. Activating this direction will bring wealth or even the chance to meet a partner through the workplace. For students, use the above directions to energize learning and success in exams.

Stoves and Toilets

The best directions for stove knobs, buttons, or controls are North, Northwest, or Southeast. If there is a stove or toilet located in your +90, +80, or +70 sector of the house, health and money loss are at a high risk. Select a toilet located in one of your negative sectors: -90, -80, -70, or -60. This section applies to the head(s) of household or breadwinner. This house *cannot* have a kitchen or fireplace in the center of the home (5, 9 combination); it can bring serious health issues such as heart attacks and high blood pressure.

Excellent Doors

Always use and activate good doors; the best ones for this chart are facing North, Northwest, Northeast, and Southeast. This applies to all exterior doors as well as an interior garage door used to enter the house. In modern homes, an interior garage door is often the main entry into the house, making it extremely important. In this chart, a South-facing door is the worst of the worst; avoid if at all possible. It has the evil 5 facing star and it's quite powerful in the South. If this is a well-used door, you will need to cure it with lots of metal next to or directly on the door. Brass, bronze, copper, pewter, and stainless steel are some high-vibrating metals to use, or you can hang large metal wind chimes. These doors can never be fully cured—only weakened—as movement/use will always keep the negative energy activated. Review the years it becomes aggressive in the Health Alerts of the Chart section.

PERIOD 7

Northwest 1 (292.6° to 307.5°)
Facing Name: *Xu* and the *Dog*

Chart: ***Prosperous Sitting and Facing*** (*Wang Shan Wang Shui*)

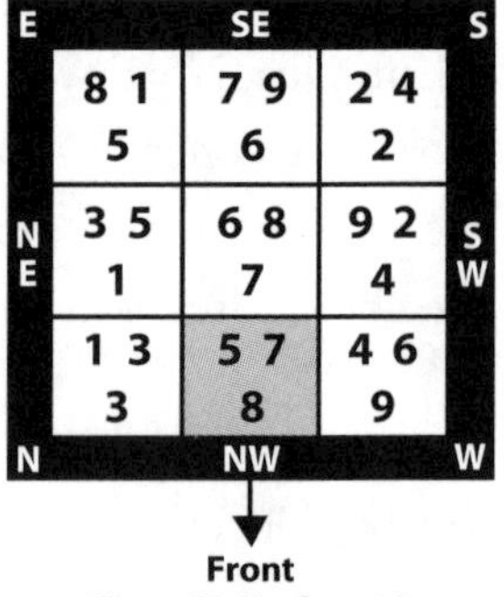

Figure 43: Northwest 1

Health Alerts of the Chart

This chart has two negative areas to pay attention to regarding health; in certain years they become more dangerous. They are the *Northeast* (5 facing star) and the *Southwest* (2 facing star). The Northeast becomes more serious for illness in the years of 2016, 2019, and 2021. The Southwest can bring more sickness in the years of 2015, 2020, and 2022. No water (pools, fountains, etc.) or fire (stoves, fireplace/pits, or grills) should be placed in either area no matter the year—it will activate the negative energy in these areas.

Activating the External Environment

Enhancements: Needs Water and Mountain in East
Cures: Paint the front door red, and place a birdbath near it

This property is known as ***Prosperous Sitting and Facing*** and in Period 7, the stars were perfectly placed; money- and people-luck would have been abundant. However, since February 4, 2004, the energy has turned harmful. The Northwest–facing structures are famous for turning almost everything to an advantage; this is especially true involving business *if* they are activated accordingly.

In order to re-energize this chart, now that we are in Period 8, you will need to install a tall, stone water fountain in the East. Moreover, the water should not be located between 82° and 97° as this can attract affairs; the water may be better placed in the Southeast (center of your back garden). If you already have a swimming pool there, this is very auspicious and becomes more so as we approach Period 9 (begins February 4, 2024). Alternatively, creating a rock waterfall with a collection pool in the East corner of your back garden would also fulfill the criteria.

If you are unable to activate this chart exterior to your site, then place a tall, heavy water fountain indoors in the East corner or on the back wall inside which is the Southeast. Place a heavy armoire or tall bookcases on the Southwest wall or in the North corner for additional supporting energy. The front door has negative energy, so paint it red and place still water such as a birdbath near it.

There is a possible *Robbery Mountain Sha* formation if there is a jagged cliff, electrical tower, huge dead tree, lamppost, or a broken mountain in the Southwest; they indicate everyone in the household getting an unusual disease, injury by knives, and disasters.

Activating the Interior Environment

Master Bedroom + Family

There are two ways activate great energy in the bedroom—location and direction; the direction of the bed will give you the most powerful results. Locate your master bedroom in the North, Southwest, or East as these sectors have good mountain stars. ***Bed Directions:*** Place your headboard to the East or West (all Guas). These bed directions have a good mountain and facing star combination with excellent energy. Use the above directions when placing the bed for other family members; get their Life Gua in the Eight Mansions chart in chapter 4.

Home Office + Study

Face your desk/body to the South, East, or West (all Guas), or Southeast (1, 3, 4, or 9 Guas only). The South direction is particularly good for 1 Guas as this is their unique relationships direction (+70) and the 4 facing star known for its romance energy. For 9 Life Guas, East is their +90, and it has very prosperous energy. For students, use the above directions to energize learning and success in exams.

Stoves and Toilets

The best directions for the stove knobs, buttons, or controls are East, South, or the Southeast. You will struggle with money, health, and relationships if there is a stove or toilet located in your +90, +80, or +70 sector of the house. Select a toilet located in one of your negative sectors of the house (-90, -80, -70, or -60). This section applies to the head(s) of household or breadwinner.

Excellent Doors

Always use and activate good doors; the best ones for this chart are facing to the South, East, West, and Southeast. This applies to all exterior doors as well as any interior garage door used to enter the house. In modern homes, an interior garage door is often the main entry into the house, making it extremely important. A Northeast-facing door, in this chart, is the worst of the worst; avoid if at all possible. It has the evil 5 facing star, which is quite powerful in the Northeast.

If this is a well-used door, you will need to cure it with lots of metal next to or directly on the door. Brass, bronze, copper, pewter, and stainless steel are some high-vibrating metals to use, or large metal wind chimes.

Unfortunately, these doors can never be fully cured, only weakened, as the movement/use will always keep the energy activated. Review the years it becomes seriously dangerous in the Health Alerts of the Chart section.

PERIOD 7

Northwest 2 (307.6° to 322.5°)
Facing Name: *Chien*

Northwest 3 (322.6° to 337.5°)
Facing Name: *Hai* and the *Pig*

Chart: *Pearl String Formation*
(*Lin Cu San Poon Gua*)

E		SE		S
	4 6 5	5 7 6	1 3 2	
NE	9 2 1	6 8 7	3 5 4	SW
	2 4 3	7 9 8	8 1 9	
N		NW		W

Front

Figure 44: Northwest 2 & 3

Health Alerts of the Chart

This chart has two negative areas to pay attention to regarding health; in certain years they become more dangerous. They are the ***Southwest*** (5 facing star) and the ***Northeast*** (2 facing star). The Southwest becomes more serious for illness in the years of 2015, 2019, and 2022. The Northeast can bring more sickness in the years of 2016, 2019, and 2021. No water (pools, fountains, etc.) or fire (stoves, fireplace/pits, or grills) should be placed in either area no matter the year—it will activate the negative energy in these areas.

Activating the External Environment

***Enhancements:** Water in Northwest, Mountain in West*

***Cures:** Place a birdbath near the back door and paint it red*

This special energy, known as a ***Pearl String*** (aka Continuous Bead), is one of the most unique charts in the Flying Star system but are only potent for twenty years. It was very lucky in Period 7 but now has lost much of its vitality as of February 4, 2004. The Northwest-facing properties are famous for turning almost everything to an advantage; this is especially true involving business *if* they are activated accordingly. Now that we are in Period 8, this chart will need to be re-energized by placing a mountain and water in the West. This may be accomplished by installing a rock waterfall (water must flow towards the house), or place a tall stone fountain. An alternative water feature may be located in the front of the property (Northwest); this direction is auspicious and becomes more so as we approach Period 9 (begins February 4, 2024). However, you will still need to create a mountain in the West with high ground, landscape mounds (like the ones at golf courses), or boulders (no sharp or jagged edges). This property's back door has negative energy and should be painted red. Additionally, a birdbath or small water feature should be placed near it to exhaust the energy.

For homes that face ***Northwest 2***, there is a possible *Eight Roads of Destruction* if you have a road coming to the house from either the West or North directions; they will activate ill health, kill good business deals/relationships, bankruptcy, and divorce. There is a possible *Robbery Mountain Sha* formation if there is a jagged cliff, electrical tower, huge dead tree, lamppost, or a broken mountain in the North; they indicate everyone in the household getting an unusual disease, hurt by knives and disasters.

For the ***Northwest 3*** facing homes if mountain energy/chi comes to the home from the South direction you could have an *Eight Killing Forces* formation, known for the harm it can cause such as blood-related accidents. There is a possible *Robbery Mountain Sha* formation if there is a jagged cliff, electrical tower, huge dead tree, lamppost, or a broken mountain in the West.

Activating the Interior Environment

Master Bedroom + Family

There are two ways to activate great energy in the bedroom—location and direction; the direction of the bed will give you the most powerful results. Locate your master bedroom in the South, West, or Northeast as these sectors have good mountain stars. ***Bed Directions:*** For homes facing *Northwest 2,* place your headboard/bed to the West (2, 6, 7, or 8 Guas only) or East (1, 3, 4, or 9 Guas only). For homes facing *Northwest 3,* place your headboard/bed to the West or East (all Guas). These bed directions have a good mountain and facing star combination with excellent energy. Use the above directions when placing the bed for other family members; get their Life Gua in the Eight Mansions chart in chapter 4.

Home Office + Study

For the *Northwest 2* homes, place your desk/face Northwest or West (2, 6, 7, or 8 Guas only), or East or North (1, 3, 4, or 9 Guas only). For the *Northwest 3* homes, place your desk/face North (1, 3, 4, or 9 Guas only), Northwest, West, or East (all Guas). North is especially good for 9 Guas as this is their unique relationships direction (+70) and the 4 facing star known for its romance energy. For the 2 Life Gua, the West is their +80 and has prosperous energy; activating this direction indicates being protected by Tien Yi (the Heavenly Doctor) and unexpected wealth from the heavens. For students, use the above directions to energize learning and success in exams.

Stoves and Toilets

The best directions for stove knobs, buttons, or controls are West, North, or Northwest. You will struggle with money, health, and relationships if there is a stove or toilet located in your +90, +80, or +70 sector of the house. Select a toilet located in one of your negative sectors of the house (-90, -80, -70, or -60). This section applies to the head(s) of household or breadwinner.

Excellent Doors

Always use and activate good doors; the best ones for this chart face Northwest, North, West, and East. This applies to all exterior doors as well as an interior garage door used to enter the house. In modern homes, an interior garage door is often the main entry into the house, making it extremely important. In this chart, a Southwest-facing door is the worst of the worst; avoid if at all possible. It has the evil 5 facing star and is quite powerful in the Southwest. If this is a well-used door, you will need to cure it with lots of metal next to or directly on the door. Brass, bronze, copper, pewter, and stainless steel are some high-vibrating metals to use, or you can hang large metal wind chimes. Unfortunately, these doors can never be fully cured, only weakened, as the movement/use of it will always keep the energy activated. Review the years it becomes particularly pernicious in the Health Alerts of the Chart section.

PERIOD 7

North 1 (337.6° to 352.5°)
Facing Name: ***Ren***

Chart: ***Double Stars Meet at Sitting***
(*Shuang Xing Dao Zuo*)

SE	S	SW
3 2 6	7 7 2	5 9 4
4 1 5	2 3 7	9 5 9
8 6 1	6 8 3	1 4 8
NE	N	NW

E (left side), W (right side)

Front

Figure 45: North 1

Health Alerts of the Chart

This chart has two negative areas to pay attention to regarding health; in certain years they become more dangerous. They are the ***West*** (2, 5) and the ***Southeast*** (2 facing star). The West becomes more serious for illness in the years of 2015, 2018, and 2020. The Southeast can bring more sickness in the years of 2015, 2017, and 2021.

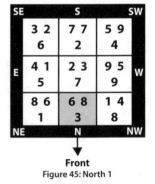

No water (pools, fountains, etc.) or fire (stoves, fireplace/pits, or grills) should be placed in either area no matter the year—it will activate the negative energy in these areas.

Activating the External Environment

Enhancements: *Water in North, Mountain in Northeast*

Cures: *Paint the back door red, and place a birdbath near it*

This property has the two 7s at the back, called ***Double Stars Meet at Sitting.*** It was quite auspicious for relationships and health until February 4, 2004, when much of its vitality was diminished, however, it's the *only* Period 7 chart with the *8* facing star in the front. The North-facing charts are known to produce people who are charismatic and very successful in business *if* activated accordingly. Now that we are in Period 8, you will need to install a gorgeous water feature in the front (North) in order to re-energize the chart. This can be a koi pond, tall stone fountain, a stream, or waterfall (the water must flow towards the house).

Water located in the *North* ushers in the most benevolent and prosperous energy and should be placed there. Also, there should be a mountain in the Northeast area of your front garden. This can be done with landscape mounds (like the ones you see on golf courses), basalt pillars, or large boulders (no sharp or jagged edges). If you are unable to activate the energy exterior to your site, then place a fountain inside near your front door. Also place a tall armoire or bookcases in the Northeast corner indoors. Alternative or additional water may be placed in the East (indoors or out).

There is a possible *Eight Roads of Destruction* if you have a road/driveway coming from and exiting the Northwest direction; this formation will activate ill health, bankruptcy, and divorce. There is a possible *Robbery Mountain Sha* formation if there is a jagged cliff, electrical tower, huge dead tree, lamppost, or a broken mountain in the West; they indicate everyone in the household getting an unusual disease, injury by knives, and disasters.

Activating the Interior Environment

Master Bedroom + Family

There are two ways to activate great energy in the bedroom—location and direction; the direction of the bed will give you the most powerful results. Locate your master bedroom in the East, Northwest, North (second floor), or Northeast as these sectors have good mountain stars. ***Bed Directions:*** Place your headboard/bed to the Northwest or East (all Guas), Northeast (2, 6, 7, or 8 Guas only), or North (1, 3, 4, or 9 Guas only). These bed directions have a good mountain and facing star combination with excellent energy.

Take special caution regarding the Southwest and West; do not use either if at all possible. If the master bedroom is already located there, make sure that the bed direction is not also Southwest or West; if so, reposition immediately—activating this direction indicates cancer, bankruptcy, leukemia, divorce, death, and all types of disasters. Place high-quality metal in the room such as wall art or statues made of bronze, brass, copper, pewter, or stainless steel. Additionally, use a soft neutral color palette such as whites, creams, taupes, and metal colors like silver and bronze. Do not use fire colors (reds, pinks, purple, or oranges) in the artwork, rugs, bedding, or wall color. These precautions will ensure that you are extracting the best energy possible and keep the aggressive 5 star calm. Use the above directions when placing the bed for other family members; get their Life Gua in the Eight Mansions chart in chapter 4.

Home Office + Study

Face your desk/body the Northwest, Southwest, or East (all Guas), Northeast (2, 6, 7, or 8 Guas only), or North (1, 3, 4, or 9 Guas only). Choose one of these facing directions coupled with your +80 to enhance health, +70 for relationships, or +90 for wealth if possible. For example, if you are a 4 Gua, choose East; it has wealth and romance energy and is your +70 (relationships).

If you are an 8 Gua, choose Northwest; it has scholarly energy and is your +80 (health direction). For students, use the above directions to energize learning and success in exams; the East and Northwest have the most potent scholarly chi.

Stoves and Toilets

The best direction for stove knobs, buttons, or controls are North, Northwest, East, or Southwest. If there is a stove or toilet located in your +90, +80, or +70 sector of the house, health and money loss are at a high risk. Select a toilet located in one of your negative sectors of the house (-90, -80, -70, or -60). This section applies to the head(s) of household or breadwinner. This house *cannot* have a kitchen or fireplace in the center of the home (2, 3 combination); it can bring serious health problems such as heart attacks, extreme tension/stress, reproductive issues, and high blood pressure.

Excellent Doors

Always use and activate good doors; the best ones for this chart are facing Southwest, North, Northwest, East, and Northeast; this applies to all exterior doors as well as any interior garage doors used to enter the house. In modern homes, an interior garage door is often the main entry into the house, making it extremely important. In this chart, a West-facing door is the worst of the worst; avoid if at all possible.

It has the evil 5 facing star, whose energy attracts all types of disasters. If this is a well-used door, you will need to cure it with lots of metal next to or directly on the door. Brass, bronze, copper, pewter, and stainless steel are some high-vibrating metals to use, or you can hang large metal wind chimes. Unfortunately, these doors can never be fully cured, only weakened, as the movement/use will always keep the energy activated. Review the years it becomes seriously dangerous in the Health Alerts of the Chart section.

PERIOD 7

North 2 (352.6° to 7.5°)

Facing name: *Tzi* and the *Rat*

North 3 (7.6° to 22.5)

Facing name: *Kwei*

Chart: *Combination of Ten* (*He Shih Chu*)

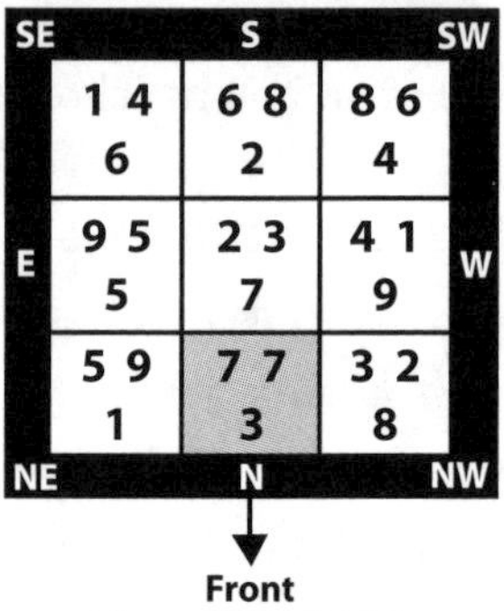

SE	S	SW
1 4 6	6 8 2	8 6 4
E: 9 5 5	2 3 7	4 1 9 :W
5 9 1	7 7 3	3 2 8
NE	N	NW

Front

Figure 46: North 2 & 3

Health Alerts of the Chart

This chart has two negative areas to pay attention to regarding health; in certain years they become more dangerous. They are the ***East*** (9, 5) and the ***Northwest*** (2 facing star). The East becomes more serious for illness in the years of 2016, 2020, and 2023. The Northwest can bring more sickness in the years of 2017, 2019, and 2023. No water (pools, fountains, etc.) or fire (stoves, fire place/pits, or grills) should be placed in either area no matter the year—it will activate the negative energy in these areas.

Activating the External Environment

Enhancements: *Water in the South, Mountain Southwest*

Cures: *Place small water near the front door and paint it red*

This property had the prestigious chart known as the ***Combination of Ten*** or *Sum of Ten* although since February 4, 2004, much of its vitality has been lost. However, North-facing charts can produce occupants who can successfully run their own businesses; they also may enjoy good fortune with their career taking them all over the world, *if* it is activated accordingly. Now that we are in Period 8, you will need to create a mountain in the Southwest corner of the back garden to re-energize this property; a mountain could be created with large boulders (no sharp or jagged edges), basalt pillars, landscape mounds (like the ones at golf courses), or tiered/terraced garden beds.

Install a grand water feature in the South of your garden to usher in the most benevolent and prosperous energy. This can be a swimming pool, koi pond, waterfall, or large stone fountain depending on the size of the structure. If you are unable to activate the exterior of your site, install an indoor fountain near your back door (South). Place a tall armoire or bookcases in the Southwest corner; these are good "mountain" simulations.

The front of the property (North) has the double 7s and this indicates robbery by guns or knives, theft, and "things being taken away"; you will need to cure this by painting the door red and placing a small water feature such as a birdbath near the door.

The *North 2* homes may have a possible *Robbery Mountain Sha* formation if there is a jagged cliff, electrical tower, huge dead tree, lamppost, or a broken mountain in the West; they indicate everyone in the household getting an unusual disease, hurt by knives and disasters.

For homes that face *North 3*, there is a possible *Eight Roads of Destruction* if you have a road/driveway coming from and exiting the Northeast direction and will activate ill health, bankruptcy, and divorce. There is a possible *Robbery Mountain Sha* formation if there is a jagged cliff, electrical tower, huge dead tree, lamppost, or a broken mountain in the Northeast.

Activating the Interior Environment

Master Bedroom + Family

There are two ways to activate great energy in the bedroom—location and direction; the direction of the bed will give you the most powerful results. Locate your master bedroom in the West, Southeast, South, or Southwest as these sectors have mountain stars. ***Bed Directions:*** For homes that face *North 2*, place your headboard/bed West, Southwest (2, 6, 7, or 8 Guas only), Southeast, or South (1, 3, 4, or 9 Guas only). For homes that face *North 3*, place your headboard/bed to the Southeast, West, Southwest, or South (all Guas). These bed directions have a good mountain and facing star combination with excellent energy.

Take special caution regarding the East and Northeast; do not use either if at all possible. If the master bedroom is already located there, make sure that the bed direction is not also East or Northeast. If so, reposition immediately; activating this direction indicates cancer, bankruptcy, leukemia, divorce, death, and all types of disasters. Place high quality metal in the room such as wall art or statues made of bronze, brass, copper, pewter, or stainless steel. Also make sure to use a soft neutral color palette such as whites, creams, taupes, and metal colors like silver and bronze. Do not use fire colors (reds, pinks, purple, or oranges) in the artwork, rugs, bedding, or wall color. These precautions will ensure that you are extracting the best energy possible and keep the aggressive 5 star calm. Use the above directions when placing the bed for other family members; get their Life Gua in the Eight Mansions chart in chapter 4.

Home Office + Study

For the *North 2* homes, place your desk/face Northeast, West, or Southwest (2, 6, 7, or 8 Guas only), South, or Southeast (1, 3, 4, or 9 Guas only). For the *North 3* homes, place your desk/face Northeast, West, Southwest, Southeast, and South (all Guas). Choose one of these facing directions coupled with your +80 to enhance health, +70 for relationships, or +90 for wealth if possible. For example, the Southeast direction is especially good for 3 Guas as this is their unique relationship direction (+70) *and* it has romance energy. For 4 Life Guas, the South has prosperous energy and it's their +80; this is their unique health direction in which the Heavenly Doctor, Tien Yi, protects you. For students, use the above directions to energize learning and success in exams; the Southeast and West have the most potent scholarly chi.

Stoves and Toilets

The best directions for stove knobs, buttons, or controls are the Southeast, South, West, or Northeast. You will struggle with money, health, and relationships if there is a stove or toilet located in your +90, +80, or +70 sector of the house. Select a toilet located in one of your negative sectors of the house (-90, -80, -70, or -60). This section applies to the head(s) of household or breadwinner. This house *cannot* have a kitchen or fireplace in the center of the home (2, 3 combination); it can bring serious health problems such as heart attacks, extreme tension/stress, reproductive issues, and high blood pressure.

Excellent Doors

Always use and activate good doors; the best ones for this chart are facing Southeast, Northeast, West, Southwest, and South. This applies to all exterior doors as well as any interior garage doors used to enter the house. In modern homes, an interior garage door is often the main entry into the house, making it extremely important. In this chart, an East-facing door is the worst of the worst; avoid if at all possible. It has the evil 5 facing star and its energy attracts all types of disasters. If this is a well-used door, you will need to cure it with lots of metal next to or on the door itself. Brass, bronze, copper, pewter, and stainless steel are some high-vibrating metals to use, or you can hang large metal wind chimes. Keep in mind that these doors can never be fully cured, only weakened, as movement/use will always keep the energy activated. Review the years it becomes aggressive in the Health Alerts of the Chart section.

PERIOD 7

Northeast 1 (22.6° to 37.5°)
Facing name: *Chou*

Chart: *Double Stars Meet at Sitting* (*Shuang Xing Dao Zuo*)

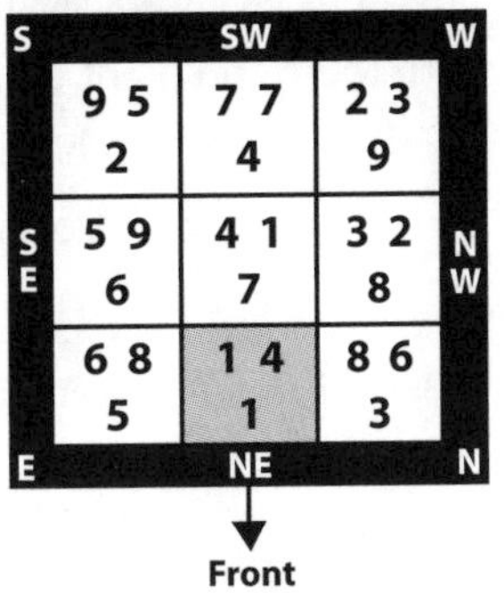

Figure 47: Northeast 1

Health Alerts of the Chart

This chart has two negative areas to pay attention to regarding health; in certain years they become more dangerous. They are the ***South*** (9, 5) and the ***Northwest*** (2 facing star). The South becomes more serious for illness in the years of 2017, 2020, and 2022. The Northwest can bring more sickness in the years of 2016, 2019, and 2023. No water (pools, fountains, etc.) or fire (stoves, fireplace/pits, or grills) should be placed in either area no matter the year—doing so will activate the negative energy in these areas.

Activating the External Environment

Enhancements: Place Water in the East, Mountain in North
Cures: Place small water near the back door and paint it red

This property has the two 7s at the back known as ***Double Stars Meet at Sitting;*** it was lucky for health/money until February 4, 2004, when much of its vitality was reduced. Northeast charts can produce people of noble energy *if* they are activated accordingly. Now that we are in Period 8, you will need to install a large water feature in the East of your front garden, such as a fountain, waterfall (must flow towards the house), or koi pond in order to re-energize this chart. Water located in the East ushers in the most benevolent and prosperous energy and should be placed there. Also, simulate a "mountain" in the North using large boulders (no sharp or jagged edges), basalt pillars, courtyard walls, or landscape mounds (like the ones in golf courses). If you're unable to place the water and mountain exterior on your site, install a fountain indoors in the East corner. Place a tall armoire or bookcases in the North corner inside your home. The back door is very negative and has robbery energy; place small water such as a fountain or birdbath there and paint the door red to exhaust the energy. It is very dangerous for this property to have big water *anywhere* in the backyard/garden; it will activate money loss, cancer, disasters, illicit affairs, robberies, and lawsuits.[38]

---

38. If there is big water located in the South *(this is the left-hand corner as you are looking out the backdoor)* such as a swimming pool, it will activate extremely disastrous events such as bankruptcy, divorce, and cancer. Moreover, it will activate a *Peach Blossom Sha* that indicates sexual misconduct such as affairs, incest, "sexting," and other things causing scandals for the household.

There is a possible *Robbery Mountain Sha* formation if there is a jagged cliff, electrical tower, huge dead tree, lamppost, or a broken mountain in the North; they indicate everyone in the household getting an unusual disease, injury by knives, and disasters.

Activating the Interior Environment

Master Bedroom + Family

There are two ways to enhance relationships, harmony and prosperity in the bedroom—location and direction; the direction of the bed will give you the most powerful results. Locate your master bedroom in the North, Northeast, or East as these sectors have good mountain stars with great energy. ***Bed Directions:*** Place your headboard/bed to the North (1, 3, 4, or 9 Guas only), East (all Guas), or Northeast (2, 6, 7, or 8 Guas only). These bed directions have a good mountain and facing star combination with excellent energy.

Take special caution regarding the Southeast and South; do not use either if at all possible. If the master bedroom is already located there, make sure that the bed direction is not also Southeast or South.

If so, reposition immediately; activating this direction indicates cancer, bankruptcy, leukemia, divorce, death, and all types of mishaps and disasters. Place high-quality metal in the room such as wall art or statues made of bronze, brass, copper, pewter, or stainless steel.

Also, make sure to use a soft neutral color palette such as whites, creams, taupes, and metal colors like silver and bronze. Do not use fire colors (reds, pinks, purple, or oranges) in the artwork, rugs, bedding, or wall color.

These precautions will ensure that you are extracting the best energy possible and calm the aggressive 5 star. Use the above directions when placing the bed for other family members; get their Life Gua in the Eight Mansions chart in chapter 4.

Home Office + Study

Face your desk/body North or Southeast (1, 3, 4, or 9 Guas only), Northeast (2, 6, 7, or 8 Guas only), or East (all Guas). Choose one of these facing directions coupled with your +80 to enhance health, +70 for relationships, or +90 for wealth if possible.

For example, Northeast is excellent for 7 Guas as this is their unique relationship direction (+70) *and* the stars support very romantic energy.

For 1 Life Guas, East is their +80 (health), Tien Yi (Heavenly Doctor who supports your health and grants "unexpected wealth from the heavens"), and this direction also has very prosperous energy.

For students, use the above directions to energize learning and success in exams; the Northeast is superior for this.

Stoves and Toilets

The best directions for stove knobs, buttons, or controls are East, Southeast, or Northeast.

If there is a stove or toilet located in your +90, +80, or +70 sector of the house, health and money loss are at a high risk. Select a toilet located in one of your negative sectors (-90, -80, -70, or -60).

This section applies to the head(s) of household or breadwinner.

Excellent Doors

Always use and activate good doors; the best ones for this chart are facing North, Northeast, Southeast, and East.

This applies to all exterior doors as well as an interior garage door used to enter the house.

In modern homes, an interior garage door is often the main entry into the house, making it extremely important.

If one of these directions is also your +80, you will be very lucky with your health.

PERIOD 7

Northeast 2 (37.6° to 52.5°)
Facing name: *Gen*

Northeast 3 (52.6° to 67.5°)
Facing name: *Yin* and the *Tiger*

Chart: ***Double Stars Meet at Facing***
(*Shuang Xing Dao Xiang*)

S	SW	W
8 6 2	1 4 4	6 8 9
SE: 3 2 6	4 1 7	5 9 8 :NW
2 3 5	7 7 1	9 5 3
E	NE	N

Front

Figure 48: Northeast 2 & 3

Health Alerts of the Chart

This chart has *three* negative areas to pay attention to regarding health; in certain years they become more dangerous. They are the ***North*** (9, 5) and the ***Southeast*** (2 facing star). The North becomes more serious for illness in the years of 2018, 2021, and 2024. The Southeast can bring more sickness in the years of 2015, 2017, and 2021. It is also unsafe for health to sleep to the ***Northwest*** (5, 9). No water (pools, fountains, etc.) or fire (stoves, fireplace/pits, or grills) should be placed in either the North or Southeast no matter the year—it *will* activate the negative energy in these areas.

Activating the External Environment

Enhancements: *Place Water in the West, Mountain in the South*
Cures: *Place small water near the front door and paint it red*

This property is known as ***Double Stars Meet at Facing*** with the once prominent 7s located in the front; since February 4, 2004, this chart's luck has been diminished a great deal. However, Northeast-facing sites can produce people who can accumulate wealth with a worldwide business *if* they are activated accordingly. Now that we are in Period 8, to reenergize this property you will need to simulate a mountain in the South corner of your back garden. This can be done with clever use of large boulders (no sharp or jagged edges), basalt pillars, landscape mounds (like the ones at golf courses), or tiered/terraced garden beds. Moreover, you will need to install a large water feature in the West corner of your garden. This can be a swimming pool, koi pond, waterfall, or large stone fountain. Water located in the West ushers in the most benevolent and prosperous energy and should be placed there. If you are unable to activate this chart on the exterior, install a large indoor water fountain in the West corner. Place a tall armoire or bookcases in the South corner; these are good representations of a mountain for indoors. The front door (Northeast-facing) is problematic; place small water such as a birdbath and paint the door red to exhaust the negative energy of the 7s.

For homes facing *Northeast 2* there is a possible *Eight Roads of Destruction* formation if you have a road/driveway coming from and exiting the North and East directions and will activate ill health, bankruptcy, and divorce. There is also a possible *Robbery Mountain Sha* formation if there *is* a jagged cliff, electrical tower, huge dead tree, lamppost, or a broken mountain in the East; they indicate everyone in the household getting an unusual disease, injury by knives, and disasters.

For the *Northeast 3* facing properties there is a possible *Eight Killing Forces* if there is a mountain in front of the property on the left-hand side; this formation will attract blood-related accidents. There is also a possible *Robbery Mountain Sha* formation if there is a jagged cliff, electrical tower, huge dead tree, lamppost, or a broken mountain in the North.

Activating the Interior Environment

Master Bedroom + Family

There are two ways activate great energy in the bedroom—location and direction; the direction of the bed will give you the most powerful results. Locate your master bedroom in the South, Southwest, or West as these sectors of the house have good mountain stars. ***Bed Directions:*** For homes that face *Northeast 2*, place your headboard/bed to the South (1, 3, 4, or 9 Guas only), Southwest or West (2, 6, 7, or 8 Guas only). For homes that face *Northeast 3*, place your headboard/bed facing South, West, or

Southwest (all Guas). These bed directions have a good mountain and facing star combination with excellent energy.

Take special caution regarding the North and Northwest; do not use either if at all possible. If the master bedroom is already located there, make sure that the bed direction is not also North or Northwest. If so, reposition immediately; activating this direction indicates cancer, bankruptcy, leukemia, divorce, death, and all types of mishaps and disasters. Place high-quality metal in the room such as wall art or statues made of bronze, brass, copper, pewter, or stainless steel. Also, make sure to use a soft neutral color palette such as whites, creams, taupes, and metal colors like silver and bronze. Do not use fire colors (reds, pinks, purple, or oranges) in the artwork, rugs, bedding, or wall color. These precautions will ensure that you are extracting the best energy possible and keep the aggressive 5 star calm. Use the above directions when placing the bed for other family members; get their Life Gua in the Eight Mansions chart in chapter 4.

Home Office + Study

For the *Northeast 2* homes, place your desk/face to the South, (1, 3, 4 or 9 Guas only), Southwest, West, or Northwest (2, 6, 7, or 8 Guas only). For the *Northeast 3* homes, place your desk/face South, Southwest, West, or Northwest (all Guas). Choose one of these facing directions coupled with your +80 to enhance health, +70 for relationships, or +90 for wealth if possible. For example, the Southwest direction is especially good for 6 Guas as this is their unique relationship direction (+70) and the stars indicate good romance energy as well. For 2 Life Guas, the West is their +80 (health) direction and the stars indicate lots of wealth.

Stoves and Toilets

The best directions for stove knobs, buttons, or controls are the Southwest, West, or Northwest. You will struggle with money, health, and relationships if there is a stove or toilet located in your +90, +80, or +70 sector of the house. Select a toilet located in one of your negative sectors of the house (-90, -80, -70, or -60). This section applies to the head(s) of household or breadwinner.

Excellent Doors

Always use and activate good doors; the best ones for this chart are facing South, Southwest, West, and Northwest; this applies to all exterior doors as well as an interior garage door used to enter the house. In modern homes, this is often the main entry into the house, making it extremely important. If one of these directions is also your +80, you will be very lucky with your health. In this chart, a North-facing door is the worst of the worst; avoid if at all possible. It has the evil 5 facing star whose energy attracts all types of disasters. If this is a well-used door or your only door in and out, you will need to cure it with lots of metal next to or directly on the door. Brass, bronze, copper, pewter, and stainless steel are some high-vibrating metals to use, or you can hang large metal wind chimes. Keep in mind that these doors can never be fully cured, only weakened, as movement/use will always keep the energy activated. Review the years it becomes seriously dangerous in the Health Alerts of the Chart section.

PERIOD 7

East 1 (67.6° to 82.5°)

Facing name: *Jia*

Chart: *Reverse Formation*

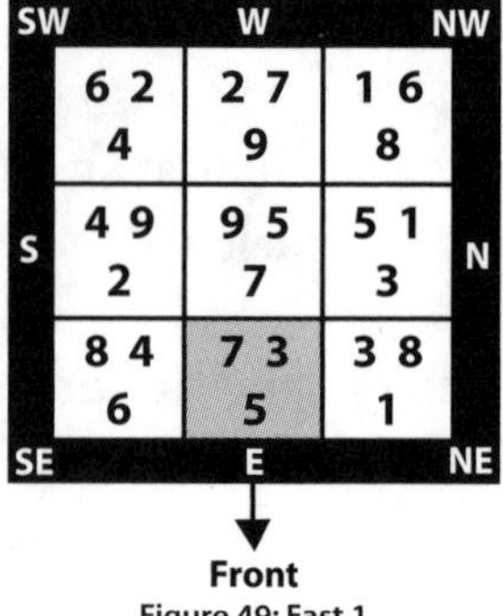

Figure 49: East 1

Health Alerts of the Chart

This chart has one negative area to pay attention to regarding health; in certain years it becomes more dangerous. It is the *Southwest*

(2 facing star) and it becomes more serious for illness in the years of 2015, 2019, and 2022. No water (pools, fountains, etc.) or fire (stoves, fireplace/pits, or grills) should be placed in this area no matter the year—the energy will be activated.

Activating the External Environment

Enhancements: *Need Water in the Northeast, Mountain in Southeast*
Cures: *The front and back doors need to be painted red*

This chart is known as a ***Reverse Formation;*** it was not considered that auspicious even in Period 7 and has become less so since February 4, 2004. However, the East-facing properties can produce those who excel in the world of academia if they are activated accordingly. Now that we are in Period 8, this property needs to be reenergized by creating a mountain in the Southeast area of your front garden. A mountain can be large boulders (no sharp or jagged edges), landscape mounds (like those at golf courses), tiered or terraced garden beds, or courtyard walls. Any of these features will emulate the energy of a real mountain. Install a gorgeous water feature in the Northeast area of your front garden. It can be a koi pond, fountain, or waterfall (the water must flow towards the house). Water located in the Northeast ushers in the most benevolent and prosperous energy and should be placed there. If you are unable to activate the exterior of your site, install a water fountain indoors in the Northeast corner. Place a tall armoire or bookcases in the Southeast corner; these types of heavy furniture will serve as an excellent representation for the internal "mountain."

Unfortunately, the front door and back door are a problem. Paint both doors red, and place metal wind chimes near the front door and small water such as a birdbath near the back door. This will exhaust much of the negative energy at these important doors; while not considered a total cure, it will help. If you have an interior garage door that faces either North or South, use it and make it you *main* door (used almost a hundred percent of the time).

There is a possible *Eight Roads of Destruction* formation if you have a road/driveway coming from and exiting the Northeast direction; they will attract ill health, bankruptcy, and divorce. There is also a possible *Robbery Mountain Sha* formation if there is a jagged cliff, electrical tower, huge dead tree, lamppost, or a broken mountain in the South; they indicate everyone in the household getting an unusual disease, injury by knives, and disasters.

Activating the Interior Environment

Master Bedroom + Family

There are two ways to activate great energy in the bedroom—location and direction; the direction of the bed will give you the most powerful results. Locate your master bedroom in the Northwest, South, or Southeast as these sectors have good mountain stars. ***Bed Directions:*** Place your headboard/bed to the Northwest or South (all Guas), or Southeast (1, 3, 4, or 9 Guas only). These bed directions have a good mountain and facing star combination with excellent energy. Use the above directions when placing the bed for other family members; get their Life Gua in the Eight Mansions chart in chapter 4.

Home Office + Study

Face your desk/body to the Northwest or South (all Guas), North or Southeast (1, 3, 4, or 9 Guas only), or Northeast (2, 6, 7, or 8 Guas only). Choose one of these facing directions coupled with your +80 to enhance health, +70 for relationships, or +90 for wealth if possible.

For example, the Southeast direction is especially good for 3 Guas as this is their unique relationship direction (+70) and the stars indicate romance energy. For the 6 Life Guas, the Northeast is their +80 (health) and the energy there is very prosperous—it is also their Tien Yi, where the Heavenly Doctor protects them. For students, use the above directions to energize learning and success in exams.

Stoves and Toilets

The best directions for stove knobs, buttons, or controls are Northeast, South, Southeast, or North. If there is a stove or toilet located in your +90, +80, or +70 sector of the house, health, and money loss are at a high risk. This house *cannot* have a kitchen or fireplace in the center of the home (9, 5 combination); it can bring serious health issues such as heart attacks and high blood pressure; it may also indicate hazardous fires in certain years. Select a toilet located in one of your negative sectors of the house (-90, -80, -70, or -60). This section applies to the head(s) of household or breadwinner.

Excellent Doors

Always use and activate good doors; the best ones for this chart are facing Northwest, South, Southeast, North, and Northeast. This applies to all exterior doors as well as an interior garage door used to enter the house. In modern homes, an interior garage door is often the main entry into the house, making it extremely important. If one of these directions is also your +80, you will be very lucky with your health.

PERIOD 7

East 2 (82.6° to 97.5°)

Facing name: *Mao* and the ***Rabbit***

East 3 (97.6° to 112.5°)

Facing name: *Yi*

Chart: ***Prosperous Sitting and Facing*** (*Wang Shan Wang Shui*)

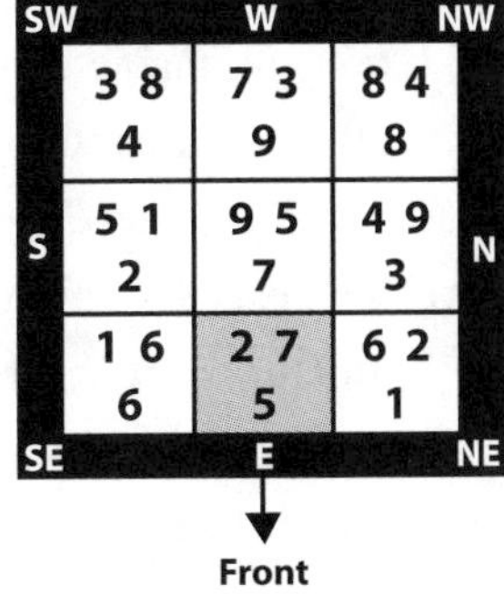

Figure 50: East 2 & 3

Health Alerts of the Chart

This chart has one negative area to pay attention to regarding health; in certain years it becomes more dangerous. It is the *Northeast* (2 facing star) and it becomes more serious for illness in the years of 2016, 2019 and 2021. No water (pools, fountains, etc.) or fire (stoves, fireplace/pits, or grills) should be placed in this area, no matter the year—it will active the negative energy.

Activating the External Environment

Enhancements: Place Water in Southwest, Mountain in Northwest
Cures: The front and back door need to be painted red

In the day (Period 7), this was indeed an excellent chart known as ***Prosperous Sitting and Facing*** and would have been very lucky for money and people; alas, its decline in vitality began February 4, 2004. However, the East-facing properties are known to produce charismatic, loyal, faithful professionals such as doctors, lawyers, and philosophers who are both wealthy and noble *if* it is activated accordingly. Now that we are in Period 8, you will need to install a stunning water feature in the Southwest corner of your backyard/garden to reenergize this chart. This can be a swimming pool, fountain, koi pond, or waterfall. Water located in the Southwest ushers in the most benevolent and prosperous energy and should be placed there. Moreover, create a mountain in the Northwest corner of your back garden using boulders (no sharp or jagged edges), tiered or terraced beds, basalt pillars, or landscaping mounds (like the ones at golf courses).

If you are unable to activate the exterior of your site, put a water fountain in the Southwest corner indoors. Place a heavy armoire or tall bookcases in the Northwest corner inside; these types of heavy furniture will serve as an excellent representation for the internal "mountain."

Unfortunately, the front and back door are a problem. Place small water such as a birdbath near the front door and paint it red. Paint the back door red and place some metal wind chimes near it as well. This will exhaust much of the negative energy at these important doors; while not considered a total cure, it will help. If you have an interior garage door that faces North or South, use it and make it your main door, used almost a hundred percent of the time.

For homes facing ***East 2*** there is a possible *Eight Killings* formation if there is a mountain from the Southwest direction; this formation will unsettle relationships and health in the house. For homes that face to *East 3*, there is a possible *Eight Roads of Destruction* if there is a road/driveway coming from and exiting from the Southeast direction; these formations will attract ill health, bankruptcy, and divorce. There is also a possible *Robbery Mountain Sha* formation for both facings, if there is a jagged cliff, electrical tower, huge dead tree, lamppost, or a broken mountain in the Northeast; they indicate everyone in the household getting an unusual disease, injury by knives, and disasters.

Activating the Interior Environment

Master Bedroom + Family

There are two ways to activate great energy in the bedroom—location and direction; the direction of the bed will give you the most powerful results. Locate your master bedroom in the Northwest or Southeast as these locations have good mountain stars. ***Bed Directions:*** For homes that face ***East 2***, place your headboard/bed to the North or Southeast (1, 3, 4, or 9 Guas only), or Northwest (2, 6, 7, or 8 Guas only). For homes that face ***East 3***, place your headboard/bed to the Northwest or Southeast (all Guas), or North (1, 3, 4, or 9 Guas only). These bed directions have a good mountain and facing star combination with excellent energy. Use the above directions when placing the bed for other family members; get their Life Gua in the Eight Mansions chart in chapter 4.

Home Office + Study

For the ***East 2*** homes, face to the Northwest or Southwest (2, 6, 7, or 8 Guas only), North, Southeast, or South (1, 3, 4, or 9 Guas only). For the ***East 3*** homes, face Northwest, Southwest, Southeast, or South (all Guas) or North (1, 3, 4, or 9 Guas only). Choose one of these facing directions coupled with your +80 to enhance health, +70 for relationships, or +90 for wealth if possible. For example, the Northwest direction is especially good for 2 Guas as this is their unique relationships direction (+70) and the stars indicate romance energy. For 8 Life Guas, choose Southwest: it's your +90 (wealth), and the stars have extremely prosperous energy there.

Stoves and Toilets

The best directions for stove knobs, buttons, or controls are South, North, Northwest, or Southwest. This house *cannot* have a kitchen or fireplace in the center of the home (9, 5 combination); it can bring serious health issues such as heart attacks and high blood pressure; it may also indicate hazardous fires in certain years. You will struggle with money, health, and relationships if there is a stove or toilet located in your +90, +80, or +70 sector of the house. Select a toilet located in one of your negative sectors of the house (-90, -80, -70, or -60). This section applies to the head(s) of household or breadwinner.

Excellent Doors

Always use and activate good doors; the best ones for this chart are facing Southwest, North, Northwest, Southeast, and South. This applies to all exterior doors as well as any interior garage doors used to enter the house. In modern homes, an interior garage door is often the main entry into the house, making it extremely important. If one of these directions is also your +80, you will be very lucky with your health.

PERIOD 7

Southeast 1 (112.6° to 127.5°)
Facing name: *Chen* and the *Dragon*

Chart: *Prosperous Sitting and Facing* (Wang Shan Wang Shui)

W		NW		N
	6 4 9	7 5 8	3 1 3	
SW	2 9 4	8 6 7	5 3 1	NE
	4 2 2	9 7 6	1 8 5	
S		SE		E

Front

Figure 51: Southeast 1

Health Alerts of the Chart

This chart has two negative areas to pay attention to regarding health; in certain years they become more dangerous. They are the ***Northwest*** (5 facing star) and the South (2 facing star). The Northwest becomes more serious for illness in the years of 2017, 2019, and 2023.

The ***South*** can bring more sickness in the years of 2017, 2020, and 2022. No water (pools, fountains, etc.) or fire (stoves, fireplace/pits, or grills) should be placed in either area no matter the year—it will activate the negative energy in these areas.

Activating the External Environment

Enhancements: *Place Water in East or North, Mountain in Southeast*
Cures: *Paint the front door red, and "metal up" the back door*

In the day (Period 7), this was indeed an excellent chart known as ***Prosperous Sitting and Facing*** and would have been very lucky for money and people; alas, its decline in vitality began February 4, 2004. However, the Southeast-facing properties can produce great talent in all types of sports and the children can excel in sciences, especially those requiring technical expertise *if* it is activated accordingly.

Now that we are in Period 8, you will need to reenergize this property by installing a striking water feature in the East area of the front garden. This can be a fountain, koi pond, or waterfall (must flow towards the house). Water located in the *East* ushers in the most benevolent and prosperous energy and should be placed there; however, if you are not able to place it there, an alternate area for water is the North.

In addition to water, you will need to create a "mountain" in front (Southeast) without blocking the front door. This can be done by clever use of boulders (no sharp or jagged edges), basalt pillars, or landscaping mounds (like the ones at golf courses).

You may also accomplish this with two very heavy, tall stone planters or pots on either side of the front door. If you are unable to activate the exterior of your site, then put a water fountain in the East corner indoors and place two heavy objects (not metal) on both sides of the front door, inside or out. A swimming pool located in the West of the back garden will activate sexual misconduct.[39]

Unfortunately, the front and back doors are problematic and must be cured. Paint the front door red and place a small birdbath near it; this will help exhaust the energy. The back door needs a great deal of high-quality metal (brass, copper, or bronze) and is best not used.

An *Eight Killings* formation is possible if there is a mountain bringing energy to the house from the North direction; this formation indicates blood-related accidents. There is also a possible *Robbery Mountain Sha* formation if there is a jagged cliff, electrical tower, huge dead tree, lamppost, or a broken mountain in the Northeast; they indicate everyone in the household getting an unusual disease, injury by knives, and disasters.

Activating the Interior Environment

Master Bedroom + Family

There are two ways to activate great energy in the bedroom—location and direction; the direction of the bed will give you the most powerful results. Locate your master bedroom in the West or East, or Southeast (upstairs) as these sectors all have good mountain stars. ***Bed Directions:*** Place your headboard/bed to the East or West (all Guas), and the North is acceptable (1, 3, 4, or 9 Guas only). These bed directions have a good mountain and facing star combination with excellent energy. Use the above directions when placing the bed for other family members; get their Life Gua in the Eight Mansions chart in chapter 4.

39. If there is big water located in the West *(this is the left-hand corner as you are looking out the back door)* such as a swimming pool, it will activate a *Peach Blossom Sha* that indicates sexual misconduct such as affairs, incest, unwelcome advances, and other things causing scandals for the household.

Home Office + Study

Face your desk/body East, West, or Southwest (all Guas), or North (1, 3, 4, or 9 Guas only). Choose one of these facing directions coupled with your +80 to enhance health, +70 for relationships, or +90 for wealth if possible. For example, the West direction is especially good for 8 Guas as this is their unique relationship direction (+70) and the stars indicate good romance energy. For 1 Life Guas, East is their +80 (health) and the stars indicate extremely prosperous energy. Also, because this is their Tien Yi direction, the Heavenly Doctor protects them. For students, use the above directions to energize learning and success in exams.

Stoves and Toilets

The best direction for stove knobs, buttons, or controls are the East, Southwest, West, or North. If there is a stove or toilet located in your +90, +80, or +70 sector of the house, health and money loss are at a high risk. Select a toilet located in one of your negative sectors of the house (-90, -80, -70, or -60). This section applies to the head(s) of household or breadwinner.

Excellent Doors

Always use and activate good doors; the best ones for this chart are facing East, West, North, and Southwest. This applies to all exterior doors as well as an interior garage door used to enter the house. In modern homes, an interior garage door is often the main entry into the house, making it extremely important. In this chart, a Northwest-facing door is the worst of the worst; avoid if at all possible. It has the evil 5 facing star and its energy attracts all types of disasters. If this is a well-used door or your only door in and out, you will need to cure it with lots of metal next to or directly on the door. Brass, bronze, copper, pewter, and stainless steel are some high-vibrating metals to use, or you can hang large metal wind chimes. Keep in mind that these doors can never be fully cured, only weakened, as the movement/use of it will always keep the negative energy activated. Review the years it becomes particularly aggressive in the Health Alerts of the Chart section.

PERIOD 7

Southeast 2 (127.6° to 142.5°)
Facing name: *Xun*

Southeast 3 (142.6° to 157.5°)
Facing name: *Su* and the *Snake*

Chart: *Pearl String* (*Lin Cu San Poon Gua*)

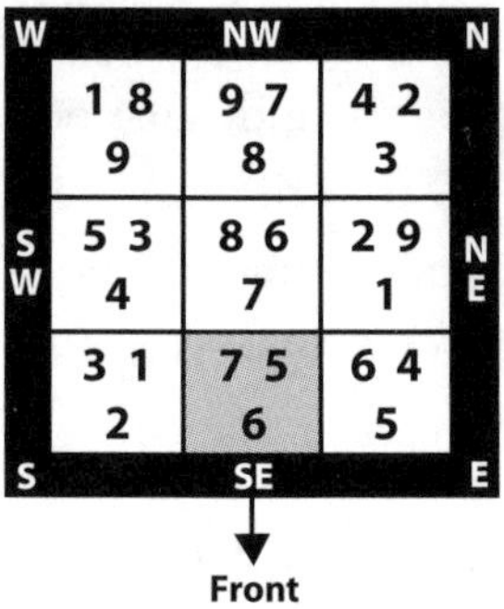

W	NW	N
1 8 9	9 7 8	4 2 3
SW: 5 3 4	8 6 7	NE: 2 9 1
3 1 2	7 5 6	6 4 5
S	SE	E

Front

Figure 52: Southeast 2 & 3

Health Alerts of the Chart

This chart has two negative areas to pay attention to regarding health; in certain years they become more dangerous. They are the ***Southeast*** (5 facing star) and the ***North*** (2 facing star). The Southeast can bring more sickness in the years of 2015, 2017, and 2021. The North becomes more serious for illness in the years of 2018, 2021, and 2024. No water (pools, fountains, etc.) or fire (stoves, fireplace/pits, or grills) should be placed in either area, no matter the year—it will activate the negative energy in these areas.

Activating the External Environment

Enhancements: *Place Water in West or South, Mountain in Northwest*
Cures: *"Metal up" the front door; paint the back door red and place a birdbath near it*

This property was a very special star chart called the ***Pearl String*** aka Continuous Bead; since February 4, 2004, however, it is no longer prestigious. The Southeast-facing charts can produce people who have good morals, nobility, trustworthiness, and the Southeast is suited for philosophers, performers, singer, and artists *if* they are activated accordingly. Now that we are in

Period 8, you will need to reenergize this property by creating a mountain in the Northwest. This can be accomplished by using boulders (no sharp or jagged edges), landscape mounds (like the ones at golf courses), tiered or terraced garden beds against a fence or significant, or solid fencing comprised of stucco, stone, or brick at the back. Moreover, you will need a grand water feature in the West corner of your back garden such as a waterfall, swimming pool, or tall, heavy stone fountain. Water located in the West ushers in the most benevolent and prosperous energy and should be placed there. If you are unable to activate the exterior, put an indoor fountain in the West corner of your interior living space. Also, place two heavy stone statues or planters on either side of your back door.

Unfortunately, the front and back doors are problematic and must be cured. The front door needs a great deal of high-quality metal (brass, copper, or bronze) and is best not used. Paint the back door red and place a small birdbath near it; this will help exhaust the energy.

There is a possible *Eight Roads of Destruction* if the house faces ***Southeast 2*** and if a road/driveway enters/exits the South or East; they are notorious for bringing ill health, bankruptcy, and divorce.

An *Eight Killings* formation is possible for homes facing ***Southeast 3*** if there is a mountain bringing energy to the house from the West direction; this formation indicates blood-related accidents. There is also a possible *Robbery Mountain Sha* formation for both facings if there is a jagged cliff, electrical tower, huge dead tree, lamppost, or a broken mountain in the East; they indicate everyone in the household getting an unusual disease, injury by knives, and disasters.

Activating the Interior Environment

Master Bedroom + Family

There are two ways to activate great energy in the bedroom—location and direction; the direction of the bed will give you the most powerful results. Locate your master bedroom in the West, Northwest, or East as these sectors all have good mountain stars. ***Bed Directions:*** For homes that face

Southeast 2, place your headboard/bed to the West (2, 6, 7, or 8 Guas only) or East (1, 3, 4, or 9 Guas only). For homes that face ***Southeast 3***, place your headboard/bed to the East or West (all Guas). These bed directions have a good mountain and facing star combination with excellent energy. Use the above directions when placing the bed for other family members; get their Life Gua in the Eight Mansions chart in chapter 4.

Home Office + Study

For the ***Southeast 2*** homes, place your desk/face to the West or Northeast (2, 6, 7, or 8 Guas only), East or South (1, 3, 4, or 9 Guas only). For the ***Southeast 3*** homes, place your desk/face East, West, Northeast, or South (all Guas). Choose one of these facing directions coupled with your +80 to enhance health, +70 for relationships, or +90 for wealth if possible. For example, the East direction is especially good for 4 Guas as this is their unique relationships direction (+70); the stars indicate good romance energy. For the 3 Life Guas, choose the South, it is your +90 (wealth) and the stars indicate money and success.

Stoves and Toilets

The best directions for stove knobs, buttons, or controls are the East, West, Northeast, or South. You will struggle with money, health, and relationships if there is a stove or toilet located in your +90, +80, or +70 sector of the house. Select a toilet located in one of your negative sectors of the house (-90, -80, -70, or -60). This section applies to the head(s) of household or breadwinner.

Excellent Doors

Always use and activate good doors; the best ones for this chart are facing West, Northeast, East, and South; this applies to all exterior doors as well as any interior garage doors used to enter the house. In modern homes, an interior garage door is often the main entry into the house, making it extremely important. Unfortunately, the Southeast-facing front door is the worst of the worst in this chart; avoid if at all possible. It has the evil 5 facing star and its energy attracts all types of disasters. If this is a well-used door or your only door in and out, you will need to cure it with lots of metal next to or directly on the door. Brass, bronze, copper, pewter, and stainless steel are some high-vibrating metals to use, or you can hang large metal wind chimes. Keep in mind that these doors can never be fully cured, only weakened, as the movement/use will always keep the negative energy activated. Review the years it becomes seriously dangerous in the Health Alerts of the Chart section.

Conclusion

Health is so essential to living a quality life, we must do all we can to secure, improve, and treasure it. Long ago, Feng Shui was devised to improve all areas of life, including health. Today, it is more essential than ever to have this ancient knowledge working for us in our living environments. Our homes should be our havens, and our workplace safe and supportive. Take the time to implement the recommendations for your home so it produces vibrant energy. Remember, the correct placement of water and fire in the home is essential for good health.

Review the section on your Life Gua's predisposition to certain illnesses, diseases, and body organs that need special attention. Take precautions using the Health Alerts for your home's unique Star Chart found in chapter 6 or 7. If you are ill or recovering from a disease, activate the Heavenly Doctor position (your +80 direction). By using all the information available in Feng Shui systems, you will be miles ahead in supporting your health.

Additionally, take full advantage of countermeasures such as anti-EMF products to protect your body, mind, and home environment from our beloved conveniences such as televisions, cell phones, and computers. Don't use microwave ovens (they alter your food and can harm your health) or poison your body with aspartame and fluoride-treated water.

Use natural products (vitamins, herbs, minerals, water, salt) and simple body work modalities (massage, hydrotherapy, and natural springs) to soothe and support the body. Select/adjust homes to support good health using the wisdom of Classical Feng Shui. Correct, sell, or pass on properties that can make you sick such as T-intersections, dirty canals, electrical towers, and broken mountains—to name a few.

Eat fresh food that is close to nature (no hormones, chemicals, or anything that has been genetically engineered) and regularly move the body (martial arts, walking, Tai Chi, and Yoga) to keep it agile and strong. These are areas where we can choose; the environment of our cities and countries, not as much. I admire those who *passionately* protest the pollution of and the lowered quality of our water, air, and food; many modern-day diseases are caused by compromising or neglecting these crucial elements. A lifestyle of "green living" is worth considering as well, leaving a small footprint on the earth's resources is responsible and respectful.[40]

We may not see the complete cleanup of toxic waste—so freely dumped at one time—in our lifetime but perhaps in our children's or grandchildren's. As the world moves forward with more astonishing technology, let us pray that it rescues our beautiful planet on which our health and existence depend.

May vibrant health, prosperity, and many loving relationships always find you!

40. Green living means making sustainable choices about what we eat, how we travel, what we buy, and how we use and dispose of it. We can implement sustainability in our workplace practices, and by greening the buildings we inhabit. Our everyday choices can create a sustainable lifestyle.

Appendix

See chart on next page.

Life Gua Determination if You Were Born on February 3, 4, or 5th *Use dates/times based on Universal Time—the time at the Greenwich Meridian—to avoid the confusion that can be caused by different time zones and the International Date Line.*											
Animal	Year	Feb.	Time The Year Began	Animal	Year	Feb.	Time The Year Began	Animal	Year	Feb.	Time The Year Began
Rooster	**1933**	4	2:10 p	Dragon	**1964**	5	3:05 a	Pig	**1995**	4	3:14 p
Dog	**1934**	4	8:04 p	Snake	**1965**	4	8:46 a	Rat	**1996**	4	9:08 p
Pig	**1935**	5	1:49 a	Horse	**1966**	4	2:38 p	Ox	**1997**	4	3:04 a
Rat	**1936**	5	7:30 a	Goat	**1967**	4	8:31 p	Tiger	**1998**	4	8:53 a
Ox	**1937**	4	1:26 p	Monkey	**1968**	5	2:08 a	Rabbit	**1999**	4	2:42 p
Tiger	**1938**	4	7:15 p	Rooster	**1969**	4	7:59 a	Dragon	**2000**	4	8:32 p
Rabbit	**1939**	5	1:11 a	Dog	**1970**	4	1:46 p	Snake	**2001**	4	2:20 a
Dragon	**1940**	5	7:08 a	Pig	**1971**	4	7:26 p	Horse	**2002**	4	8:08 a
Snake	**1941**	4	12:50 p	Rat	**1972**	5	1:20 a	Goat	**2003**	4	1:57 p
Horse	**1942**	4	6:49 p	Ox	**1973**	4	7:04 a	Monkey	**2004**	4	7:46 p
Goat	**1943**	5	12:41 a	Tiger	**1974**	4	1:00 p	Rooster	**2005**	4	1:34 a
Monkey	**1944**	5	6:23 a	Rabbit	**1975**	4	6:59 p	Dog	**2006**	4	7:25 a
Rooster	**1945**	4	12:20 p	Dragon	**1976**	5	12:40 a	Pig	**2007**	4	1:14 p
Dog	**1946**	4	6:05 p	Snake	**1977**	4	6:34 a	Rat	**2008**	4	7:03 p
Pig	**1947**	4	11:55 p	Horse	**1978**	4	12:27 p	Ox	**2009**	4	12:52 a
Rat	**1948**	5	5:43 a	Goat	**1979**	4	6:13 p	Tiger	**2010**	4	6:42 a
Ox	**1949**	4	11:23 a	Monkey	**1980**	5	12:10 a	Rabbit	**2011**	4	12:32 p
Tiger	**1950**	4	5:21 p	Rooster	**1981**	4	5:56 a	Dragon	**2012**	4	6:40 p
Rabbit	**1951**	4	11:14 p	Dog	**1982**	4	11:46 a	Snake	**2013**	4	12:24 a
Dragon	**1952**	5	4:54 a	Pig	**1983**	4	5:40 p	Horse	**2014**	4	6:21 a
Snake	**1953**	4	10:46 a	Rat	**1984**	4	11:19 p	Goat	**2015**	4	12:09 p
Horse	**1954**	4	4:31 p	Ox	**1985**	4	5:12 a	Monkey	**2016**	4	6:00 p
Goat	**1955**	4	10:18 p	Tiger	**1986**	4	11:09 a	Rooster	**2017**	3	11:49 p
Monkey	**1956**	5	4:13 a	Rabbit	**1987**	4	4:52 p	Dog	**2018**	4	5:38 a
Rooster	**1957**	4	9:55 a	Dragon	**1988**	4	10:43 p	Pig	**2019**	4	11:28 a
Dog	**1958**	4	3:50 p	Snake	**1989**	4	4:27 a	Rat	**2020**	4	5:18 p
Pig	**1959**	4	9:43 p	Horse	**1990**	4	10:15 a	Ox	**2021**	3	11:08 p
Rat	**1960**	5	3:23 a	Goat	**1991**	4	4:08 p	Tiger	**2022**	4	4:58 a
Ox	**1961**	4	9:23 a	Monkey	**1992**	4	9:48 p	Rabbit	**2023**	4	10:47 a
Tiger	**1962**	4	3:18 p	Rooster	**1993**	4	3:38 a	Dragon	**2024**	4	4:37 p
Rabbit	**1963**	4	9:08 p	Dog	**1994**	4	9:31 a	Snake	**2025**	3	10:27 p

Figure 53: Eight Mansions February Chart.

Glossary of Terms

This book includes Feng Shui terms using both Wade-Giles and Pinyin; in several instances the glossary gives both spellings. The Chinese-to-English translations also include some in Mandarin and others in Cantonese; I've chosen the ones most used by Grandmaster Yap Cheng Hai and their spellings.

24 Mountains: This is the single most important ring on the Chinese Luo Pan/compass; all homes and buildings will be one of these facing directions. Each of the eight directions has three divisions, comprising a total of twenty-four.

81 Combinations: There are nine (9) stars and when combined each with the other, they create the famous *81 combinations* or sets (9x9=81). The eighty-one combinations have a unique description for each set; they are an extraction from various, distinctive Feng Shui classic texts, including the Purple White Scripts (*Tzi Bai Jue*), Ode of Time and Space (*Xuan Kong Mi Zi*), Heavenly Jade Classics (*Tien Yue Jing*), and the Time Space Mysticism (*Xuan

Kong Jie). While each star has a meaning, when they combine they can indicate very specific outcomes and results. Keep in mind that timing, activation, and landforms often determine whether these "descriptions" will actually occur.

Acupuncture: The stimulation of specific acupoints along the skin of the body involving various methods such as the application of heat, pressure, or laser or penetration of thin needles; most often used in the treatment of pain.

Age of Eight: This is part of the Flying Star system (*Xuan Kong Fei Xing*). Also known as Period 8; it is a twenty-year period of time that affects the luck of people and influences the world with its energy. These twenty-year periods were first tracked and recorded by Chinese astronomers in about 2500 BCE. They observed that the planets in our solar system line up every 180 years. It was further noted that every twenty years, the Milky Way shifts and influences the events of humankind. These periods number one to nine every twenty years and then start over again. The current Age of Eight began February 4, 2004.

Alchemy, Chinese: Chinese alchemy mainly focuses on the purification of one's spirit and body with the goal of attaining immortality through the practice of Qigong and/or consumption and use of various concoctions known as alchemical medicines or elixirs, each of which has a different purpose. Pao Chi refers to the alchemy of processing Traditional Chinese medicines, such as honey or wine frying and roasting with toxic metals such as mercury, lead, and arsenic. The Taoist *Quest for Immortality*, had two distinct parts: the classical *Tao Chia*, mystical in nature and stemming primarily from Lao Tzu and Zhuangzi; and the more popular *Tao Chiao*, the well-loved, magical, and alchemical side of Taoism.

Auspicious: Feng shui favors the term *auspicious* when referring to something as lucky and from which good events will ensue.

Ayurvedic Medicine: A system of traditional medicine native to the Indian subcontinent and a form of alternative medicine. By the medieval period, Ayurvedic practitioners developed a number of medicinal preparations and surgical procedures for the treatment of various ailments.

Ba Gua: Also spelled as *Pa Kua*. An octagonal arrangement of the eight trigrams or Guas of Taoist mysticism; used as a basic tool of energy assessment in Feng Shui.

Big Dipper Casting Golden Light: Known as *Jin Guang Dou Lin Jing* in Chinese and also spelled as *Kam Kwong Dou Lam King*. This style of Eight Mansions is used in this book; it is also called Golden Star Classic.

Black Hat Sect aka BTB: A new school of Feng Shui created in the 1980s. It was brought to the Western world by Professor Thomas Lin Yun, a Buddhist monk of the Black Hat Order of Tibetan Buddhism. Although not considered an authentic system of Feng Shui, Black Hat is the most recognized style in the world except in Asia, where people are most familiar with more traditional schools of Feng Shui. Feng Shui is neither a religion nor spiritual practice, and has no roots in Buddhism.

Book of Changes: Also known as the *I Ching*.

Book of the Nine Elixirs: The *Book of the Nine Elixirs* (Jiudan jing), written around 649 to 686 BCE, is the main extant text of the Great Clarity, the earliest identifiable tradition of Chinese alchemy. It describes the preparation of nine elixirs with particular attention paid to the ritual context and sequencing. The main stages are the transmission from master to disciple, the establishment of the ritual area, the choice of an auspicious time, the compounding of the elixir, its offering to the gods, and its ingestion.

Broken mountain: This is a term used in Feng Shui to depict a mountain that has been excavated, scarred, or destroyed in any fashion. If such a mountain is in view of a home site or business, it is considered extremely inauspicious.

Buddhism: A nontheistic religion that encompasses a variety of traditions, beliefs, and practices largely based on the teachings attributed to Siddhartha Gautama, who is commonly known as the Buddha, meaning "the awakened one." According to the religion's tradition, the Buddha lived and taught in the eastern part of India sometime between the sixth and fourth centuries BCE.

Canal: An artificial waterway for boats or irrigation. In Feng Shui, canals are considered rivers; they can be particularly ruinous if they run behind your home.

Cardinal directions: Points of geographic orientation—North, South, East, and West. The specific and exact points of these directions are 0/360, North; 90 degrees, East; 180 degrees, South; and 270 degrees, West. Keep in mind that the directions in this book are used differently from the more common "north, south, east, west" applications. For example, when the indication is to "face the bed North," it means within the 24-degree range of North 1, North 2, and North 3. *See also* 24 Mountains.

Chai: House, also spelled *Zhai*.

Chen: One of the eight trigrams of the Ba Gua. It represents the eldest son, thunder, and spring. In the Later Heaven arrangement of the Ba Gua, the Chen trigram is located in the East.

Cheuh Ming: In the Eight Mansions system, this represents total loss, divorce, and bankruptcy. According to Master Yap's numeric representation, it is the -90.

Chi: The vital life-force energy of the universe and everything in it; sometimes chi is referred to as "cosmic breath." It is also spelled *ch'i* or *qi* and is pronounced *chee*.

Chien: One of the eight trigrams of the Ba Gua also spelled *Qian*. It represents the father, the heavens, and late autumn. In the Later Heaven arrangement of the Ba Gua, the Chien trigram is located in the Northwest.

Chinese Lunar and Solar Calendars: The Solstices and Equinoxes were used to fix the calendar in China. 15° Aquarius is exactly halfway between the Winter Solstice and the Spring Equinox (on the Northern Hemisphere). In the past, Chinese Lunar New Year started around the Winter Solstice. In 104 BCE, Emperor Han Wu Di moved the beginning of the year so that the Winter Solstice occurs in the eleventh month. Winter Solstice falls on the fifteenth day of Zi/Rat month, the middle of the winter, 15° Aquarius is the Sun's position. Whenever the sun reaches that position will dictate the Solar New Year, typically February 3, 4, or 5. 15° Aquarius was chosen as the starting point of the spring season and the New Year. The Spring Equinox falls exactly in the middle of the Spring season; always on the fifteenth day of Mao/Rabbit month.

The Lunar calendar defines the lunar month on the first day of the appearance of the New Moon, so a Lunar New Year begins on the first day of this new "moon"; a lunar month is from one new moon to the next new moon. The ancients divided the ecliptic into twelve equal segments. The Chinese Solar year is based on these twenty-four divisions; they are called twenty-four solar terms. The year, then, is divided into twenty-four periods lasting fifteen days each. Li Chun is the first of the twenty-four terms, and the names of these divisions date back to the late Chou Dynasty (10450–221 BCE).

By far the most important of the twenty-four terms is the New Year. All Feng Shui experts worth their salt use the Solar Calendar as the basis for their practice. This is not to say they don't celebrate the Lunar New Year; they do. Nearly every Asian country celebrates the Lunar New Year (in the West usually called the Chinese New Year), and it is extremely popular and important.

Chinese Zodiac: Called *Sheng Xiao* ("Birth resemblance") in Chinese, a system of astrology that relates each year to an animal and its reputed attributes according to a 60-year cycle calculated by the movements of Jupiter (the "Grand Duke") and the Stem and Branch system (*Liu Shi Hua Jia*). It is popular in several Asian countries, such as China, Vietnam, Korea, and Japan.

Classical Feng Shui: Also known as Traditional Feng Shui. It is the authentic, genuine Feng Shui that has been developed and applied for hundreds, even thousands, of years in Asia. Sophisticated forms are practiced in Hong Kong, Taiwan, Malaysia, and Singapore. Classical Feng Shui is only being introduced and practiced in Western countries and has not yet reached mainstream status. The traditional systems of Feng Shui are the *San He* ("three combinations") and *San Yuan* ("three cycles"). All techniques, methods, and formulas will be under one or the other. Feng Shui masters and practitioners will use both systems as one comprehensive body of knowledge.

Combination of 10: A wealth-producing chart in the Flying Star system where the stars add to ten in all nine palaces. In Chinese it is translated as *He Shih Chu*.

Compass, Chinese: See Luo Pan.

Cosmic Trinity: Known in Chinese as *Tien-Di-Ren*. The three categories of luck are Heaven Luck, Man Luck, and Earth Luck. The

Chinese believe Heaven Luck is fixed, but people have control over Feng Shui (Earth Luck) and personal effort (Man Luck).

Dao: Also spelled *Tao*, is a Chinese concept signifying the way, path, or route; sometimes known as the doctrine or principle. Within the context of traditional Chinese philosophy and religion, Tao is a metaphysical concept originating with Lao Tzu that gave rise to a religion and philosophy, Taoism. The concept of Tao was shared with Confucianism and Zen Buddhism. Within these contexts, Tao is the primordial essence or fundamental nature of the universe. In Taoism, Chinese Buddhism, and Confucianism, the object of spiritual practice is to become one with the Tao or harmonize one's will with Nature in order to achieve effortless action; this involves meditative and moral practices.

Direction: One of the most important aspects of determining the energy of a site or structure is taking a compass direction. Generally, the direction is read at the main door of the structure.

Double Stars Meet at Facing: Shuang Xing Dao Xiang in Chinese means that two stars in the Flying Star system are in the front of the house or building.

Double Stars Meet at Sitting: Shuang Xing Dao Zuo in Chinese means that two stars in the Flying Star system are at the back of the house or building.

Dragon: In Feng Shui a "dragon" is a mountain and can also refer to something powerful or curving (land or water) that brings to mind the mythical creature's body. Above all other creatures, the dragon is the most revered in China, and references to it have multiple applications and meanings.

Drain: An opening in the ground usually covered with a grate that moves water away from an area. Uncovered, rectangular drains are sometimes seen in subdivisions. In Feng Shui, drains are considered water exits and can bring wealth or disaster. A drain near a main door of a home or business is always bad. Only exposed drains are important in Feng Shui; underground and invisible formations do not count.

Early Heaven Ba Gua: This is the first arrangement of the eight trigrams; known as the *Ho Tien* or *Fu Xi* Ba. It can be easily recognized as the Chien trigram (three solid lines) and is always placed on the top. This is the arrangement used in Ba Gua mirrors to deter sha ("killing") chi.

Earth Luck: One of the three categories of luck that humans can experience; your luck will increase by using Feng Shui, also known as Earth Luck. The Chinese word for Earth is *Di.*

East Life Group: In the Eight Mansions system, people are divided into the East or West group. The 1, 3, 4, and 9 Life Guas are part of the East Life Group.

Eight House: This is another name for the Eight Mansions; in Chinese it is *Pa Chai* or *Ba Zhai.*

Eight House Bright Mirror: In Chinese, *Pa Chai Ming Jing* is one of the eight different styles of the Eight Mansions system. This style uses the sitting direction of the house instead of the facing.

Eight Killing Forces: A formation where the door direction and the energy of a nearby mountain are in disharmony. The Eight Killings should be taken very seriously as it will bring disaster to the household.

Eight Life Aspirations: Also known as the *Eight Life Stations*, these stations correspond to a point on the Ba Gua and an aspect of life—South is fame, Southwest is marriage, Southeast is wealth, North is career, and so forth. This is the work of Black Hat Sect founder Lin Yun. The Eight Life Stations as a philosophy is not found in classic texts, nor is it part of genuine Feng Shui's ancient practice and principles. Though it may sound related, it is not an aspect of the Eight Mansions system and does not even derive from it. Some popular Feng Shui books promoting Classical Feng Shui also include the Eight Life Aspirations, only adding to the confusion.

Eight Roads of Destruction: Also known as the Eight Roads to Hell, this formation is based on a road or driveway's egress from a property in correlation to the front door. Roads and driveways are considered virtual water, so the direction they exit are called *water exits*. This unlucky formation can have disastrous results; remedial measures must be taken.

Eight Wandering Stars: Also known as the *Big Wandering Sky*, these stars are matched with the nine stars of Ursa Major, the Big Dipper. They are as follows:

- Tan Lang (*Greedy Wolf* or *Ravenous Wolf*) is matched with ***Sheng Chi***
- Jue Men *(Huge Door* or *Great Door)* is matched with ***Tien Yi***
- Wu Chu *(Military Arts)* is matched with ***Yen Nien***
- Tso Fu and Fu Pi *(Left/Right Assistant* or the Big Dipper's handle) are is matched with ***Fu Wei***
- Lu Chun *(Rewards/Salary)* is matched with ***Wo Hai***
- Lien Zheng *(Five Ghosts* or *Chastity)* is matched with ***Wu Gwei***
- Wen Qu *(Literary Arts* or *The Scholar)* is matched with ***Lui Sha***
- Tien Kong *(Broken Soldier* or *Destructive Army)* is matched with ***Cheuh Ming***

These nine stars and their unique energy are very important in many Feng Shui systems. More information on the nine stars appears in chapter 5; the Chinese names above are also the "secret names" of the nine stars.

Energy: The Chinese call energy chi (also spelled *qi*, pronounced *chee*.) Our entire universe is energy; there are many types of chi—human, environmental, and heavenly or celestial (as in the solar system, not the afterlife).

Esoteric: Any knowledge available only to a narrow circle of enlightened or initiated people or a specially educated group. Feng Shui is part of Chinese metaphysics and is considered esoteric.

External environment: Refers to the terrain and topography, including mountains, water, and other natural formations. It also encompasses man-made features, such as roads, pools, retaining walls, highways, poles, drains, washes, tall buildings, stop signs, fire hydrants, and other structures.

Facing direction: The front side of the home or building, generally where the front or main door is located and faces the street.

Facing Star: Also known as the water star, this star is located in the upper right-hand corner of a Flying Star chart in all nine palaces or sectors. The facing star is in charge of wealth-luck.

Feng: The Chinese word for "wind" pronounced *fung,* although *foong* is a more accurate sound.

Feng Shui: Pronounced *fung shway.* Also known as *Kan Yu* (translated as "the way of heaven and earth") until about a hundred years ago, the Chinese system of maximizing the accumulation of beneficial chi improves the quality of life and luck of the occupants of a particular building or location. The literal translation is "wind and water," but it refers to wind as it means *direction* and water as it means *energy.*

Feng Shui master: One who has mastered the skills of Classical Feng Shui and/or has been declared as such by a teacher, or both. It is also said that practitioners become masters when their clients refer to them as such. Most Feng Shui masters from Classic traditions will belong to a lineage of teachers. Masters may also be referred to as "lineage carriers," meaning they continue and pass down the teachings and practices of their education. Feng Shui masters generally oversee their own schools and students as well.

Feng Shui schools: There are two major schools or branches (systems rather than physical locations) of Classical Feng Shui: San He and San Yuan. Hundreds of formulas, techniques, and systems serve as subsets of either school. If you practice Classical Feng Shui, you use the San He and the San Yuan systems as one collective body of knowledge. *See* entries San He and San Yuan for details about each school.

Flying Stars: Known as *Xuan Kong Fei Xing* in Chinese, which means mysterious void or the subtle mysteries of time and space. It is a popular Feng Shui system that is superior in addressing the time aspect of energy. Refer to chapter 4 for additional information on this vast system.

Fu Wei: The direction and location for stability as it applies to the Eight Mansions system. According to Master Yap's numeric representation, it is the +60.

Fu Xi: A sage, king, and shaman who was responsible for discovering and arranging the Early Heaven Ba Gua.

Gen: One of the eight trigrams of the Ba Gua also spelled as *Ken*. It represents the youngest son, the mountain, and early spring. In the Later Heaven arrangement of the Ba Gua, the Gen trigram is located in the Northeast.

Golden Pill: Taoist masters tried for centuries to create this, believing that ingesting it would grant spiritual transcendence and immortality.

Golden Star Classic: From the Chinese *Kam Kwong Dou Lam King*; also spelled as *Jin Guang Dou Lin Jing*. It translates as "Big Dipper Casting Golden Light" and refers to the style of Eight Mansions used in this book.

Grandmaster: To receive this recognition, the person must have been practicing and teaching for many years, belong to a respected lineage of masters, and have at least one master among his or her pupils.

Grandmaster Datuk Chee Kim Thong: A martial arts teacher of Grandmaster Yap Cheng Hai.

Grandmaster Yap Cheng Hai (GMY) 1927–2014: Master Yap was born and raised in Singapore and lived in Xiamen, China, for four years. He moved to Kuala Lumpur, Malaysia, in 1963 to manage his uncle's business and soon became a citizen. Although his life was full, he pursued two passions: Feng Shui and Martial Arts. He began practicing Feng Shui professionally in the early 1960s. He has consulted with prominent figures such as members of royalty, ministers, corporations, banks, and developers. A loyal client since the 1960s, Paramount Garden consulted him to plan their townships that included SEA Park, Damansara Utama, and Bandar Utama. GMY is quite famous in Southeast Asia for his Water Dragon techniques that he learned from Grandmaster Chan Chuan Huai in Taiwan who created several billionaires there. He began teaching in the late 1990s to those wishing to learn authentic, Classical Feng Shui. I graduated in 2001 as a Master right after 9/11.

Great Cycle: 180 years in length. *See* Age of Eight.

GYM Code: this is a code devised by Grandmaster Yap Cheng Hai to easily identify your good and bad directions in the Eight Mansions system. +90, +80, +70, and +60 are your *good* directions representing wealth, health, relationships/longevity, and stability respectively. -90, -80, -70, and -60 represent your *bad* directions. If activated, the bad directions will cause divorce/bankruptcy, bad health/betrayals, affairs/lawsuits and setbacks, respectively.

Gua: Alternatively spelled *Kua* and also known as a trigram. It represents one of eight Guas of the Ba Gua, defined by a combination of three solid or broken lines.

Gua Number: Also referred to as *Ming Gua* (nothing to do with the Ming Dynasty). To determine your personal Life Gua number, use your birthday. See chapter 4 for specific instructions.

Heaven Luck: One of the three categories of luck that humans can experience. The Chinese believe every human has a destiny and a fate determined by the heavens (*Tien*). This category cannot be changed and is considered *fixed.*

High-rise building: In the external environment, high-rise buildings and skyscrapers function as virtual or urban mountains.

Ho: The Chinese word for fire.

Ho Hai: Also known as *Wo Hai,* part of the Eight Mansions system. It can bring mishaps—nothing goes smoothly. According to Master Yap's numeric representation, this is the -60.

Hsia: Pronounced *she-ah*; this is the name for the Chinese solar calendar based on the cycles of the sun. The solar calendar regulates agriculture because the sun determines the seasons; it is used in all Feng Shui techniques for its accuracy. The solar year begins on February 4 or 5; there are two possible dates not because of uncertainty but due to the fact that the Gregorian calendar "wobbles" due to the insertion of the extra day during leap years.

I Ching: A philosophical and divinatory book based on the sixty-four hexagrams of Taoist mysticism. It is also known as the *Classic of Changes* or *Book of Changes*.

Incoming dragon: The energy of a mountain that comes directly to your home or building. If a mountain range is nearby, the highest peak is measured with a Luo Pan because it has the most powerful energy. An entire science is based on determining the effects of mountain energy on any given site. In Feng Shui, the terms "mountain" and "dragon" are used interchangeably.

Intercardinal directions: Northwest, Southwest, Northeast, and Southeast.

Interior environment: The Interior environment encompasses anything that falls within the walls of a structure, including kitchen, staircase, Master Bedroom + Family, fireplaces, bathrooms, hallways, dining room, bedrooms, appliances, furniture, and so on.

Kan: One of the eight trigrams. It represents the middle son, the moon, and mid-winter. In the Later Heaven Arrangement of the Ba Gua, it is located in the North.

Kurzweil, Ray: An American author, inventor, futurist, and a director of engineering at Google. Aside from futurology, he is involved in fields such as optical character recognition (OCR), text-to-speech synthesis, speech recognition technology, and electronic keyboard instruments. He has written books on health, artificial intelligence (AI), transhumanism, the technological singularity, and futurism. In his public talks, he has shared his primarily optimistic outlooks on life extension technologies and the future of nanotechnology, robotics, and biotechnology.

Kun: One of the eight trigrams. It represents the mother, the earth, and late summer. In the Later Heaven Arrangement of the Ba Gua, it is located in the Southwest.

Later Heaven Ba Gua: The second arrangement of the trigrams known as the *Wen Wang* or *Xien Tien* Ba Gua. This is used extensively in the application of Classical Feng Shui.

Li: One of the eight trigrams. It represents the middle daughter, fire, and full summer. In the Later Heaven Arrangement of the Ba Gua, it is located in the South.

Life Gua Number: A number assigned to people, based on birthday and gender, in the Eight Mansions system (*Ba Zhai*).

Life Gua Personalities: A trademarked description of personality types based on the Life Gua numbers in the Eight Mansions system expanded on and first seen in *Classical Feng Shui for Wealth and Abundance* (2013).

Life Gua Zodiac Personalities: A trademarked, expanded version of the Life Gua Personalities that include the Zodiac animal year of birth. First appeared in *Classical Feng Shui for Romance, Sex & Abundance* (2015).

Liu Sha: In the Eight Mansions system, it is also known as the *Six Killings* direction and can bring backstabbing, affairs, and lawsuits. According to Master Yap's numeric representation, it is the -80.

Location: A particular place or position, differing from the concept of direction. For example, your living room might be located on the South side of your home (location), but your desk faces North (direction).

Lunar calendar: A calendar based on the cycles of the moon.

Lung: The Chinese word for dragon.

Luo Pan: The Luo Pan is the quintessential tool of a Feng Shui practitioner. It is a compass that contains four to forty concentric rings of information. The most popular model is approximately ten inches across, square, and often constructed of fine woods. The circle part of the Luo Pan is made of brass and rotates to align with the compass itself, which is located in the center. There are three major types of Luo Pans—the *San Yuan* Luo Pan, the *San He* Luo Pan, and the *Chung He* Luo Pan (also known as *Zong He* or *Zhung He*), which is a combination of the first two. Though Luo Pans have similar basic components, Feng Shui masters do customize their own with secret information for them and their students.

Luo Shu: A square that contains nine palaces or cells with a number in each; it adds to fifteen in any direction. The Luo Shu is also known as the *Magic Square of 15.*

Main door: This is usually the front door of the home or business. If the occupants always enter the residence from the garage, this may also be considered a main door.

Man luck: One of the three categories of luck a person can experience, does not refer to the male gender exclusively. This area of fortune is mutable and defined by individual effort such as hard work, study, education, experience, and good deeds. The Chinese word for man is *Ren.*

Martial arts: Codified systems and traditions of combat practices, which are practiced for a variety of reasons: self-defense, competition, physical health and fitness, entertainment, as well as mental, physical, and spiritual development.

Massage: The manipulation of superficial and deeper layers of muscle and connective tissue using various techniques, to enhance function, aid in the healing process, decrease muscle reflex activity, inhibit motor-neuron excitability, promote relaxation and well-being, and as a recreational activity.

Metal Cures: The best metals are bronze, copper, brass, pewter, stainless steel, and wrought iron to weaken the 2 or 5 star.

Ming Dynasty: A ruling dynasty of China, which lasted from 1368 to 1644 CE.

Mountains: Includes real mountains and virtual mountains, such as tall buildings, landscape mounds, retaining walls, huge boulders, or any object of mass in the environment. See *dragon*.

Nanotechnology: Also known as *nanotech,* is the manipulation of matter on an atomic, molecular, and supramolecular scale. The earliest, widespread description of nanotechnology referred to the particular technological goal of precisely manipulating atoms and molecules for fabrication of macroscale products, also now referred to as molecular nanotechnology.

Nien Yen: This is the incorrect spelling of the *Yen Nien* (+70) in the Eight Mansions system; you will see this mistake in many Feng Shui books.

Parent String Formation: Known in Chinese as *Fu Mu San Poon Gua* and sometimes referred to as the *Three Combinations*, these are special wealth-producing Flying Star charts. This formation of energy applies to certain structures—which are activated by a mountain in the front of the property and water in the back—on intercardinal directions. They only last for twenty years and are unlucky if not activated properly.

Pa Sha Hwang Chuen: The Chinese translation of the Eight Killing Forces.

Pearl String Formation: Known in Chinese as *Lin Cu San Poon Gua* and sometimes referred to as the *Continuous Bead Formations,* these are special wealth-producing Flying Star charts that only show up in homes that face an intercardinal direction. Though excellent energy for prosperity, this formation only lasts for twenty years and is unlucky if not activated properly.

Period: The twenty-year increment of the Flying Star system; currently the world is in Period 8. Nine periods comprise a megacycle of 180 years.

Period 7: This is part of the Flying Star system; Period 7 began February 4, 1984, and ended February 3, 2004. Each Period is twenty years in duration.

Period 8: This is part of the Flying Star system; Period 8 began February 4, 2004 and will end on February 3, 2024. Each Period is twenty years in duration.

Prosperous Sitting and Facing: Known in Chinese as *Wang Shan Wang Shui*; a Flying Star chart that means "*good for people, good for money.*" These charts have the perfect placement of the current prosperous stars—the facing star is at the facing (good for money), and the mountain star is at the sitting (good for people).

Qi Gong: Also spelled *Qigong, chi kung,* or *chi gung*; traditional Chinese Qi Gong is a practice of aligning body, breath, and mind for health, meditation, and martial arts training. With roots in Chinese medicine, philosophy, and martial arts, qigong is traditionally viewed as a practice to cultivate and balance qi (chi) or what has been translated as "life energy."

Retaining walls: High walls, at least three to six feet in height, which can be used to secure a site and prevent loss of energy. The more dynamic the landscape, the more walls are needed to protect sloping areas or sharp drop-offs.

Road: A route, path, or open way for vehicles. In Feng Shui, roads are *rivers* of energy and play a huge part in analyzing a site because energy is powerful. These virtual, or urban, rivers are calculated when assessing, designing, enhancing, or implementing counter measures or enhancements for a site.

San He: Also known as *San Hup*. One of the two major schools of study in Classical Feng Shui—the other is San Yuan. The San He system is excellent for tapping natural landforms, primarily addresses large-scale projects, land plots, urban developments, city planning, and master-planned communities. The system is extensive and has several practical techniques for new and existing residential spaces as well. When assessing and altering a site or a structure, San He and San Yuan can be blended for maximum results.

San Yuan: One of the two major schools of Classical Feng Shui. The Flying Stars is part of this system; it excels in techniques of timing. See the Schools of Feng Shui section in the compendium for more details.

Sector: An area inside or outside a building: South sector, North sector, and so on.

Sha chi: Also known as *shar chi*. Extremely negative energy, or killing chi.

Shan: The Chinese word for mountain.

Sheng Chi: Part of the Eight Mansions system. It can bring life-generating energy, wealth, and opportunities. Using Master Yap's numeric representation, this is the +90.

Shui: The Chinese word for water; pronounced *shway*.

Sitting: In Feng Shui it refers to the back of the house, as if the structure is sitting in a chair on the land or property. It is the heavy part of the house; also considered a mountain.

Sitting Star: Also known as the Mountain Star in the Flying Star system. It influences people-luck, such as fertility, employees, and health.

Solar calendar: A calendar based on the movements of the sun.

Southeast Asia: Countries south of China and east of India, including Thailand, Vietnam, Cambodia, Laos, Myanmar, the Philippines, and Singapore.

Tai Chi: The black and white symbol of Taoist philosophy; a sphere with two semi-circles intertwined showing the division of yin and yang energy. An alternate spelling is Taiji.

Tai Chi Martial Arts: Also spelled *t'ai chi*, *tai chi chuan*, or *taijiquan*, and is nicknamed "meditation in motion" for its slow, beautiful movements. It is an internal Chinese martial art practiced for both its defense training and its health benefits. It is also typically practiced for a variety of other personal reasons; namely, longevity. As a result, a multitude of training forms exist, both traditional and modern, corresponding to those aims.

Tao: Also known as "the Way." It is the core of Taoism (pronounced with a D sound).

Tapping the energy or chi: A technique that invites the available energy from the external environment to support the occupants of a structure.

Tien Yi: Part of the Eight Mansions system. It can bring excellent health and wealth. In Chinese it means "heavenly doctor" or "the doctor from heaven watches over you." Using Master Yap's numeric representation, it is the +80.

Tilting a door: A time-honored tradition used by Feng Shui masters and practitioners to change the degree of a door and the energy of a space. The doorframe and threshold are re-angled toward the desired degree. When the door is re-hung, it is tilted at a different degree.

Time Star: Also known as the *Base Star* in the Flying Star system; it is the single star below the mountain and facing star of the chart.

T-juncture: When two roads meet perpendicularly to create a T. The formation is toxic when a home or business sits at the top and center of that *T*.

Traditional Feng Shui: Another term for Classical Chinese Feng Shui.

Tui: Also spelled *Dui.* One of the eight trigrams that represents the youngest daughter, the lake, and mid-fall. In the Later Heaven Ba Gua it is located in the West.

Twelve animals: Together, they are the Chinese zodiac and comprise Chinese astrology's earthly branches. They are also used extensively in Classical Feng Shui. The animals are: Rat, Ox, Tiger, Rabbit, Dragon, Snake, Horse, Goat, Monkey, Rooster, Dog, and Pig.

Virtual mountains: High-rise structures, such as apartments, office buildings, and skyscrapers, are considered virtual or urban mountains that influence the energy of nearby structures accordingly.

Virtual water: Roads, sidewalks, driveways, low ground, highways, and other similar formations that are purveyors of chi.

Washes: In the external environment, these natural and man-made channels whisk away water from a site.

Water: In Feng Shui, water is the secret to enhancing wealth, prosperity, longevity, nobility, and relationships. The Chinese word is *shui,* and it represents energy and life force. Feng Shui considers water the most powerful element on the planet.

Water exits: The location or direction where water leaves a site. Water exits are used in Feng Shui to bring good results, but if not placed well can usher in disasters.

Waterfalls: Used to enhance wealth-luck; the direction of the waterfall is important.

Water Star: Also called the *Facing Star* in the Flying Star system; it rules wealth-luck.

Western Feng Shui: In addition to the Black Hat Sect, other schools cropped up that incorporated the principles (but not the rituals) associated with Lin Yun's followers. As the masters of Classical Feng Shui started to teach around the world, some of the most well-acclaimed instructors and authors of Western Feng Shui began to learn Classical Feng Shui. Unwilling to give up the Western-style Feng Shui that made them famous, they mixed the old with the new, adding to the confusion over what is "authentic" Feng Shui in the process. More than half of the books written about Feng Shui include a hodgepodge of both theories.

West Life Group: In the Eight Mansions system, people are divided into the East or West group. The 2, 6, 7, and 8 Life Guas are part of the West Life Group.

Wu Gwei: Part of the Eight Mansions system that can attract lawsuits, bad romance, and betrayals. Using Master Yap's numeric representation, it is the -70. This is also known as the Five Ghosts direction.

Wu Xing: The five elements of Feng Shui: wood, fire, earth, metal, and water.

Xing Fa: An approach to assessing form and shape in the environment.

Xun: One of the eight trigrams of the Ba Gua, also spelled *Sun*. It represents the eldest daughter, the wind and early summer. In the

Later Heaven arrangement of the Ba Gua, the Xun trigram is located in the Southeast.

Yang: Alive, active, and moving energy; the world of the living. Considered the male energy of the yin yang symbol.

Yang Feng Shui: Feng Shui was first practiced for the selection of a perfect gravesite, or what is commonly known by the Chinese as Yin Feng Shui—Feng Shui for the dead. Later, techniques were developed to increase luck and opportunities for homes of the living.

Yan Shou Gong: A style of martial arts for longevity devised by Grandmaster Yap Cheng Hai and his teacher, Grandmaster Datuk Chee Kim Thong. It is easy to use and master. Grandmaster Yap has written a trilogy of books on the techniques to master.

Yellow Spring: A term used by the Chinese to describe Hell or the underworld.

Yen Nien: Part of the Eight Mansions system that can bring longevity, good relationships, and love. Using Master Yap's numeric representation, it is the +70. It is a common mistake to spell this term as Nen Yien.

Yin: Passive, slow, and flowing energy; the world of the dead. Considered the female energy of the yin yang symbol.

Bibliography & References

Alexandersson, Olof. *Living Water: Viktor Schauberger and the Secrets of Natural Energy*. Dublin, Ireland: Gill & MacMillan, 1990.

Batmanghelidj, F., M.D. *ABC of Asthma, Allergies, and Lupus*. Global Health Solutions, Inc., 2005:

———. *Obesity, Cancer, Depression: Their Common Cause & Natural Cure.*

———. *Water: For Health, For Healing For Life*

———. *Water Cures: Drugs Kill*

———. *Your Body's Many Cries for Water*

Begich, Nick and Manning, Jeane. *Angels Don't Play This Haarp: Advances in Tesla Technology*. Earthpulse Press; 1st edition (September 1995)

Connett, Paul, PhD; Beck, James, MD, PhD; and Micklem, H.S., DPhil. *The Case Against Fluoride*. White River Junction, VT: Chelsea Green Publishing, 2010.

Ellis, Richard. "Poaching for Traditional Chinese Medicine" author of *Tiger Bone and Rhino Horn*, for the EAZA Rhino Campaign 2005-6 Info Pack. www.savetherhino.org/rhino_info/threats_to_rhino/poaching_for_traditional_chinese_medicine.

Gerstung, Wilhelm and Jens Mehlhase. *The Complete Feng Shui Health Handbook.* Twin Lakes, WI: Lotus Press-Shangri-La, 2000.

Guilford, Gwynn. "There's a Country That Will Pay $300,000 Per Rhino Horn to Cure Cancer and Hangovers and It's Wiping out Rhinos" @sinoceros. May 14, 2013. qz.com/82302/theres-a-country-that-will-pay-300000-per-rhino-horn-to-cure-cancer-and-hangovers-and-its-wiping-out-rhinos.

Huang, Alfred. *The Numerology of the I Ching: A Sourcebook of Symbols, Structures, and Traditional Wisdom*. Rochester, VT: Inner Traditions, 2000.

Kurzweil, Ray and Grossman, Terry, MD. *The Age of Spiritual Machines: When Computers Exceed Human Intelligence.* New York: Penguin Books.

———. *Fantastic Voyage: Live Long Enough to Live Forever.* New York: PLUME (Penguin Group), 2005.

———. *The Singularity is Near: When Humans Transcend Biology*. New York: Penguin Books, 2005.

———. *Transcend: Nine Steps to Living Well Forever.* New York: Rodale, Inc., 2009.

Mercola, Joseph. *Why Did the Russians Ban an Appliance Found in 90% of American Homes?* http://articles.mercola.com/sites/articles/archive/2010/05/18/microwave-hazards.aspx. May 18, 2010. May 18, 2010.

Sitchin, Zecharia. *The Stairway to Heaven.* Santa Fe: Bear & Co., 1992.

Skinner, Stephen. *Guide to the Feng Shui Compass: A Compendium of Classical Feng Shui*. Woodbury, MN: Llewellyn Publishing, 2010.

———. *The Living Manual of Feng Shui: Chinese Geomancy.* London: Arkana Penguin Books, 1982.

Too, Lillian. *The Illustrated Encyclopedia of Feng Shui*. New York: Barnes & Noble, 1999.

———. *Total Feng Shui: Bring Health, Wealth and Happiness Into Your Life*. San Francisco: Chronicle Books, 2005.

Wong, Eva. *Harmonizing Yin and Yang: the Dragon-Tiger Classic.* Boston: Shambhala, 1997.

———*The Shambhala Guide to Taoism.* Boston: Shambhala, 1997.

———*The Tao of Health, Longevity, and Immortality: The Teachings of Immortals Chung and Lü.* Boston: Shambhala, 2000.

———. *Teaching of the Tao*. Boston: Shambhala, 1997.

Vercammen, Dan K. J. "Chinese Taoist Alchemy and the Tradition Taught at the China Arts College." 2014. www.taoiststudies.org/taoist_studies_web/downloads_en_files/chinese%20alchemy%20and%20our%20tradition.pdf.

Yiamouyiannis, Dr. John. *Fluoride the Aging Factor*. Delaware, OH: Health Action Press, 1993.

Feng Shui Resources

Classical Feng Shui Classes

If you're interested in learning Classical Feng Shui, there are a number of excellent Feng Shui masters around the world who offer classes on one or more of the Five Chinese Metaphysical Arts. You can receive training on Classical Feng Shui (*San He* and *San Yuan*), Face Reading (*Mian Xiang*), Chinese Astrology (*Ba Zi* also known as *Four Pillars of Destiny* and *Zi Wei Dou Shu*), and Oriental medicine (acupuncture, herbology). For an extensive list refer to *Classical Feng Shui for Wealth and Abundance: Activating Ancient Wisdom for a Rich and Prosperous Life.*

Master Denise Liotta Dennis
The American College of Classical Feng Shui (ACCFS)
Dragon-Gate Feng Shui, LLC Consulting
Houston, Texas USA
Phone: 480-241-5211

Email:
denise@dragongatefengshui.com

Website:
www.dragongatefengshui.com

Offers books, consulting services (residential and commercial, training classes, one-on-one mentoring, and specializes in mixed-use projects, master-planned communities/shopping centers and urban development. ACCFS has thirty-six different modules; live classes are offered in Houston, Phoenix, Los Angeles, and Chicago.